FRISCH

A German Course for the

BY

W. B. SAVIGNY, M.A.
*Formerly Senior Modern Language Master
Wigan Grammar School*

AND

W. C. MITCHELL, B.A.
*Formerly Senior Modern Language Master
Workington Grammar School*

Illustrated by
CHRISTOPHER BROOKER

Nelson

Thomas Nelson and Sons Ltd
Nelson House   Mayfield Road
Walton-on-Thames   Surrey
KT12 5PL   UK

51 York Place
Edinburgh
EH1 3JD   UK

Thomas Nelson (Hong Kong) Ltd
Toppan Building 10/F
22A Westlands Road
Quarry Bay   Hong Kong

Distributed in Australia by

Thomas Nelson Australia
480 La Trobe Street
Melbourne   Victoria 3000
and in Sydney, Brisbane, Adelaide and Perth

© W.B. Savigny and W.C. Mitchell 1959

First published by George G. Harrap and Co. Ltd 1959
(under ISBN 0-245-53107-6)

Reprinted twelve times
This impression published by Thomas Nelson and Sons Ltd 1985
Reprinted 1987

ISBN 0-17-444592-X

Print No. 03

Printed in Hong Kong

All Rights Reserved. This publication is protected in the United
Kingdom by the Copyright Act 1956 and in other countries by
comparable legislation. No part of it may be reproduced or recorded by
any means without the permission of the publisher. This prohibition
extends (with certain very limited exceptions) to photocopying and
similar processes, and written permission to make a copy or copies must
therefore be obtained from the publisher in advance. It is advisable to
consult the publisher if there is any doubt regarding the legality of any
proposed copying.

ACKNOWLEDGMENTS

Thanks are due to the following authors and publishers for their kind permission to reproduce copyright material: C. Bertelsmann Verlag, Gütersloh (*Bahnwärter Thiel*); Verlag Kurt Desch, München (*Die Reise*); Dörnersche Verlagsanstalt Düsseldorf (*Spuk in St. Pauli*); S. Fischer Verlag, Frankfurt a.M. (*Der Tod in Venedig* from *Erzählungen* by Thomas Mann); H-J. Laturner (*Capitano Terrore*); Neue Illustrierte, Köln (*Liebe hinter dem Ladentisch*); R. Piper and Co Verlag, München (*Tante Frieda*); Ullstein Taschenbücher-Verlag GmbH, Frankfurt a.M. (*Mordkommission Hollywood* and *Tanger-nach Mitternacht*).

The publishers and authors regret that in spite of every effort they have been unable to trace the trustees or other representatives of C. O. Windecker and Heinrich Lersch, extracts from whose works are included in this book.

CONTENTS

SECTION	PAGE
1. Summary of Grammar	9
2. Exercises on Grammar	62
3. Prose Passages for Translation into German	83
4. German Prose Extracts for Translation	111
5. German Prose Extracts for Dictation, Oral and Aural Practice	139
6. Free Composition	157
7. Passages for Comprehension & Multiple Choice Exercises	170
8. German–English Vocabulary	195
English–German Vocabulary	223

PLATES IN HALF-TONE

Im Schwarzwald   *page* 64

Köln: Blick vom rechten Rheinufer   65

Rheindampfer   65

Hannover: Brunnen am Holzmarkt   96

Hameln: zwei Bürgerhäuser am Rathausplatz   97

*The photographs are reproduced by courtesy of the
German Tourist Bureau*

SECTION 1

Summary of Grammar

		Page	Exercise page
1.	Conjugation of weak verbs	10	62
2.	Verbs with prefixes	11	63
3.	Conjugation of strong verbs	11	
4.	**Sein** and **haben** as auxiliaries	12	65
5.	List of strong verbs	12	
6.	Passive voice	15	66
7.	Reflexive verbs	16	67
8.	Modal verbs	17	67
9.	Impersonal verbs	19	68
10.	Conjugation of the subjunctive	19	
11.	Uses of the subjunctive	20	68
12.	Word order	22	63
13.	Declension of nouns	23	69
14.	Declension of adjectives	27	69
15.	Uses of cases	30	71
16.	Comparison of adjectives	32	72
17.	Comparison of adverbs	32	72
18.	Personal pronouns	33	73
19.	Relative pronouns	34	73
20.	Interrogative pronouns	35	74
21.	Possessive pronouns	35	74
22.	Demonstrative pronouns	36	74
23.	Translation of the English present participle	36	74
24.	Numerals	38	75
25.	Times, dates, age	40	75
26.	Prepositional phrases	43	
27.	Other useful phrases	49	
28.	Difficult translations	50	76
29.	The family	58	
30.	The nation	59	
31.	Punctuation	60	

1. CONJUGATION OF WEAK VERBS

A. The simpler tenses. Model: **machen** — to make

Present: **mach-e, -st, -t, -en, -t, -en**
Imperative: **mache! macht! machen Sie!**
Imperfect: **mach-te, -test, -te, -ten, -tet, -ten**
Perfect: **ich habe ... gemacht**
  (*cf.* verbs with **sein, ich bin gekommen**)
Pluperfect: **ich hatte ... gemacht**
Future: **ich werde ... machen**

Note:
(a) the three forms in German for the English *you*.
  du machst — familiar form, singular
  ihr macht — plural of **du machst**
  Sie machen — singular and plural of the polite form

(b) the different tenses used in English and German with the word *since*—**seit**.
  Seit wann wohnen Sie hier? How long have you been living here?
  Ich wohne seit zwei Jahren hier. I have been living here for two years.
  Ich wohnte seit zwei Jahren in der Stadt. I had been living in the town for two years.

B. More difficult tenses.

Conditional: **ich würde ... machen,** I should make
Future Perfect: **ich werde ... gemacht haben,** I shall have made
Conditional perfect: **ich würde ... gemacht haben,** I should have made

Note: **ich werde ... gekommen sein, ich würde ... gekommen sein**

C. Verbs to watch. The present, imperative, imperfect, and perfect of verbs whose infinitives end in **-ten.**

antworten — to answer

Present: **antwort-e, -est, -et, -en, -et, -en**
Imperative: **antworte! antwortet! antworten Sie!**

Imperfect:	**antwort-ete, -etest, -ete, -eten, -etet, -eten**
Perfect:	**ich habe ... geantwortet**

2. VERBS WITH PREFIXES

Many verbs have prefixes. In the conjugation of the verb, it is necessary to know whether the prefix is separable or inseparable.

A. Inseparable Prefixes

be-, emp-, ent-, er-, ge-, miß-, ver-, zer-

verstehen — to understand

Present:	**ich verstehe**
Imperfect:	**ich verstand**
Perfect:	**ich habe ... verstanden**
Future:	**ich werde ... verstehen**
With **zu**:	**ich hoffe ... zu verstehen**

B. Separable Prefixes. Most prepositions can be used as prefixes and in this case are usually separable. The prefix must be at the end of the clause.

aufstehen — to get up, to rise

Present:	**ich stehe ... auf (wenn ich ... aufstehe)**
Imperative:	**steh(e) ... auf! steht ... auf! stehen Sie ... auf!**
Imperfect:	**ich stand ... auf (wenn ich ... aufstand)**
Perfect:	**ich bin ... aufgestanden**
Future:	**ich werde ... aufstehen**
With **zu**:	**ich hoffe ... aufzustehen**

3. CONJUGATION OF STRONG VERBS

A. Strong verbs usually change the infinitive stem-vowel in the Present (2nd and 3rd singular), Imperative (singular, familiar form, usually same vowel as 3rd singular Present), Imperfect and Perfect.

B. In the verb tables, the 3rd singular of the main tenses is given, so as to show these changes.

nehmen — to take

Present:	**nehme, nimmst, nimmt, nehmen, nehmt, nehmen**

Imperative: **nimm! nehmt! nehmen Sie!**
Imperfect: **nahm, nahmst, nahm, nahmen, nahmt, nahmen**
Perfect: **ich habe ... genommen**

4. **Sein** AND **haben** AS AUXILIARIES

   A. **sein** (a) Always with **sein, werden, geschehen, gelingen, bleiben, kommen, gehen, verschwinden, erscheinen**

   (b) With intransitive verbs indicating change of place or state

   B. **haben** (a) With all transitive verbs
   (b) With all reflexive verbs

   Note: Some verbs can be used transitively or intransitively, *e.g.*:—

   Er hat das Pferd geritten.
   Er ist durch das Dorf geritten.

5. *LIST OF STRONG VERBS*

   (For Modal verbs—see separate section)

   Note (i) Most strong verbs have an optional **-e** in Imperative singular, thus **stehe!** or better **steh!**

   (ii) Verbs marked with an asterisk (*) have **haben** as auxiliary when used transitively.

Infinitive	Meaning	Present	Imperfect	Perfect
befehlen	command	er befiehlt	befahl	er hat befohlen
beginnen	begin	er beginnt	begann	er hat begonnen
beißen	bite	er beißt	biß	er hat gebissen
biegen	bend, turn	er biegt	bog	er hat gebogen
bieten	offer	er bietet	bot	er hat geboten
binden	bind, fasten	er bindet	band	er hat gebunden
bitten	request	er bittet	bat	er hat gebeten
blasen	blow	er bläst	blies	er hat geblasen
bleiben	remain	er bleibt	blieb	er ist geblieben
brechen	break	er bricht	brach	er hat gebrochen
brennen	burn	er brennt	brannte	er hat gebrannt
bringen	bring	er bringt	brachte	er hat gebracht
denken	think	er denkt	dachte	er hat gedacht
empfehlen	recommend	er empfiehlt	empfahl	er hat empfohlen
erschrecken	be frightened	er erschrickt	erschrak	er ist erschrocken
essen	eat	er ißt	aß	er hat gegessen
*fahren	go, drive	er fährt	fuhr	er ist gefahren
fallen	fall	er fällt	fiel	er ist gefallen
fangen	catch	er fängt	fing	er hat gefangen

SUMMARY OF GRAMMAR

Infinitive	Meaning	Present	Imperfect	Perfect
fechten	fight, fence	er ficht	focht	er hat gefochten
finden	find	er findet	fand	er hat gefunden
fliegen	fly	er fliegt	flog	er ist geflogen
fliehen	flee, escape	er flieht	floh	er ist geflohen
fließen	flow	er fließt	floß	er ist geflossen
frieren	freeze	er friert	fror	er hat gefroren
geben	give	er gibt	gab	er hat gegeben
gehen	go (on foot)	er geht	ging	er ist gegangen
gelingen (*impersonal*)	succeed	es gelingt ihm	gelang ihm	es ist ihm gelungen
gelten	be worth	er gilt	galt	er hat gegolten
genesen	recover (from illness)	er genest	genas	er ist genesen
genießen	enjoy (sth)	er genießt	genoß	er hat genossen
geschehen (*impersonal*)	happen	es geschieht	geschah	es ist geschehen
gewinnen	win, gain	er gewinnt	gewann	er hat gewonnen
gießen	pour	er gießt	goß	er hat gegossen
gleichen	resemble	er gleicht	glich	er hat geglichen
gleiten	slide	er gleitet	glitt	er ist geglitten
graben	dig	er gräbt	grub	er hat gegraben
greifen	seize, grab	er greift	griff	er hat gegriffen
haben	have	er hat	hatte	er hat gehabt
halten	hold, stop	er hält	hielt	er hat gehalten
hängen	hang	er hängt	hing	er hat gehangen
heben	raise, lift	er hebt	hob	er hat gehoben
heißen	be called, bid, mean	er heißt	hieß	er hat geheißen
helfen	help	er hilft	half	er hat geholfen
kennen	know	er kennt	kannte	er hat gekannt
klingen	sound, ring (of things)	es klingt	klang	es hat geklungen
kommen	come	er kommt	kam	er ist gekommen
kriechen	creep, crawl	er kriecht	kroch	er ist gekrochen
laden	load	er lädt (ladet)	lud	er hat geladen
lassen	let, cause	er läßt	ließ	er hat gelassen
laufen	run	er läuft	lief	er ist gelaufen
leiden	suffer	er leidet	litt	er hat gelitten
leihen	lend	er leiht	lieh	er hat geliehen
lesen	read	er liest	las	er hat gelesen
liegen	be lying	er liegt	lag	er hat gelegen
lügen	tell a lie	er lügt	log	er hat gelogen
meiden	avoid	er meidet	mied	er hat gemieden
nehmen	take	er nimmt	nahm	er hat genommen
nennen	name	er nennt	nannte	er hat genannt
pfeifen	whistle	er pfeift	pfiff	er hat gepfiffen
raten	advise	er rät	riet	er hat geraten
reißen	tear	er reißt	riß	er hat gerissen
*reiten	ride (animals)	er reitet	ritt	er ist geritten
*rennen	run, race	er rennt	rannte	er ist gerannt
riechen	smell	er riecht	roch	er hat gerochen

Infinitive	Meaning	Present	Imperfect	Perfect
ringen	wrestle	er ringt	rang	er hat gerungen
rufen	call	er ruft	rief	er hat gerufen
schaffen	create	er schafft	schuf	er hat geschaffen
scheiden	separate (depart with sein)	er scheidet	schied	er hat geschieden
scheinen	shine, seem	er scheint	schien	er hat geschienen
schelten	scold	er schilt	schalt	er hat gescholten
schieben	shove, push	er schiebt	schob	er hat geschoben
schießen	shoot	er schießt	schoß	er hat geschossen
schlafen	sleep	er schläft	schlief	er hat geschlafen
schlagen	strike, hit	er schlägt	schlug	er hat geschlagen
schleichen	creep	er schleicht	schlich	er ist geschlichen
schließen	shut	er schließt	schloß	er hat geschlossen
schneiden	cut	er schneidet	schnitt	er hat geschnitten
schreiben	write	er schreibt	schrieb	er hat geschrieben
schreien	cry out	er schreit	schrie	er hat geschrie(e)n
schreiten	stride	er schreitet	schritt	er ist geschritten
schweigen	be silent	er schweigt	schwieg	er hat geschwiegen
schwimmen	swim	er schwimmt	schwamm	er ist geschwommen
schwören	swear, promise	er schwört	schwor (schwur)	er hat geschworen
sehen	see	er sieht	sah	er hat gesehen
sein	be	er ist	war	er ist gewesen
senden	send	er sendet	sandte (sendete)	er hat gesandt (gesendet)
singen	sing	er singt	sang	er hat gesungen
sinken	sink	er sinkt	sank	er ist gesunken
sitzen	sit	er sitzt	saß	er hat gesessen
sprechen	speak	er spricht	sprach	er hat gesprochen
springen	jump	er springt	sprang	er ist gesprungen
stechen	sting	er sticht	stach	er hat gestochen
stehen	stand	er steht	stand	er hat gestanden
stehlen	steal	er stiehlt	stahl	er hat gestohlen
steigen	climb	er steigt	stieg	er ist gestiegen
sterben	die	er stirbt	starb	er ist gestorben
stoßen	push, nudge	er stößt	stieß	er hat gestoßen
streiten	fight, quarrel	er streitet	stritt	er hat gestritten
tragen	carry, wear	er trägt	trug	er hat getragen
treffen	meet, hit	er trifft	traf	er hat getroffen
treiben	drive, carry on	er treibt	trieb	er hat getrieben
treten	tread, step	er tritt	trat	er ist getreten
trinken	drink	er trinkt	trank	er hat getrunken
tun	do	er tut	tat	er hat getan
verbergen	hide	er verbirgt	verbarg	er hat verborgen
*verderben	spoil, go bad	er verdirbt	verdarb	er ist verdorben
vergessen	forget	er vergißt	vergaß	er hat vergessen
verlieren	lose	er verliert	verlor	er hat verloren
verschwinden	disappear	er verschwindet	verschwand	er ist verschwunden
wachsen	grow, increase	er wächst	wuchs	er ist gewachsen
waschen	wash	er wäscht	wusch	er hat gewaschen
weisen	point	er weist	wies	er hat gewiesen
wenden	turn	er wendet	wandte (wendete)	er hat gewandt (gewendet)

Infinitive	Meaning	Present	Imperfect	Perfect
werden	become	er wird	wurde	er ist geworden
werfen	throw	er wirft	warf	er hat geworfen
winden	wind, twist	er windet	wand	er hat gewunden
wissen	know, realise	er weiß	wußte	er hat gewußt
*ziehen	go, march, pull	er zieht	zog	er ist gezogen

6. *PASSIVE VOICE*

A. Formed by using the Past Participle of the verb with the appropriate tense of **werden**.

Infinitive — **geschlagen werden**

Present:	**ich werde ... geschlagen**
Imperfect:	**ich wurde ... geschlagen**
Perfect:	**Ich bin ... geschlagen worden**
Pluperfect:	**ich war ... geschlagen worden**
Future:	**ich werde ... geschlagen werden**
Conditional:	**ich würde .. geschlagen werden**
Future Perfect:	**ich werde ... geschlagen worden sein**
Conditional Perfect:	**ich würde ... geschlagen worden sein**

B. Only an accusative object in the Active Voice can become the subject of a sentence in the Passive Voice.

Mein Bruder schlägt den Ball.   Der Ball wird von meinem Bruder geschlagen.

C. The Passive Voice is frequently used in German and it is not necessary to avoid it. Where it is impossible to translate directly with the Passive Voice (*e.g.* with verbs taking a dative direct object), the following methods may be used:

either (*a*) Turn the sentence into the Active Voice:

    The book was given to me by my brother.
    Mein Bruder gab mir das Buch.

or   (*b*) Use **man** with the Active Voice:

    The book was given to me. **Man gab mir das Buch.**

or   (*c*) Use **es** with the Passive:

    He must be helped. **Es muß ihm geholfen werden.**

D. The English *by* with the Passive Voice is translated by **von**.

> **Er wurde von seinem Bruder gesehen.**

by means of is sometimes translated by **durch**.

> **Es wurde ihm durch die Post mitgeteilt.**

E. Note these constructions:
  (a) *There is (was)* + verbal noun ending with -ing:

  > There is (was) a great deal of singing. **Es wird (wurde) viel gesungen.**

  (b) *Can (could)* + passive infinitive:

  > He can (could) not be found. **Er ist (war) nicht zu finden.**

7. REFLEXIVE VERBS

A. With reflexive pronoun in the Accusative.

ich wasche mich	wir waschen uns
du wäschst dich	ihr wascht euch
er wäscht sich	sie waschen sich

B. With reflexive pronoun in the Dative.

ich wasche mir die Hände	wir waschen uns die Hände
du wäschst dir die Hände	ihr wascht euch die Hände
er wäscht sich die Hände	sie waschen sich die Hände

C. Imperative.

wasche dich!	wasch(e) dir die Hände!
wascht euch!	wascht euch die Hände!
waschen Sie sich!	waschen Sie sich die Hände!

D. Position of reflexive pronoun is as near as possible to the beginning of the sentence.

  (a) Take the infinitive phrase — **sich die Hände mit Seife waschen.**

  > *e.g.* **Wenn wir uns die Hände mit Seife waschen,** ...

(b) It often precedes the noun subject in the inverted word order.

Dann wusch sich mein Vater die Hände.

E. Note the reciprocal pronoun **sich** or **einander**.

Sie schreiben sich (or **einander**) **jede Woche.**
They write to each other every week.

F. The emphatic pronoun **selbst** is not a reflexive.

Ich werde es selbst tun.
I will do it myself.

8. *MODAL VERBS*

A. **müssen** — **er muß,   mußte,   hat gemußt**
   wollen — **er will,   wollte,   hat gewollt**
   können — **er kann,   konnte,   hat gekonnt**
   dürfen — **er darf,   durfte,   hat gedurft**
   mögen — **er mag,   mochte, hat gemocht**
   sollen — **er soll,   sollte,   hat gesollt**

Note:
(a) The infinitive form is used instead of the normal Past Participle if another infinitive is present.

Er hat es gekonnt.
Er hat es tun können.

(b) In subordinate clauses, the auxiliary precedes two infinitives.

Ich weiß, daß er morgen wird kommen können.

B. Uses of Modal verbs.

(a) **Müssen** implies compulsion, necessity.

Ich mußte gehen.   I had to go.
Ich mußte lachen.   I could not help laughing.
Ich muß es getan haben.   I must have done it.
Ich habe es tun müssen.   I have had to do it.

Note: must + negative is translated by **dürfen** + negative.

(b) **Wollen** implies wish, intention.

Ich will gehen.   I intend to go, I want to go.

(*cf.* **Ich werde gehen** — future indicative of **gehen** — a statement of what will happen, without any reference to intention.)

Er wollte eben (gerade) gehen. He was about to go.
Er will reich sein. He says he is rich.
Wir wollen gehen. Let's go.
Wollen wir gehen? Shall we go?

(c) **Können** implies ability.

Ich kann es tun. I am able to do it.
Ich konnte nicht umhin zu lachen. I could not help laughing.
Können Sie Deutsch? Do you speak German?
Es kann regnen. It may rain.
Er könnte kommen. He might come.
Ich kann nichts dagegen tun. I can do nothing about it.

(d) **Dürfen** implies permission (sometimes to dare).

Er darf gehen. He is allowed to go.
Wie darf er so frech sein? How dare he be so cheeky?

(e) **Mögen** implies liking, wish.

Ich mag es nicht. I do not like it.
Ich möchte gern wissen. I should like to know, I wonder.

Note: With **wie, wer, was, wo, wieviel** (plus usually **auch**) it often translates the English *ever*.

Wie groß er auch sein mag
Wie groß er auch sein möge } However big he is, may be
Wie groß er auch sei

(f) **Sollen** implies duty, moral obligation.

Du sollst nicht stehlen. Thou shalt not steal.
Note also: **Er soll reich sein.** He is said to be rich.
Ought is always the past tense of **sollen**.

(g) Difficult constructions:

Er hätte gehen können. He could have gone, would have been able to go.

Er hätte gehen müssen. He would have had to go.
Er hätte gehen wollen. He would have wanted to go.
Er hätte gehen dürfen. He would have been allowed to go.
Er hätte gehen mögen. He would have liked to go.
Er hätte gehen sollen. He ought to have gone.

9. *IMPERSONAL VERBS*

   A. All verbs connected with the weather, *e.g.* **es regnet, es schneit, es donnert, es blitzt, es dunkelt.**

   B. *There is.*
      (*a*) **es gibt**+*acc.* makes a general statement:
      Es gibt viele Leute in England.
      (*b*) **es ist**+*nom.* restricts locality or number (note also its plural):
      Es sind zwei Männer in meinem Garten.

   C. There are many other impersonal verbs and impersonal uses of verbs.

   es klopft, someone is knocking
   es klingelt, the bell is ringing
   es gelingt mir, I succeed
   es wundert mich, I am surprised
   es tut mir leid, I am sorry
   es tut mir weh, it hurts me, gives me pain
   es friert mich, I am cold
   mir ist (**zumute**), I feel
   mir wird kalt, I am getting cold
   es fehlt (**mangelt**) **mir an Geld,** I have no money
   es gefällt mir, it pleases me, I like it
   es schmeckt mir, I like it (the taste)

10. *CONJUGATION OF THE SUBJUNCTIVE*

    A. Endings for all tenses, all types of verbs: **-e, -est, -e, -en, -et, -en**

    B. *Present* (*a*) weak: **mach-e, -est, -e, -en, -et, -en**
                  (*b*) strong: **nehm-e, -est, -e, -en, -et, -en**

Imperfect (a) weak: **macht-e, -est, -e, -en, -et, -en**
(b) strong: **nähm-e, -est, -e, -en, -et, -en**

To form the Imperfect Subjunctive of strong verbs, take the 1st pers. Imperfect Indicative, add an Umlaut (¨) if possible and the Subjunctive endings.

C. Irregularities.
   (a) The only irregular present tense is **sein**:
   sei, seiest, sei, seien, seiet, seien
   (b) Of the few irregular Imperfect Subjunctives, there are:
   beginnen — begönne: brennen — brennte: helfen — hülfe; rennen — rennte; stehen — stünde; sterben — stürbe; werfen — würfe.

D. When the Present Subjunctive is identical with the Present Indicative, the Imperfect Subjunctive is often used (and vice versa).

11. *USES OF THE SUBJUNCTIVE*

A. Reported Speech.
   (a) In all reported speech, *e.g.* after such verbs as saying, hoping, thinking, fearing, asking.
   Er sagt, daß er krank sei.
   (b) The tense of the Subjunctive is that of the original speech.
   Er sagte: „Ich bin krank." Er sagte, daß er krank sei.

   The Perfect Subjunctive is often used for the Imperfect Indicative.
   Er sagte: „Ich war krank." Er sagt , daß er krank wäre or **Er sagte, daß er krank gewesen sei.**

   (c) The **daß** may be omitted, especially after **sagen**.
   Er sagte, er sei krank.
   (d) If there is certainty in the mind of the speaker that what he reports is definitely true, then the Indicative is retained. (If you are in doubt which form to use, use the Subjunctive.)
   Er sagte, er war krank.

(e) Imperative in Reported Speech.

Er sagte mir: „Gehen Sie ins Haus!" Er sagte, daß ich ins Haus gehen solle (or **möge**).

B. For the Imperative of 3rd pers. singular, use Present Subjunctive or **sollen**.

Er komme morgen. } Tell him to come
Er soll morgen kommen. } tomorrow.

C. Main Clauses.

(a) The Present Subjunctive expresses a wish you hope will be fulfilled.

Es lebe die Königin! Long live the Queen!

(b) The Imperfect Subjunctive expresses an unfulfillable wish. (Note the omission of **wenn**.)

Wäre er nur hier! If only he were here!

D. In Conditional sentences, the subordinate clause uses the Subjunctive; the main clause uses the Conditional.

Wenn ich es könnte, würde ich es tun. If I could, I would do it.

Strong verbs may use the Imperfect Subjunctive in the main clause instead of the Conditional.

Wenn ich ein Vöglein wäre, flöge ich zu dir.

Note: *If* plus a Present tense in English is translated by the same tense in German.

Wenn er nicht kommt, bleibe ich hier. If he does not come, I shall stay here.

E. With **wer, was, wie, wieviel, wo** (plus usually **auch**).

Wer er auch sei ... Whoever he may be ...
Was es auch koste ... Whatever it may cost ....

F. In clauses introduced by **als ob** or **als wenn** (*as if*); **damit** (*in order that*); **damit ... nicht** (*lest*); **so daß** (*in order that*).

Er rannte, damit er möglichst früh ankäme. He ran in order that he might arrive as early as possible.

Note:

(a) In modern German, **damit** tends to take an Indicative when used with the Present tense.

(b) When **so daß** means *with the result that* it is followed by the Indicative.

Er lief schnell, so daß er früh ankam. He ran quickly, with the result that he arrived early.

12. *WORD ORDER*

A. Main Clause. In the main clause, the verb is always the second idea in the whole sentence. If anything but the subject of the main verb begins the whole sentence (even if it is a long subordinate clause, but not an exclamation or the Vocative) the main verb precedes its subject (inverted order).

Der Garten liegt hinter dem Hause.
Hinter dem Hause liegt der Garten.
Ach, der Garten liegt hinter dem Hause!
Wo ich wohne, liegt der Garten hinter dem Hause.

B. In subordinate clauses the verb is at the end of its clause (transposed order).

Wir setzen ein Komma ein, wenn wir eine Pause machen.
Wenn wir eine Pause machen, setzen wir ein Komma ein.

Exceptions:

(a) When **wenn** is omitted, especially in conditional clauses. In that case the main clause is introduced by **so** or **dann**.

Machen wir eine Pause, dann setzen wir ein Komma ein.

Hätte er geschrieben, so wären wir nicht gekommen.

(b) Omission of **wenn** or **ob** after **als**.

Er sieht aus, als sei er krank.

(c) Omission of **daß** in reported speech.

Er sagt, er sei krank.

SUMMARY OF GRAMMAR

C. Co-ordinating conjunctions (**und, aber, allein, denn, sondern, oder**) join clauses of identical value, whether main or subordinate, so that the verbs in these clauses must be in identical positions.

Er kam früh nach Hause und brachte einen Freund mit.
Er fragte, ob er früh nach Hause kommen könne und einen Freund mitbringen dürfe.
Ich muß jetzt nach Hause gehen, denn ich will meine Aufgaben machen.

D. Objects. The Dative precedes the Accusative unless the Accusative is a pronoun.

Er gab mir das Buch.
Er gab es mir.
Er gab es seinem Bruder.

E. Adverbs. The normal order of adverbs is Time, Manner, Place. The adverb of Time often precedes the direct object.

Wir werden heute zu Fuß nach Freiburg wandern.
Ich werde heute nachmittag einen Spaziergang auf das Land machen.

13. *DECLENSION OF NOUNS*

FIRST DECLENSION

	Singular	*Plural*
N.	-	- or ¨
A.	-	- or ¨
G.	-s	- or ¨
D.	-	-n or ¨n

E.g.

N.	der Onkel	die Onkel
A.	den Onkel	die Onkel
G.	des Onkels	der Onkel
D.	dem Onkel	den Onkeln

or

N.	der Bruder	die Brüder
A.	den Bruder	die Brüder
G.	des Bruders	der Brüder
D.	dem Bruder	den Brüdern

To this group belong:

(a) All masculine and neuter nouns ending in **-el, -er, -en.**

(b) All neuters ending with **-chen, -lein.**

(c) All neuters beginning with **Ge-** and ending with **-e.**

(d) Only two feminines — **die Mutter** and **die Tochter.***
(both add Umlaut)

* Remember that no feminines change in the singular.

Note: Some masculines add an Umlaut in the plural, *e.g.*
Apfel, Bruder, Garten, Vogel, Laden, Vater, Kasten.

The only neuter to add the Umlaut is **das Kloster**, the monastery.

SECOND DECLENSION

Singular	Plural
N. -	-e or ⸚e
A. -	-e or ⸚e
G. -(e)s	-e or ⸚e
D. -(e)	-en or ⸚en

E.g.

N. **der Hund**	**die Hunde**
A. **den Hund**	**die Hunde**
G. **des Hunds**	**der Hunde**
D. **dem Hund(e)**	**den Hunden**

or

N. **der Baum**	**die Bäume**
A. **den Baum**	**die Bäume**
G. **des Baumes**	**der Bäume**
D. **dem Baum(e)**	**den Bäumen**

To this group belong:

(a) Most masculines of one syllable.

(b) All masculines ending in **-ich, -ig, -ing, -icht.** (Never add Umlaut in the plural)

(c) Feminines and neuters ending in **-nis** (*pl.* **-nisse**).

(d) A number of feminines of one syllable, *e.g.* **Bank, Hand, Kuh, Maus, Nacht, Stadt, Wand, Wurst.**

Note: Most masculines of one syllable add Umlaut. Examples of those that do not are **Hund, Tag.**

The only neuter to add Umlaut is **das Floß**, the raft.

THIRD DECLENSION

	Singular	Plural	
N.	-	-er	or ⸚er
A.	-	-er	or ⸚er
G.	-(e)s	-er	or ⸚er
D.	-(e)	-ern	or ⸚ern

E.g.

N.	das Buch	die Bücher
A.	das Buch	die Bücher
G.	des Buches	der Bücher
D.	dem Buch(e)	den Büchern

To this group belong:

(a) Most neuters of one syllable.

(b) Words ending in **-tum** (all neuter except **der Reichtum**, riches; **der Irrtum**, mistake).

(c) A few masculines of one syllable (**Wald, Mann, Rand**).

(d) *No Feminines*

Note: Most words add Umlaut in the plural.

FOURTH DECLENSION

	Singular	Plural
N.	-	(e)n
A.	-	(e)n
G.	-(e)s	(e)n
D.	-(e)	(e)n

E.g.

N.	die Frau	die Frauen
A.	die Frau	die Frauen
G.	der Frau	der Frauen
D.	der Frau	den Frauen

or

N.	das Ohr	die Ohren
A.	das Ohr	die Ohren

G. **des Ohres**	**der Ohren**
D. **dem Ohr(e)**	**den Ohren**

To this group belong:

(a) *All* feminines not in First or Second declensions.

(b) The following masculines: **Bauer***, **Motor**, **Nachbar***, **Staat**, **See**, **Strahl**, **Schmerz**, **Vetter**.

(c) The following neuters: **Auge**, **Bett**, **Ende**, **Hemd**, **Insekt**, **Interesse**, **Ohr**.

* Sometimes follows the first of the irregular declensions.

Note: No Umlaut is added in the plural.

IRREGULAR DECLENSION (1)

	Singular	Plural
N.	**-(e)**	**-en**
A.	**-en**	**-en**
G.	**-en**	**-en**
D.	**-en**	**-en**

E.g.

N.	**der Junge**	**die Jungen**
A.	**den Jungen**	**die Jungen**
G.	**des Jungen**	**der Jungen**
D.	**dem Jungen**	**den Jungen**

To this group belong:

(a) All masculine nouns ending in **-e**.

(b) Most masculine foreign nouns, *e.g.* **Kamerad**, **Polizist**, **Soldat**, **Student**.

(c) Most masculine titles, *e.g.* **Fürst**, **Graf**, **Herr***, **Oberst**, **Prinz**.

* **Herr** adds **-n** in the singular, **-en** in the plural.

Note: No Umlaut is added in the plural.

IRREGULAR DECLENSION (2)

	Singular	Plural
N.	**-e**	**-en**
A.	**-en**	**-en**
G.	**-ens**	**-en**
D.	**-en**	**-en**

E.g.

N. **der Name**	**die Namen**
A. **den Namen**	**die Namen**
G. **des Namens**	**der Namen**
D. **dem Namen**	**den Namen**

To this group belong:

(*a*) The following masculines: **Buchstabe, Friede, Name, Gedanke, Glaube, Wille.**

(*b*) neuter, **das Herz** (*Acc. sing.* **das Herz**).

Note: No Umlaut is added in the plural.

14. *DECLENSION OF ADJECTIVES*

A. After: **alle** (*plur.*) all **jener** that
der the **solcher** such
dieser this **welcher** which
jeder (*sing.*) each, every

	Masc.	*Fem.*	*Neut.*	*Plur.*
N.	-e	-e	-e	
A.		-e	-e	
G.				
D.				

Except in the above cases, the adjective ending is always **-en.**

	Masc.	*Fem.*
N.	**der junge Mann**	**die junge Frau**
A.	**den jungen Mann**	**die junge Frau**
G.	**des jungen Mannes**	**der jungen Frau**
D.	**dem jungen Mann(e)**	**der jungen Frau**

	Neut.	*Plur.*
N.	**das junge Kind**	**die jungen Leute**
A.	**das junge Kind**	**die jungen Leute**
G.	**des jungen Kindes**	**der jungen Leute**
D.	**dem jungen Kind(e)**	**den jungen Leuten**

B. After: **mein** my **euer** your (*plur.* of **dein**)
dein your **Ihr** your (polite form
sein his, its (her) *sing.* and *plur.*)
ihr her, its, their **ein** a
unser our **kein** no, not a

	Masc.	Fem.	Neut.	Plur.
N.	-er	-e	-es	
A.		-e	-es	
G.				
D.				

Except in the above cases, the adjective ending is always **-en.**

Masc.

- N. **mein kleiner Bruder**
- A. **meinen kleinen Bruder**
- G. **meines kleinen Bruders**
- D. **meinem kleinen Bruder**

Fem.

- N. **meine kleine Schwester**
- A. **meine kleine Schwester**
- G. **meiner kleinen Schwester**
- D. **meiner kleinen Schwester**

Neut.

- N. **mein kleines Kind**
- A. **mein kleines Kind**
- G. **meines kleinen Kindes**
- D. **meinem kleinen Kind(e)**

Plur.

- N. **meine kleinen Kinder, Brüder, Schwestern**
- A. **meine kleinen Kinder, Brüder, Schwestern**
- G. **meiner kleinen Kinder, Brüder, Schwestern**
- D. **meinen kleinen Kindern, Brüdern, Schwestern**

C. The adjective alone in front of a noun adds the case endings themselves, except for two Genitives.

	Masc.	Fem.	Neut.	Plur.
N.	-er	-e	-es	-e
A.	-en	-e	-es	-e
G.	**-EN**	-er	**-EN**	-er
D.	-em	-er	-em	-en

	Masc.	*Fem.*
N.	**roter Wein**	**rote Tinte**
A.	**roten Wein**	**rote Tinte**
G.	**roten Weines**	**roter Tinte**
D.	**rotem Wein(e)**	**roter Tinte**

	Neut.	*Plur.*
N.	**grünes Gras**	**rote Äpfel**
A.	**grünes Gras**	**rote Äpfel**
G.	**grünen Grases**	**roter Äpfel**
D.	**grünem Gras(e)**	**roten Äpfeln**

D. Note the adjective declension after numerals and plural words of quantity:

einige some	**viele** many
einzelne single	**wenige** very few
mehrere several	**ein paar** a few

N.	**viele gute Leute**	**zwei hohe Bäume**
A.	**viele gute Leute**	**zwei hohe Bäume**
G.	**vieler guten Leute**	**zweier hoher Bäume**
D.	**vielen guten Leuten**	**zwei hohen Bäumen**

(The Genitive form **vieler guter Leute** is possible but not advised.)

E. After **etwas, nichts, viel, wenig** the adjective has a capital letter and is declined:

N.	**etwas Gutes**
A.	**etwas Gutes**
G.	**etwas Guten**
D.	**etwas Gutem**

ander does not normally take a capital nowadays: **etwas anderes**.

F. Names of towns and districts used as adjectives usually add **-er** (in which case they are not declined). Otherwise use **von**.

Die Berliner Straßen but **die Straßen von Manchester.**

G. Most adjectives can be used as nouns, in which case they begin with a capital letter and must be declined according to the preceding article.

Die Alte spricht mit dem Blinden.
Er tut sein Bestes, sein Möglichstes.
Das ist das Beste, was ich gehört habe.

15. *USES OF CASES*

   A. *Nominative*

   (a) Subject of the sentence and the Vocative.

   Lieber Freund, Ihr Bruder ist nicht hier.

   (b) The complement of **sein, werden, bleiben, heißen** (*to be called*), **scheinen**.

   Er ist ein bekannter Arzt.
   Er scheint ein großer Mann (**zu sein** understood).

   B. *Accusative*

   (a) Direct object of most verbs.

   (b) After prepositions: **durch, für, ohne, gegen, um, bis, wider.**

   (c) Two object accusatives are used after **heißen** (*to call*), **lehren, nennen**.

   Er nennt mich seinen Freund.

   (d) In phrases of definite time or time how long.

   Den nächsten Tag reisten wir ab.

   (e) With compounds of prepositions with **hin-** or **her-**.

   Wir ruderten den Fluß hinauf.

   (f) In phrases of weights, measures, prices.

   Es kostet eine Mark das Pfund.

   (g) Sometimes to replace the English *with*.

   Den Hut in der Hand, ging er ins Haus.
   With his hat in his hand. . . .

   C. *Genitive*

   (a) To show possession: **Das Haus meines Vaters** or **meines Vaters Haus**.

   (b) After prepositions: **anstatt, trotz** (also takes Dative), **während, um . . . willen** (**um meines Bruders willen**), **wegen**.

SUMMARY OF GRAMMAR

Note: Other prepositions taking the Genitive but not so frequently met are:

ausserhalb, outside   **unterhalb,** below
innerhalb, inside   **diesseits,** on this side of
oberhalb, above   **jenseits,** beyond

(c) Phrases of indefinite time:

eines Tages, eines Abends. (*Note:* also **eines Nachts.**)

(d) After weights and measures when the noun is preceded by an adjective:

eine Flasche Wein but **eine Flasche roten Weins.**

D. *Dative*

(a) After prepositions: **mit, nach, bei, seit, von, zu, gemäß, zuwider, gegenüber, entgegen, außer, aus.**

(b) The indirect object, *e.g.* after **bringen, erzählen, geben, sagen.**

Er gab seinem Bruder das Buch.

(c) The direct object of certain verbs. The most usual are:

antworten, to answer   **gehören,** to belong to
befehlen, to command   **gelingen** (*impers.*),
begegnen, to meet   to succeed
danken, to thank   **glauben,** to believe
dienen, to serve   **gleichen,** to resemble
drohen, to threaten   **helfen,** to help
fehlen (*impers.*),   **sich nähern,** to approach
   to lack   **schmecken,** to taste
folgen, to follow   **raten,** to advise
gefallen, to please   **trauen,** to trust
gehorchen, to obey   **trotzen,** to defy

(d) Dative pronoun and the definite article often used with parts of the body, or articles of clothing.

Ich habe mir den Arm verletzt.
Ziehe dir den Regenmantel an.

E. The following prepositions take either the Accusative or the Dative. If change of place is indicated, the Accusative is used, otherwise the Dative:

an, auf, hinter, neben, in, über, unter, vor, zwischen.

Er lief in den Garten. He ran into the garden.
Er lief in dem Garten herum. He was running about inside the garden.

16. *COMPARISON OF ADJECTIVES*

A. All adjectives add **-er** in the comparative and **-st** in the superlative. Those of one vowel usually add the Umlaut.

lang	**länger**	**längst**
weise	**weiser**	**weisest**
interessant	**interessanter**	**interessantest**

B. Irregular.

groß	**größer**	**größt**
gut	**besser**	**best**
hoch	**höher**	**höchst** (drops **c** when a vowel follows the second **h**)
nah	**näher**	**nächst**
viel	**(mehr)**	**meist**

C. When a noun is after or understood after the comparative or superlative, the adjective ending is added.

Dieser Apfel ist der süßeste von allen.

D. *Note:* as ... as: **so groß wie,** as big as
-er than: **größer als,** bigger than
-er and -er: **immer heißer,** hotter and hotter

17. *COMPARISON OF ADVERBS*

A. **schön, schöner, am schönsten**

B. When no noun is possible after the comparative or superlative, the adverbial form is used.

Hier ist der Fluß am breitesten.
Er studiert am fleißigsten.

SUMMARY OF GRAMMAR

C. Irregular.

bald	eher	am ehesten
gern	lieber	am liebsten
wenig	weniger ⎫	am wenigsten
	minder ⎭	am mindesten

D. Special forms.

äußerst, extremely   **jüngst,** lately
erstens, first of all   **meistens,** usually
frühestens, at the earliest   **mindestens,** at least
höchst, extremely   **spätestens,** at the latest
höchstens, at the most   **wenigstens,** at least

E. The ... the ...: **je ... desto (um so, je)**

Je höher wir steigen, desto (um so, je) kälter wird es.

18. PERSONAL PRONOUNS

A.
N. **ich**	**du**	**er**	**sie**	**es**
A. **mich**	**dich**	**ihn**	**sie**	**es**
G. **meiner**	**deiner**	**seiner**	**ihrer**	**seiner**
(mein)	**(dein)**	**(sein)**	**(ihr)**	**(sein)**
D. **mir**	**dir**	**ihm**	**ihr**	**ihm**
N. **wir**	**ihr**	**sie**	**Sie** (polite form)	
A. **uns**	**euch**	**sie**	**Sie**	
G. **unser**	**euer**	**ihrer**	**Ihrer**	
D. **uns**	**euch**	**ihnen**	**Ihnen**	

B. The short forms of the Genitive are used in poetry and a few fixed expressions.

C. When the third person refers to things and is governed by a preposition, a compound is formed with **da-** (**dar-** before a vowel).

Wo ist mein Tennisschläger? Ich will damit spielen.
Er deckte den Tisch mit einem Tuch und stellte die Teller darauf.

(*Note:* **darnach** is found as well as **danach**.)

D. The pronoun takes its gender from the noun it refers to.

Ich kann diesen Apfel nicht essen, er ist noch nicht reif.

19. *RELATIVE PRONOUNS*

A.
	Singular			Plural
	Masc.	Fem.	Neut.	
N.	der	die	das	die
A.	den	die	das	die
G.	dessen	deren	dessen	deren
D.	dem	der	dem	denen

B. The relative pronoun takes its number and gender from the noun or pronoun it refers back to (the antecedent); the case comes from its function in its own clause. A relative pronoun introduces a subordinate clause.

Der Bruder des Jungen, der gestern bei Ihnen war, ist wieder hier.
In dem Roman, den ich eben gekauft habe, ist etwas sehr Interessantes.

Die Frau, in deren Haus ich wohne, ist Witwe.
Die Reisenden, denen ich zehn Mark lieh, haben mir das Geld zurückgegeben.

C. **Welcher, welche, welches, welche** may be used for the relative pronoun in all cases except the Genitive, but it is not usually considered good style.

D. He who ... } **wer** or { **derjenige, der** ...
   Those who ... }   { **diejenigen, die** ...

E. A relative pronoun referring to things and governed by a preposition, usually contracts to **wo-** (**wor-** before a vowel).

Der Ball, mit dem ich spiele ...
   womit ich spiele ...

F. Relative pronoun of time.

Eines Tages, als ...

G. **Was** is used as the relative pronoun in the following cases:

(a) After **alles, etwas, nichts, wenig.**

Alles, was er sagt, ist gut.

SUMMARY OF GRAMMAR 35

(b) After an adjective used as a neuter noun.

Das ist das Beste, was ich tun kann.

(c) When the pronoun refers to a whole clause.

Er arbeitet tüchtig, was uns erfreut.

20. *INTERROGATIVE PRONOUNS*

A.
	Masc. and *Fem.*	*Neut.*
N.	**wer**	**was**
A.	**wen**	**was**
G.	**wessen**	
D.	**wem**	

B. Neuter interrogative pronoun preceded by a preposition usually combines with **wo-** (**wor-** before a vowel).

Womit spielst du denn?
Woran denken Sie?

C. A subordinate clause introduced by an interrogative pronoun must use the Subjunctive (indirect question).

21. *POSSESSIVE PRONOUNS*

A. There are three forms:

1. **der meinige, die meinige, das meinige, die meinigen** (declined like the definite article and an adjective), **der deinige, der seinige, der ihrige, der unsrige, der eurige, der Ihrige.** This is old-fashioned.

2. **der meine, die meine, das meine,** etc. (declined like definite article and an adjective).

3. **meiner, meine, meines** (declined like **dieser**). This form is the best.

Mein Buch ist rot, das Ihrige
                      das Ihre   **⎬ ist blau.**
                      Ihres

B. *Note:* A friend of mine. **Ein Freund von mir.**

C. **die Meinigen, die Deinigen,** etc. (*i.e.* plural and spelt with a capital letter) means *family*.

Die Meinigen kommen heute abend zurück.
My family are returning to-night.

22. DEMONSTRATIVE PRONOUNS

A. der, die, das, die, etc.
dieser, diese, dieses, diese, etc.
Das ist mein Hut, wem gehört dieser?

B. derselbe, dieselbe, dasselbe, dieselbe, etc.
Jene Frau trägt immer denselben Mantel.

C. derjenige, diejenige, dasjenige, diejenigen, etc.
Diejenigen, die es nicht wissen, müssen es jetzt lernen.

(Better **Wer es nicht weiß, muß es jetzt lernen.**
   Die, die es nicht wissen, müssen es jetzt lernen.)

23. TRANSLATION OF THE ENGLISH PRESENT PARTICIPLE

Use the German Present Participle only as a simple adjective.

die aufgehende Sonne, the rising sun

In all other cases, eliminate the English Present Participle by using one of the following constructions:

1. Simple infinitive (without **zu**) after: **bleiben, fühlen, helfen, hören, lehren, lernen, machen, sehen.**
   Er sah mich kommen. He saw me coming.

2. Infinitive with **zu** when preceded by *of* and depending on a noun or when dependent on an adjective.
   Das Vergnügen, Sie zu begleiten. The pleasure of accompanying you.
   Es ist angenehm, hier zu sitzen. It is pleasant sitting here.

3. Past Participle after **kommen.**
   Er kam ins Haus gelaufen. He came running into the house.

4. A relative clause.
   Ein Mann, der im Ausland reiste. A man travelling abroad.

SUMMARY OF GRAMMAR

5. An adjective phrase.

   Ein im Ausland reisender Mann. A man travelling abroad.

6. **Ohne ... zu, anstatt ... zu.**

   Ohne ein Wort zu sagen, ging er hinaus. He went out without saying a word.

   Anstatt zu arbeiten, spielt er immer. He is always playing instead of working.

7. **Ohne daß, anstatt daß** when the Present Participle is a verbal noun.

   Er ging durch das Zimmer, ohne daß ich ihn sah. He went through the room without my seeing him.

8. Subordinate clause with **da, weil, indem, während, nachdem, ehe, bevor.**

   Ehe ich ins Bett gehe, trinke ich eine Tasse Kaffee. Before going to bed ...

   Da ich mich müde fühlte, ging ich ins Bett. Feeling tired ...

9. By a verbal noun when it is the subject or object, or sometimes after *while*.

   Das Lernen ist schwer. Learning is difficult.
   Beim Fußballspielen. While playing football.

10. By a noun with **bei** when preceded in English by *in* or *on*.

    Beim Verkauf. On selling.
    Bei unsrer Ankunft ... On arriving (*i.e.*, when we arrived ...).

11. **dadurch, daß ...** to translate *by*.

    Er verdient dadurch viel Geld, daß er den ganzen Tag arbeitet. He earns a lot of money by working all day.

12. Finite verbs to describe simultaneous or consecutive actions.

    Sie lag im Bette und las. She lay in bed reading.
    Er stieg ins Auto und machte die Tür hinter sich zu. He got into the car, shutting the door behind him.

24. NUMERALS

A. Cardinals

1	**eins**	19	**neunzehn**
2	**zwei**	20	**zwanzig**
3	**drei**	21	**einundzwanzig**
4	**vier**	22	**zweiundzwanzig**
5	**fünf**	30	**dreißig**
6	**sechs**	40	**vierzig**
7	**sieben**	50	**fünfzig**
8	**acht**	60	**sechzig**
9	**neun**	70	**siebzig**
10	**zehn**	80	**achtzig**
11	**elf**	90	**neunzig**
12	**zwölf**	100	**hundert**
13	**dreizehn**	101	**hundert(und)eins**
14	**vierzehn**	200	**zweihundert**
15	**fünfzehn**	202	**zweihundert(und)zwei**
16	**sechzehn**	1000	**tausend**
17	**siebzehn**	1003	**tausend(und)drei**
18	**achtzehn**	1100	**tausendeinhundert**

1959 **neunzehnhundertneunundfünfzig**

Notes:

(a) **ein** before a noun is declined: **Tausend und eine Nacht.**

(b) **Um ein Uhr.**
    Es hat eins geschlagen.
    Vor ein paar Tagen.

(c) *two* as an adjective is best translated by **beide**.
    Heinrich und seine beiden Brüder.
    Ihr seid beide zu jung.

(d) **Es waren Hunderte (Tausende) von Menschen da.**

B. Ordinals (*i.e.* adjectives)

der (die, das) erste
        der zweite
        der dritte
        der fünfte
        der neunzehnte
        der zwanzigste

SUMMARY OF GRAMMAR

der einundzwanzigste
der dreißigste
der hundert(und)erste

Notes:

(a) From 20 onwards add **-ste**.

(b) The ordinal numerals are treated as adjectives and must be declined.

(c) In titles the numeral is spelt with a capital letter.

Friedrich der Erste.

C. *Fractions*

$\frac{1}{2}$	**halb, die Hälfte**	$\frac{5}{8}$	**fünf Achtel**
$\frac{1}{3}$	**das Drittel**	$1\frac{1}{2}$	**anderthalb**
$\frac{1}{4}$	**das Viertel**	$2\frac{1}{2}$	**zweieinhalb**
$\frac{1}{5}$	**das Fünftel**	$3\frac{1}{2}$	**dreieinhalb**

Note: half my money, **die Hälfte meines Geldes**
half an hour, **eine halbe Stunde**
a quarter of an hour, **eine Viertelstunde**

D. **erstens,** firstly   **drittens,** thirdly
   zweitens, secondly   **viertens,** fourthly

E. **einmal,** once   **zum erstenmal,** for the first time
   zweimal, twice   **zum letztenmal,** for the last time
   dreimal, three times   **noch einmal,** once more

F. **einerlei,** of one kind   **vielerlei,** of many kinds
   zweierlei, of two kinds   **allerlei,** of all kinds
   dreierlei, of three kinds

Note: **es ist mir einerlei,** it is all the same to me.

G. **einfach,** simple, not complex   **einfältig,** simple, stupid
   zweifach, twofold   **zweifältig,** twofold
   dreifach, threefold   **dreifältig,** threefold

H. **ein paar,** a few, is undeclined.

   mit ein paar Freunden, with a few friends.

but **Er kaufte ein Paar Handschuhe.** He bought a pair of gloves.

I. **wenig, viel** are undeclined in the singular before a noun.

> **Er hat nur wenig Geld.** He has only a little (very little) money.

but **Es waren nur wenige Menschen da.** There were only a few people there.

> **Ich habe viel Zeit zu lesen.** I have lots of time to read.

but **Wir sehen viele Burgen am Rhein.** We see lots of castles on the Rhine.

(*Note:* **wenig** means *only a few, only a little*; *cf.* **einige** below.)

J. **einige**, a few, several, some.

einige seiner Freunde, several of his friends.

Note: **Ich mußte einige Zeit warten.** I had to wait a little (some) time.

K. *Measurements*

Masculine and neuter nouns do not normally take the plural form; feminine nouns do.

Die Mauer ist 10 Meter hoch und 30 Meter lang.
Zwei Kilo Fleisch zu 80 Pfennig das Pfund.
Drei Pfund Butter.
Zwei Glas Bier.
Zwei Tassen Tee.
Zwei Flaschen Wein.
Zwei Mark zwanzig Pfennig.

Note: Remember **zwei Marken** is short for **zwei Briefmarken,** two stamps.

25. *TIME, DATES, AGE*

   A. *Time of day*

Wieviel Uhr ist es?	What time is it?
Es ist ein (zwei) Uhr	It is one (two) o'clock
Es ist halb sechs	It is half past five
Es ist zwanzig Minuten nach sieben	It is twenty past seven
Es ist zwanzig Minuten vor acht	It is twenty to eight

SUMMARY OF GRAMMAR

Es ist Viertel nach zehn ⎫
Es ist Viertel elf ⎬ It is a quarter past ten
Es ist Viertel vor zehn It is a quarter to ten
Es ist Mittag (Mitter- It is midday (midnight)
  nacht)
Um wieviel Uhr? At what time?
Um sechs Uhr At six o'clock
Gegen sechs Uhr About six o'clock

B. *Kinds of time*

1. Time how long: Accusative, sometimes followed by **lang**.

   Eine Stunde (lang) For an hour
   Note: **Lange** For a long time

2. Time when: Accusative (sometimes follows the preposition **an** with the Dative).

   Jeden Tag Every day
   Zweimal die Woche Twice a week
   Letzten Mittwoch Last Wednesday
   Nächstes Jahr Next year
   Am Abend In the evening
   Den (am) nächsten ⎫
     Tag ⎬ The next day
   Den (am) folgenden ⎭
     Tag

3. Time ago: **vor** with the Dative.

   Vor einigen Jahren A few years ago
   Vor kurzem A short time ago

4. Time from now: **auf** with the Accusative.

   Auf eine Woche For a week
   Auf immer For ever
   Note: **Ab heute** From to-day

5. Time started in the past and uncompleted. **seit** with the Dative and the simple tense.

   Er ist seit einer He has been ill for a week
     Woche krank
   Er war schon seit He had been ill for a week
     einer Woche krank

6. Indefinite time: Genitive.

Eines Tages One day   **Eines Nachts** One night

C. *Other phrases of time*

morgens	A.M., every morning
abends	P.M., every evening
bei Tage (Nacht)	during the day (night)
bei Tagesanbruch **bei Sonnenaufgang**	at dawn
bei Sonnenuntergang	at dusk
morgen	to-morrow
übermorgen	the day after to-morrow
morgen über acht Tage	a week to-morrow
morgen über vierzehn Tage	a fortnight to-morrow
morgen früh	to-morrow morning
morgen abend	to-morrow evening
heute morgen (abend)	this morning (evening)
gestern	yesterday
vorgestern	the day before yesterday
gestern vor einer Woche	a week yesterday

D. *Dates*

(Der) Montag, Dienstag, Mittwoch, Donnerstag, Freitag, Sonnabend (or **Samstag**), **Sonntag**

(Der) Januar, Februar, März, April, Mai, Juni, Juli, August, September, Oktober, November, Dezember

(Der) Frühling, Sommer, Herbst, Winter

Den wievielten haben wir heute? **Der wievielte ist heute?**	What is the date to-day?
Wir haben heute den ersten Mai **Es ist heute der erste Mai**	It is May 1st
Er kommt Sonntag	He is coming on Sunday
Er kommt sonntags	He comes every Sunday
Er kommt erst Montag	He is not coming until Monday
Er bleibt bis Dienstag	He will stay until Tuesday

Im August	In August
Im Herbst	In autumn
Im Jahre 1957	In 1957
Er ist 1950 geboren	He was born in 1950
Zu Ostern (Pfingsten, Weihnachten)	At Easter (Whitsuntide, Christmas)

E. *Age*

Wie alt sind Sie?	How old are you?
Ich bin fünfzehn Jahre alt	I am fifteen

26. *PREPOSITIONAL PHRASES*

A. Prepositions with the Accusative only.

Durch

Durch einen Unfall	As a result of an accident
Durch Zufall	By chance
Die ganze Nacht hindurch	Throughout the night

Für

Man hält ihn für einen Narren	They think he is a fool
Er interessiert sich für Briefmarken	He is interested in stamps

Ohne

Ohne mich	Without me, if it had not been for me
Ohne Zweifel	Without doubt
Ohne weiteres	Without further ado

Gegen

Gegen Ende des Jahres	Towards the end of the year
Gegen seinen Bruder ist er immer gut	He is always kind to his brother
Gegen (*or* gen) **Norden (Süden)**	To the north (south)
Freundlich gegen	Friendly to
Höflich gegen	Polite to
Grausam gegen	Cruel to

Um

Es ist um ihn geschehen	It is all over with him
Um seines Bruders willen	For his brother's sake
Betteln um	To beg for
Bitten um	To ask for
Streiten um	To fight for

Bis

Wir fahren bis Hannover	We are going as far as Hanover
Er fiel bis an den Hals ins Wasser	He fell up to the neck in the water

Wider

Wider alle Erwartung	Contrary to all expectation
Wider meinen Willen	Against my wishes, against my will

B. Prepositions with Dative only.

Aus

Er stammt aus Bayern	He comes from Bavaria
Der Stuhl ist aus Holz gemacht	The chair is made of wood
Er tat es aus Liebe zu seiner Mutter	He did it for love of his mother
Aus Furcht vor der Gefahr	For fear of danger
Was ist aus ihm geworden?	What has become of him?
Aus diesem Grunde	For this reason
Bestehen aus	To consist of

Außer

Er war außer sich vor Freude	He was beside himself with joy
Außer dem Gelde	Besides (in addition to) the money
Außer Gefahr	Out of danger
Außerdem	Besides, in addition

Bei

Die Schlacht bei Waterloo	The battle of Waterloo
Das findet man bei Goethe	That is in Goethe
Er wohnt bei Frau Schmidt	He lives at Mrs Smith's (c/o Mrs Smith)
Er ist bei der Arbeit	He is at work
Beim Buchhändler	In the bookshop
Bei meiner Ankunft	On my arrival
Bei uns	At our house
Ich habe kein Geld bei mir	I have no money with me
Bei diesen Worten	At these words
Bei dieser Gelegenheit	On this occasion

Gegenüber

Er wohnt dem Rathaus gegenüber	He lives opposite the town-hall
Seinem Vater gegenüber	In the presence of (towards) his father

Gemäß

Dem Plan gemäß	According to the plan

Mit

Mit der Post	By post
Mit der Elektrischen (Straßenbahn)	By tram
Mit dem Zug (Dampfer, Fahrrad)	By train (steamer, bicycle)
Mit der Zeit	In time
Mit Tränen in den Augen	With tears in the eyes
Mit der größten Schwierigkeit	With the greatest difficulty
Mit lauter Stimme	In a loud voice

Nach

Meiner Meinung nach	In my opinion
Wir fahren nach Italien	We are going to Italy
Er fragte nach meiner Adresse	He asked for my address

Wir schickten nach dem Arzt	We sent for the doctor
Es roch nach Fisch	There was a smell of fish
Nach Tische	After the meal
Nach Hause gehen	To go home
Der Reihe nach	In turns
Nach und nach	Gradually

Seit

Ich bin seit drei Wochen hier	I have been here for three weeks
Ich lernte seit vier Jahren Deutsch	I had been learning German for four years

Von

Was denken Sie von dem Buche?	What do you think of the book?
Das versteht sich von selbst	That is obvious
Von oben bis unten	From top to bottom

Zu

Zu Mittag essen wir um Viertel nach eins	We lunch at quarter past one
Zu Ostern (Weihnachten, Pfingsten)	At Easter (Christmas, Whitsuntide)
Zwei Briefmarken zu 25 Pfennig	Two 25 Pfennig stamps
Zu Fuß (Pferde)	On foot (horseback)
Hotel zum Roten Löwen	Red Lion Hotel
Zum Beispiel	For example
Zu Hause	At home
Zum Glück	Fortunately
Zum Teil	In part
Er sprang zum Fenster hinaus	He jumped out of the window
Er war zu allem bereit	He was ready for anything

C. Prepositions with the Dative or Accusative.

An

Wir saßen am Tische	We were sitting at table
Bonn liegt am Rhein	Bonn lies on the Rhine

Am Ufer eines Flusses	On the banks of a river
Es fehlt (mangelt) mir an Gelde (*dat.*)	I have no money
Aus Mangel an (*dat.*)	For lack of
Leiden an (*dat.*)	To suffer from
Wir setzten uns an den Tisch	We sat down at the table
Denken an (*acc.*)	To think of
Erinnern an (*acc.*)	To remind of
Sich gewöhnen an (*acc.*)	To get used to
Glauben an (*acc.*)	To believe in

Auf

Auf der Straße sein	To be in the street
Auf die Straße gehen	To go into the street
Auf dem Lande sein	To be in the country
Auf das Land gehen	To go into the country
Auf dem Felde sein	To be in the fields
Auf das Feld gehen	To go into the fields
Auf der Post sein	To be at the post-office
Auf die Post gehen	To go to the post-office
Auf dem Markt sein	To be at market
Auf den Markt gehen	To go to the market
Auf englisch	In English
Auf Wiedersehen	Au revoir, good-bye
Aufs Geratewohl	At random
Auf immer (ewig)	For ever
Auf diese Weise	In this way
Auf die Jagd gehen	To go hunting
Auf frischer Tat ertappt	Caught in the act
Ich verreise auf 14 Tage	I am going away for a fortnight
Ich freue mich auf Ihren Besuch	I am looking forward to your visit
Auf einmal	Suddenly
Sich auf den Weg machen	To set off
Er kam auf mich zu	He came up to me
Er war stolz auf den Hund	He was proud of the dog
Warten auf (*acc.*)	To wait for

Achtgeben auf (*acc.*)	To take care of
Sich verlassen auf (*acc.*)	To rely on
Antworten auf (*acc.*)	To reply to (*e.g.*, a letter)
Bestehen auf (*acc.*)	To insist on

In

Ins Freie	Into the open air
Bis tief in die Nacht hinein	Far into the night
Ins Kino (Theater) gehen	To go to the pictures (theatre)
Ins Bett gehen	To go to bed
In die Schule (Kirche) gehen	To go to school (church)
In Frankreich	In France
In ganz Frankreich	In the whole of France
Im Begriffe sein	To be about to
Er kam in dem Dorfe an	He arrived in the village
Im Gegenteil	On the contrary
In dieser Weise	In this way
In Hemdsärmeln	In his shirt sleeves
Im Notfall	In case of need
Im Freien	In the open air
Die Hände in den Taschen	With his hands in his pockets

Über

Wir reisen über Köln	We are going via Cologne
Die Reise dauert über 24 Stunden	The journey lasts more than 24 hours
Er redet über die Musik	He is talking about music
Ich freue mich über Ihren Besuch	I am pleased at your visit
Klagen über (*acc.*)	To complain about
Lachen über (*acc.*)	To laugh at
Spotten über (*acc.*)	To mock at
Sich wundern über (*acc.*)	To be surprised at
Sich ärgern über (*acc.*)	To get angry about

Unter

Unter den Zuschauern	Among the onlookers (audience)

Unter der Regierung Karls des Großen	In the reign of Charles the Great
Unter dieser Bedingung	On this condition

Vor

Ich habe Furcht vor ihm / **Ich fürchte mich vor ihm**	I am afraid of him
Er rettete mich vor dem Tode	He saved me from death
Sie zitterte vor Angst	She was trembling with fear
Er schrie vor Schmerzen	He screamed with pain
Ich weinte vor Freude	I wept with joy
Er warnte mich vor dem Manne	He warned me against the man
Er war rot vor Zorn	He was red with anger
Er ging an dem Hause vorbei (vorüber)	He went past the house
Vor allen Dingen / **Vor allem**	Above all
Der Sommer ist vorbei	Summer is past
Er lächelte vor sich hin	He smiled to himself

27. *OTHER USEFUL PHRASES*

Wer (ist) da?	Who is there?
Ich bin's	It is I
Ach, Sie sind's!	Oh, it is you
All mein Geld / **Mein ganzes Geld**	All my money
Ganz Deutschland / **Das ganze Deutschland**	All Germany
Er war der Meinung, daß ...	He was of the opinion that ...
Es ist nicht der Mühe wert	It is not worth the trouble
Es war klar	It was obvious
Er lief die Straße entlang	He ran along the street
Jenseits des Berges	On the far side of the hill
Diesseits des Flusses	On this side of the river
Wie schade!	What a pity
Es tut mir leid	I am sorry
Der Fuß tut mir weh	My foot is hurting

Was ist los?	What's wrong, what's going on?
Fröhliche Weihnachten	A Merry Christmas
Ein Glückliches Neujahr	A Happy New Year
Noch nicht	Not yet
Noch nie	Never before
Noch einmal	Once more
Noch ein Glas Milch	Another glass of milk
Ein bißchen Brot	A little bit of bread
Aus dem Deutschen ins Englische	From German into English
Es war einmal ein Mann . . .	Once upon a time there was a man . . .
Nehmen Sie es mir nicht übel	Don't be cross with me
Ich bitte um Verzeihung	I beg your pardon
Sehr gerne	Willingly
Ich mache das sehr gern	I like doing that
Ich mache das sehr ungern	I do not like doing that
Ich möchte gern wissen	I would like to know, I wonder
Ich lasse mich ungern photographieren	I do not like being photographed
Ich lasse mir ein Haus bauen	I am having a house built
Ich ließ mir die Haare schneiden	I had my hair cut
Wir ließen den Arzt holen	We sent for the doctor
Wir machen einen Ausflug nach . . .	We are going on a trip to . . .
Wir hatten Glück (Pech)	We were lucky (unlucky)
Du hast recht (unrecht)	You are right (wrong)
Er hatte Durst (Hunger)	He was thirsty (hungry)
Es macht nichts	It doesn't matter
Er stellte mir viele Fragen	He asked me a lot of questions

28. *DIFFICULT TRANSLATIONS*

A. German.

Da

1. Adverb

Da steht das Haus	There is the house

SUMMARY OF GRAMMAR

2. Subordinating conjunction (verb at the end of the clause).

Da er krank ist, kann er nicht kommen   As he is ill . . .

Hin- and **her-**

Both used with verbs as prefixes of motion, and are therefore not used with such verbs as **sein, stehen, bleiben.**

Her- *hither, from that place*, e.g. **woher?** from what place?

Indicates normally movement towards the speaker, so should not be combined with **gehen.**

Where do you come from?	**Wo kommen Sie her?**
He came running downstairs	**Er kam die Treppe heruntergelaufen**
He jumped out of the window (*the speaker being outside*)	**Er sprang zum Fenster heraus**

Hin- *hence, to that place*, e.g. **wohin?** to what place?

Indicates normally movement away from the speaker, so is not usually combined with **kommen.**

Where are you going?	**Wo gehen Sie hin?** **Wohin denn?**
He jumped out of the window (*the speaker being inside*)	**Er sprang zum Fenster hinaus**
He ran downstairs (*away from the speaker*)	**Er lief die Treppe hinunter**

Wenn means either *if* or *when*.

B. English.

AFTER

Preposition: After dinner	**Nach dem Essen**
Conjunction: After he had eaten	**Nachdem er gegessen hatte, . . .**
Adverb: Twenty years after	**Zwanzig Jahre später**
He came afterwards	**Er kam nachher**

ALL

Singular: All my money	**All mein Geld, mein ganzes Geld**

Plural: All my friends — **All meine Freunde**
All the others — **Alle anderen, die übrigen**
All (everything) that he says — **Alles, was er sagt**

AS

When. As he sat down ... — **Als er sich hinsetzte ...**
Because. As he is ill ... — **Da er krank ist ...**
While. As he was walking ... — **Während er ging ...**

As big as — **So groß wie**

ASK

Questions, inquiries

He asked me who I was — **Er fragte mich, wer ich sei**

He asked the police for my address — **Er erkundigte sich bei der Polizei nach meiner Adresse**

He asked me lots of questions — **Er stellte mir viele Fragen**

Requests (also *beg* but see *beg* below)

He asked me to help him — **Er bat mich, ihm zu helfen**

He asked my pardon — **Er bat um Verzeihung**

Invite

He asked me to lunch — **Er lud mich zum Mittagessen ein**

Require, demand

He asked for the bill — **Er verlangte die Rechnung**

BE

1. German **haben**

to be { lucky / right / wrong / afraid / inclined / hungry / thirsty } { **Glück** / **recht** / **unrecht** / **Angst** / **Lust** / **Hunger** / **Durst** } **haben**

SUMMARY OF GRAMMAR

2. English Passive Voice but German reflexive verbs

to be pleased (about)	**sich freuen (über + *acc*.)**
to be afraid (of)	**sich fürchten (vor + *dat*.)**
to be interested (in)	**sich interessieren (für + *acc*.)**
to be amused (at)	**sich amüsieren (über + *acc*.)**
to be surprised (at)	**sich wundern (über + *acc*.)**
to be annoyed (with, at)	**sich ärgern (über + *acc*.)**

BEFORE

Preposition: Before his arrival	**Vor seiner Ankunft**
Conjunction: Before he arrived	**Bevor (ehe) er ankam**
Adverb: I have seen this before	**Ich habe das schon (früher) gesehen**

BEG

Plead

He begged me to go with him	**Er bat mich, ihn zu begleiten**

Asks alms, act as a beggar

He begs every day in this street	**Er bettelt jeden Tag in dieser Straße**

DOWNSTAIRS

Adverb of rest: He is downstairs	**Er ist unten**
Adverb of motion: He goes downstairs	**Er geht die Treppe hinunter**

ENJOY

How did you enjoy the opera?	**Wie hat Ihnen die Oper gefallen?**
Did you enjoy the meal?	**Hat Ihnen das Essen geschmeckt?**
Enjoy yourselves	**Amüsieren Sie sich gut!**
He enjoys good health	**Er erfreut sich guter Gesundheit**

FEW

Einige: Some, a few
Wenige: Only a few

I have bought a few books	Ich habe einige Bücher gekauft
A few (some) of his friends ...	Einige seiner Freunde ...
After some time	Nach einiger Zeit
A few pounds of pears	Einige Pfund Birnen
After a very few days	Nach wenigen Tagen
He has very few friends	Er hat wenige Freunde
He has very little money	Er hat wenig Geld

GET

Become: He is getting old	Er wird alt.
Fetch: They got the water from the well	Sie holen das Wasser aus dem Brunnen
Buy: Will you get me some things in town?	Wollen Sie mir einiges in der Stadt besorgen?
Receive: I got your letter this morning	Ich erhielt heute morgen Ihren Brief
Arrive: You got home late	Sie kamen spät nach Hause
Climb: They got into the train	Sie stiegen in der Zug ein
They got out of the tram	Sie stiegen aus der Elektrischen (aus)

Note: **kriegen** meaning *to get* is used in speech but not in good prose.

GO

We are going for a walk	⎰ Wir machen einen Spaziergang ⎱ Wir gehen spazieren
They are going for a trip	Sie machen einen Ausflug
They are going for a picnic	Sie halten ein Picknick
He is going abroad	Er reist ins Ausland
We are going (by car or train) to London	Wir fahren nach London
Our train goes at 6 o'clock	Unser Zug fährt um sechs Uhr ab

SUMMARY OF GRAMMAR

IF: When *if* means *whether* use **ob**, otherwise use **wenn**

I do not know if he will come	**Ich weiß nicht, ob . . .**
If he comes early . . .	**Wenn er früh kommt, . . .**

After **wenn** use the same tense as in English in the **wenn** clause.

If it rains, we will stay at home	**Wenn es regnet, bleiben wir zu Hause**
If it rained, we would stay at home	**Wenn es regnete, würden wir zu Hause bleiben**

INSIDE

Adverb of rest: He is inside	**Er ist drinnen**
Adverb of motion: He goes inside	**Er geht hinein**
Preposition of place: Inside the town	**Innerhalb der Stadt**
Preposition of time: Within two hours	**Binnen zwei Stunden**

KNOW

Kennen: To have met, to know by acquaintance, so followed by direct object.
Wissen: To know in the mind, to realise, to know that . . .; usually followed by a clause.

I know the man (the book)	**Ich kenne den Mann (das Buch)**
I do not know what to do	**Ich weiß nicht, was ich tun soll**
My brother is ill. Yes, I know	**Mein Bruder ist krank. Ja, ich weiß es**
Note: Do you know German?	**Können Sie Deutsch?**

LEAVE

A place: **verlassen.** He left the house at 9 o'clock	**Er verließ das Haus um neun Uhr**
Not take: **liegenlassen.** I left the book on the table	**Ich ließ das Buch auf dem Tische liegen**

Depart: **abfahren.** The train leaves at midday — **Der Zug fährt um zwölf Uhr mittags ab**

OUTSIDE

Adverb of rest: He is outside — **Er ist draußen**

Adverb of motion: He goes outside — **Er geht hinaus**

Preposition: Outside the town — **Außerhalb der Stadt**

PUT

Flat: **legen**
He put the book on the table — **Er legte das Buch auf den Tisch**

Upright: **stellen**
Put the chair in the corner — **Stellen Sie den Stuhl in die Ecke!**

Inside: **stecken**
He put the money in his pocket — **Er steckte das Geld in die Tasche**

On top of: **setzen**
He put on his cap — **Er setzte die Mütze auf**

READY

To begin, to do something:
We are ready — **Wir sind bereit**

Finished: The letter is ready — **Der Brief ist fertig**

SINCE

Conjunction of time: Since he came home he has been ill — **Seitdem er nach Hause kam, ...**

Conjunction of reason: Since he is ill he cannot play — **Da er krank ist, ...**

Preposition: Since his return ... — **Seit seiner Rückkehr ...**

Adverb: I have not seen him since — **Ich habe ihn seitdem (seither) nicht gesehen**

STAY

He stayed quietly in his seat — **Er blieb ruhig sitzen**

SUMMARY OF GRAMMAR

He is staying with his uncle	**Er ist bei seinem Onkel zu Besuch**
We stayed the night in Vienna	**Wir übernachteten in Wien**
His stay in Rome was very pleasant	**Sein Aufenthalt in Rom war sehr angenehm**
He is staying in Cologne	**Er hält sich in Köln auf**

STOP

Vehicle: He stopped the car	**Er hielt das Auto an**
The car stopped	**Das Auto hielt an**
Action: It has stopped raining	**Es hat aufgehört zu regnen**
Movement: He stopped suddenly	**Er blieb plötzlich stehen**

TAKE

I will take you in my car	**Ich fahre Sie in meinem Auto**
They took him before the judge	**Sie führten ihn vor den Richter**
Take my bag upstairs	**Tragen Sie meine Tasche hinauf!**
May I take you home?	**Darf ich Sie nach Hause begleiten?**
Take a seat	{ **Nehmen Sie Platz!** / **Setzen Sie sich!** }
Take it with you	**Nehmen Sie es mit!**
He took off his clothes	**Er zog sich aus**
He took off his coat	**Er legte den Mantel ab**

THEN

At that time: **damals**

He was then only ten years old	**Er war damals erst zehn Jahre alt**

Subsequently: **dann**

First he came in and then shut the door	**Er trat zuerst herein und machte dann die Tür zu**

UPSTAIRS

Adverb of rest: He is upstairs	**Er ist oben**
Adverb of motion: He ran upstairs	**Er lief nach oben**

WAKE

With direct object: He wakened me — **Er weckte mich**

No object: I woke at 6 o'clock
- **Ich erwachte um sechs Uhr**
- **Ich wachte um sechs Uhr auf**

To be awake: I was awake all night
- **Ich wachte die ganze Nacht**
- **Ich war die ganze Nacht wach**

WHEN

1. One definite action in the past: **als**
   He said nothing when I saw him today — **Er sagte nichts, als ich ihn heute sah**
2. Meaning *after*: **nachdem**
   He went out when he had finished — **Nachdem er fertig war, ging er hinaus**
3. Question: **wann**
   When are you coming home? — **Wann kommen Sie nach Hause?**
   He asked when I was coming home — **Er fragte, wann ich nach Hause komme**
4. Meaning *while*: **während, indem**
   He came when you were away — **Er kam, während Sie verreist waren**
5. One day when … — **Eines Tages, als …**
6. All other cases — use **wenn**

29. THE FAMILY **DIE FAMILIE**

grandfather	**der Großvater** (¨)
grandmother	**die Großmutter** (¨)
grandparents	**die Großeltern** (*plural*)
father	**der Vater** (¨)
mother	**die Mutter** (¨)
parents	**die Eltern** (*plural*)
son	**der Sohn** (¨e)
daughter	**die Tochter** (¨)
child	**das Kind** (-er)
brother	**der Bruder** (¨)
sister	**die Schwester** (-n)
brothers and sisters	**die Geschwister** (*plural*)

grandson	der Enkel (-)
granddaughter	die Enkelin (-nen)
uncle	der Onkel (-)
aunt	die Tante (-n)
nephew	der Neffe (-n, -n)
niece	die Nichte (-n)
cousin (male)	der Vetter (-s, -n)
cousin (female)	die Kusine (-n)
father-in-law	der Schwiegervater (¨)
mother-in-law	die Schwiegermutter (¨)
brother-in-law	der Schwager (¨)
sister-in-law	die Schwägerin (-nen)
son-in-law	der Schwiegersohn (¨e)
daughter-in-law	die Schwiegertochter (¨)

30. *THE NATION* **DAS VOLK (¨ER)**

Afrika	afrikanisch	der Afrikaner
Amerika	amerikanisch	der Amerikaner
Belgien	belgisch	der Belgier
Deutschland	deutsch	der Deutsche
England	englisch	der Engländer
Frankreich	französisch	der Franzose
Griechenland	griechisch	der Grieche
Indien	indisch	der Inder
Italien	italienisch	der Italiener
Österreich	österreichisch	der Österreicher
Preußen	preußisch	der Preuße
Rußland	russisch	der Russe
Schottland	schottisch	der Schotte
Spanien	spanisch	der Spanier

All the above names of countries are neuter and do not require the definite article. The following are feminine or plural and must have the article before the country's name.

die Tschechoslowakei	tschechisch	der Tscheche
die Schweiz	schweizerisch	der Schweizer
die Türkei	türkisch	der Türke
die Niederlande	niederländisch	der Niederländer

die Europäische Wirtschaftsgemeinschaft		(die EWG)
die Vereinigten Staaten	—	— (die USA)
die Vereinten Nationen	—	— (die UNO)

31. PUNCTUATION

A. *The comma*

1. Used to divide clauses. There is, however, no comma before **und** or **oder** if the subject of the two clauses joined by them is the same and is not repeated.

   Er stieg auf das Pferd, während ich bei dem Hause wartete.
   Er stieg auf das Pferd und ritt davon.
   Mein Vater war zornig, weil ich zu spät kam und meine Bücher vergessen hatte.

2. There is no comma before the simple infinitive with **zu**.

   Sie luden mich ein zu schwimmen.

   When the infinitive with **zu** is combined with **ohne** or **anstatt** or if it has a predicate, it must be preceded by a comma.

   Er will immer spielen, anstatt zu arbeiten.
   Er bat mich, heute zu kommen.

3. The comma divides words in apposition, but not titles.

   Der Löwe, der König der Tiere, stand vor uns.
   Friedrich der Große war König von Preußen.

4. A comma is used after the Vocative and an interjection.

   Karl, wo bist du?
   Ach, ich bin müde.

5. Lists of words are divided by a comma, except before **und** and **oder**.

   Ein Löwe, ein Tiger und ein Bär.

SUMMARY OF GRAMMAR

6. For decimal points and money, but *not* for ordinary numbers above the thousand.
   9,8 is the English 9.8.
   DM 1,50 is **eine Mark, fünfzig Pfennig.**
   300 000 is three hundred thousand (note the German spacing).

7. There is *no* comma before or after the word **aber** meaning *however*.

B. *Semi-colon*
Sometimes used before **denn, nämlich, doch.**
Ich tue es nicht; denn es ist verboten.

C. *Colon*
Must be used before direct speech.
Er sagte feierlich: „Es lebe der König!"

D. *Exclamation mark*
1. After an exclamation.
   Pfui! Das ist schrecklich!
2. After an imperative.
   Kommen Sie herein!
3. At the beginning of a letter.
   Lieber Hans!
   Sehr geehrter Herr Winter!

SECTION 2

A. Sentence exercises on the grammar.
B. Sentences for general revision. Each group of ten sentences introduces as many points of grammar as possible.

SECTION 2A

SENTENCE EXERCISES

1. A. *Simple tenses* (**Grammar 1A**)

   1. He is coming. 2. Will you go? (*3 forms*). 3. They were playing. 4. Have we not bought? 5. My sister used to cry a lot. 6. He will bring his friend. 7. I have not sent the book. 8. Are his parents working in the garden? 9. This girl had drawn that picture. 10. Are we not going to the pictures? 11. Our mother has bought a wireless-set. 12. When will you see your friend? (*3 forms*). 13. Where are you building your house? 14. Our uncle and aunt will arrive here to-morrow. 15. Why were those pupils not listening? 16. I have not heard that story. 17. We used to live in the country. 18. The Smith family was making a garden behind their house. 19. The girl has put her coat in the rucksack. 20. The bell had wakened me early.

B. *More difficult tenses* (**Grammar 1B**)

   1. My father would not go with me to the pictures.
   2. Will you have saved enough money by Christmas?
   3. Her brothers will not have heard the news.
   4. Why would your uncle not read that book?
   5. They will send the bill next week.
   6. I would have put those lovely flowers in a vase.
   7. These parents will not have seen their children during the holidays.

EXERCISES ON GRAMMAR 63

8. No honest man would have sold you this old car.
9. When will your mother have finished her work?
10. Any boy would like to drive a railway-engine.

2. *Verbs in* **-ten**; *separable and inseparable prefixes* (**Grammar 1C, 2**)

1. He is riding home with his brother.
2. Why do you get up so early in summer?
3. I never understood what he said.
4. This firm has not yet answered my letter.
5. He opened the door and an old man came in.
6. The steamer has not yet reached the harbour.
7. Were they working when you arrived home?
8. The boy got up slowly and dressed.
9. My sister hopes to spend her holidays in France.
10. This boy works every day in our shop.
11. He was working and trying to listen to the wireless.
12. Boys will always climb apple-trees.
13. "When does the plane arrive in Berlin?" the man asked.
14. The clerk did not answer my question immediately.
15. He dived into the stream and appeared two minutes later.

3. *Position of the verb in the sentence* (**Grammar 12**)

A. *The Past Participle at the end of its clause*

1. I have not seen the farmer to-day. 2. He has sold the house to his friend. 3. These soldiers have served in the English army. 4. This rich man has once been very poor. 5. Our neighbour has bought a new car.

B. *After most verbs the infinitive is preceded by* **zu**

1. He has decided to visit his sick mother. 2. That man wishes (**wünschen**) to go into the town. 3. This girl has the gift of making friends. 4. The doctor has advised us to go to the seaside. 5. They asked him to stay the night at the inn.

C. *The infinitive is not preceded by* **zu** *after the modal verbs* (**dürfen, können, mögen, müssen, sollen, wollen**) *and also after* **fühlen, helfen, heißen** (*to order*), **hören, lassen, lehren, lernen, machen, sehen**

1. Can you hear him coming? 2. We were obliged to go home. 3. Do you not wish to see the ship's captain? 4. He is not allowed to drive a car. 5. The clerk was unable to write with his right hand. 6. We saw the man cross the street. 7. My father will help us to write this letter. 8. They ordered me to see the doctor. 9. The sailor felt himself falling. 10. I have learnt to speak German.

D. *When the infinitive clause denotes purpose, use* **um ... zu** *with the infinitive*

1. The merchant has come to see his sick wife. 2. I must go now to get home early. 3. Our family is going to the country to enjoy the fresh air. 4. We must buy paper to write some letters. 5. They ran quickly in order not to miss the train.

E. *When anything but the subject begins the main clause (even if it is a whole clause), use inversion in the main clause*

1. Which dry wood have we not yet burnt? 2. When did you last have a swim in the sea? 3. Why have they sold that fine house? 4. In the morning I will go to the bank. 5. In November it rains a great deal.

F. *In clauses introduced by subordinating conjunctions, the verb stands at the end of its clause*

1. My friends cannot come to-morrow because their car has broken down.
2. Although he is afraid of the sea, he will come with me.
3. When they have finished their work, they will send it to us.
4. We will climb the mountain to-morrow if it is not misty.
5. As the sun is hot it will dry us quickly.
6. The weather is so beautiful that we must go out.
7. While she was ill last year, she had to stay at home in bed.
8. Whenever he goes to the theatre he returns home late.
9. I recognised the stranger as soon as I saw him.
10. Because we live in the town we want to be in the country.

Im Schwarzwald

Köln: Blick vom rechten Rheinufer

Rheindampfer

EXERCISES ON GRAMMAR

G. *The following conjunctions join clauses of equal value and do not affect the position of the verb:* **und, aber, allein** (*however*), **denn, sondern, oder**

1. My son can read for he is eight years old now.
2. His brother may go to the pictures but he will stay at home.
3. I will not accompany you but I will not stay here alone.
4. When the beggar saw me yesterday and I gave him my old coat he was very grateful.
5. We must hurry because it is already very late.
6. You may take the book now but I must have it to-morrow morning.
7. I will bring the letter to-night and he can read it then.
8. We must look after our dog although he is old and cannot walk.
9. He cannot do it or he does not want to do it.
10. When they reached the shore and undressed, they ran quickly into the sea.

4. *Verbs with* **sein** *and* **haben** (*use compound tenses*) (**Grammar 4**)
1. The trees have now become green.
2. My grandfather died when I was very young.
3. The soldiers rode their horses through the village.
4. We had been riding all day when we finally saw our camp.
5. His friend would have come with us if we had invited her.
6. The sun will have already melted the snow in the mountains.
7. The snow in the valley had melted before the end of March.
8. A great misfortune happened in our town last year.
9. The child fell asleep and slept for ten hours.
10. This morning I got up at five to see the sunrise.
11. Why did you not stay at home if you had a cold?
12. We travelled up the Rhine from Cologne to Rüdesheim by steamer.
13. Mr Brown fell from the ladder and broke his arm.
14. He has succeeded in passing his examination.
15. Our visitors will have arrived when we get home.
16. The postman did not appear until we had gone out.

17. You have stayed in the water too long if you are cold.
18. After the cold night the pond will have frozen.
19. These students have been three times to Germany.
20. We have not heard any news. What has happened?

5. A. *Passive Voice* (**Grammar 6A, B, D**)

1. His shout was not heard.
2. The old man is often seen in his garden.
3. This house was built in 1759.
4. The new toy has been broken by my little brother.
5. The money will be paid when I have sold the house.
6. The birds in the trees would be heard if you were silent.
7. Last night a thief was caught in my house by a policeman.
8. A big red car was seen in the square near the theatre.
9. The harvest will be spoilt this year by the rain.
10. The prisoners have been freed from the island.
11. The wide streets were much admired by the visitors from abroad.
12. Because the flames were too big, the castle could not be saved.
13. His house was hit twice by bombs during the last war.
14. Your work will not be done if you do not try hard.
15. If he had (**hätte**) not shouted, he would not have been heard.

B. (**Grammar 6C, E**)

1. He has been told.
2. You were helped.
3. They were not given an answer.
4. We were not believed.
5. They were threatened by the farmer.
6. We were followed by a dog.
7. After dinner there was dancing at the town-hall.
8. The children were shown the ships in the harbour.
9. She was advised to go for a long sea-voyage.
10. The shops are closed now; they are closed at 6 P.M.
11. On his birthday, Brown was given a car by his father.
12. He must be told of the death of his best friend.

13. My sister will be helped by her friend.
14. The general's order has not been obeyed.
15. Our house will be threatened by the floods

6. *Reflexive Verbs* (**Grammar 7**)

1. Please sit down.
2. Help yourself to a cup of coffee.
3. I cannot remember his name.
4. The sailors found themselves on a deserted island.
5. We will approach the village from the south.
6. While we were walking in the Black Forest, we got lost.
7. I imagine that I will never fly in an aeroplane.
8. "You are mistaken, gentlemen," the innkeeper replied.
9. Charles bent down and picked up the pretty stones.
10. You must thank yourselves for your success.
11. We must hurry, if we do not wish to miss the train.
12. He has changed his name; the weather changes frequently.
13. My younger brother has caught a cold.
14. I am looking forward to the summer holidays.
15. People often sing when they feel happy.
16. We will make it ourselves.
17. The door opened and then shut quietly.
18. The footballer broke his leg during the match.
19. These two friends write to each other every week.
20. My brother will come to see you himself.

7. *Modal Verbs* (**Grammar 8**)

1. Charles cannot come with us. 2. He has to work in the butcher's shop. 3. I wonder (*would like to know*) where he is. 4. They were not allowed to write. 5. We ought not to have laughed. 6. Will you take this newspaper? 7. The children ought to go home now. 8. My aunt may have arrived already. 9. Shall I help you? 10. I would like to do something. 11. Our guests will want to pick some flowers. 12. John could have repaired the machine himself. 13. They have had to do many unpleasant things. 14. He speaks German very well. 15. They have never been allowed to camp alone. 16. He will have to work

harder. 17. That man is supposed to be French. 18. Would you like some coffee? 19. May I ask my friend to dinner? 20. What will you want to do this evening?

8. *Impersonal Verbs* (**Grammar 9**)

1. It gets dark early in winter. 2. It often thunders and lightens during a storm. 3. There are good books and bad books in this world. 4. He cannot come because his leg hurts. 5. I am thirsty; is there any water in that glass, please? 6. If he succeeds, it will please his parents. 7. That woman has no lack of money. 8. How many birds are there in that cage? 9. It is a pity that the pond is not frozen. 10. There have been great poets in every nation. 11. We cannot climb the mountain if it snows. 12. There were seats for ten people in the bus. 13. I am surprised you have not heard the news. 14. Is there a fire in my room? 15. There were a lot of people in the Youth Hostel yesterday. 16. We are sorry. 17. I am pleased to see you. 18. It does not matter if it rains. 19. There used to be a house there. 20. There will be dancing to-night.

9. *Subjunctive* (**Grammar 10, 11**)

A. (**Grammar 11A**)

1. He said he was tired. 2. Charles tells me he will come to-morrow. 3. The doctor asked the sick man what he had eaten. 4. We hope our son will be home for Christmas. 5. The soldier reported that the camp was empty. 6. The messenger had heard that the king was ill. 7. My father thinks we are very foolish. 8. The boy insisted that he was right. 9. The girl dreamt she was a queen. 10. The farmer said he had seen a ghost. 11. His friends replied that it was his own shadow. 12. The sailor explained how they had found the treasure. 13. The boy answered that he had left his work at home. 14. The traveller asked how much the meal cost. 15. The man had told the driver that he was late. 16. They are enquiring who we are. 17. The policeman will tell you that the next village is two miles away. 18. My brother writes that

EXERCISES ON GRAMMAR

he is ill. 19. The swimmer called out that the river was very deep. 20. Do you know where he is?

B. (**Grammar 11 B, C, E, F**)

1. Long live the bride! 2. If only I were rich! 3. Would that I had heard this news earlier! 4. We might play tennis this afternoon. 5. You look as if you had been working too hard. 6. If only he had read the book earlier! 7. I shall put on a warm coat so that I shall not feel cold. 8. Tell the young man to telephone me in the morning. 9. I wish my brother would come! 10. He has bought a car in order that his family may accompany him. 11. Your sister looks as if she were ill. 12. We must hurry so that we do not miss the bus. 13. He must come home at once wherever he is. 14. Tell the waiter to bring me a glass of water. 15. However rich he may be, I do not like him.

C. (**Grammar 11D**)

1. I would have written to you if I had had the time.
2. We would buy a bigger house if we had the money.
3. My brother could have gone to the dance if he had wished.
4. If we had seen your father we would have spoken to him.
5. If I had longer holidays I should go to Italy every year.
6. Would you have come with us if you had had the chance?
7. If the pond freezes to-night we can skate.
8. If the pond had frozen we could have skated.
9. If we had not seen it we would never have believed it.
10. I wonder what he will do if he cannot play football.

10. *Declension of Nouns and Adjectives* (**Grammar 13, 14**)

A. 1. Give the gender and plural (with reasons if possible) of: König, Gebirge, Dorf, Matrose, Dampfer, Wille, Schönheit, Stiefel, Zeitung, Hemd.
2. Decline in full: dieser junge Mann; das lange Tal; Ihr neuer Schuh; ein gutes Buch; unsere kleine Schwester.

3. Complete the following sentences:
   (a) Während jen— fleißig— Schüler schwer arbeiten, spielen d— ander— immer auf d— geschäftig— Straßen.
   (b) Weder sein— alt— Tante noch sein— freundlich— Onkel wollten ihr— Kinder— erlauben, mit uns in d— Schwimmbad zu gehen.
   (c) Mein— Mutter hat mein— älter— Bruder, der im Fern— Osten lebt, ein— lang— Brief geschrieben.

B. 1. Give the gender and plural (with reasons if possible) of: Köchin, Jüngling, Tür, Brüderchen, Mantel, Neffe, Landschaft, Hund, Gebäude, Bauer.

2. Decline in full: keine schönere Blume; welches schwarze Auto; eine lustige Geschichte; rote Tinte; jener berühmte Dichter.

3. Complete the following sentences:
   (a) Wer sind jen— wohlgekleidet— Herren, die in d— groß— Autos gekommen sind?
   (b) Als d— neu— Gast in unser— klein— Wirtshaus trat, fragte mein— Mutter ihn, ob er ein— lang— Reise gemacht habe.
   (c) Wegen d— plötzlich— Sturmes mußten d— Reisend— wieder in d— nächst— Dorf zurückfahren.

C. 1. Give the gender and plural (with reasons if possible) of: Umgebung, Franzose, Insel, Tag, Königtum, Bett, Frucht, Held, Brief, Leidenschaft.

2. Decline in full: euer bekanntes Haus; das arme Tier; eine zornige Löwin; mein neuer Schwager; weißer Wein.

3. Complete the following sentences:
   (a) Unser— lustig— Kinder gingen nach jen— dicht— Wald, wo sie viel— Vogelnester zu finden hofften.
   (b) D— jung— Arzt wußte d— Schwerkrank— kein— gut— Rat zu geben.

EXERCISES ON GRAMMAR 71

(c) Mein— alt— Bedient— ist ein— ehrlich— Mann, dem ich mein— voll— Geldbeutel anvertrauen könnte.

D. 1. Give the gender and plural (with reasons if possible) of: Schiffer, Kleid, Krieg, Wahrheit, Freundschaft, Bäumlein, Käfig, Bote, Gräfin, Interesse.

2. Decline in full: Ihr buntes Hemd; diese lange Mauer; das nächste Jahr; ein wunderbarer Film; unser dankbarer Diener.

3. Complete the following sentences:

(a) Als jen— Gefangen— sah, daß d— wachsam— Soldat ihn erblickt hatte, sprang er von d— hoh— Mauer in d— tief— Fluß.

(b) Unser— Familie hat auf ein— kurz— Zeit ein— neu— Wohnung nicht weit von d— hoh— Bergen gemietet.

(c) Dies— freundlich— Wirt reichte d— müd— Wanderer ein— Glas sprudelnd— Weins.

11. *Uses of Cases* (**Grammar 15**)

1. Through the window; into the water; with his neighbour; instead of your brother; opposite the town-hall.
2. Outside the town; for his father; near the village; in spite of the snow; round the house.
3. He ran out of the house and into the garden.
4. I bought this house two years ago and since that time I have lived here alone.
5. My uncle has given my cousin a motor-bike.
6. We will meet you between our house and the village.
7. Give me the book; do not send it to my brother.
8. I got this packet from the postman; it is for you.
9. The ball rolled quickly down the hill and fell into the stream.
10. The vicar lives near the bridge opposite his church.
11. My best friend has gone abroad and now lives in the United States.
12. The doctor jumped out of his car, ran into the house and up the stairs.

13. They looked behind the door but did not see me, because I was hidden behind the cupboard.
14. Put your brother's books on the table near the window.
15. The policeman took the thief before the judge who listened to his story with great interest.
16. The doctor advised the sick man to go for a long walk every day over the hills.
17. The poor child was hit on the head by a hard ball.
18. He is living at present with his aunt in Frankfurt on the Main.
19. Except for a vase there was nothing on the table.
20. I will go with you as far as the post-office.

12. *Comparison of Adjectives and Adverbs* (**Grammar 16, 17**)

1. That lawyer is the most cunning man I know.
2. The Zugspitze is the highest mountain in Germany.
3. From the top of the hill they could see the next village more easily.
4. Goethe's dramas are better than his novels, but his poems are better still.
5. John is not as clever as Mary but he works harder.
6. The Rhine is wide at Basle, wider at Rüdesheim but widest near Cologne.
7. The sooner you are ready the better.
8. That was the most interesting film I have ever seen.
9. The most expensive things are not always the best.
10. He could at least have said that he would help you.
11. I like playing the piano but I like best to play when I am alone.
12. I like travelling by train but I prefer to fly.
13. We should arrive home at half past five at the latest.
14. Your brother can jump higher than you can.
15. The higher we climbed the colder it became.
16. It is not as cold in the south as in the north.
17. We are moving more and more quickly every day.
18. The meal should cost ten shillings at the most.
19. One works best in the morning.
20. A growing boy eats more than a man.

13. Personal and Relative Pronouns (**Grammar 18, 19**)

1. *Accusative:* I ask you; they see him; we know her; she is watching me; you (*2nd plural*) want it; you are thinking of us.
2. *Dative:* Give me the letter; answer him; will he pardon her?; tell us the news; the doctor advises them; we do not believe you.
3. I need a stick, will you buy it for me?
4. The old man in the village remembered us.
5. Who is it? It is I.
6. Will you come with us? No, I will go with them.
7. My pen is empty, it has no ink.
8. There is a table near the piano, put your cup on it.
9. Have you seen my pencil? No, I have not seen it.
10. This is the house; we were just talking about it.
11. Here is the shoemaker who mends our shoes.
12. I have just seen the picture you have sold.
13. This is the lady whom I have advised to go to the south of France.
14. Have they found the stick with which he broke the window?
15. The officer whose horse you bought last year has gone to America.
16. The customer to whom I sent the money is your friend.
17. He who is content with his lot will be happy.
18. Here are the glasses from which the guests drank.
19. The little girl with whom Mary played yesterday came again to-day.
20. Those who do not speak the truth do not deserve our confidence.
21. That is the most beautiful (thing) that I have ever seen.
22. He hopes to find work in an office which will please his parents.
23. The lady whose dog has bitten the postman lives opposite the post-office.
24. Nothing that I can do pleases him.
25. He said something that I did not quite understand.

14. Interrogative, Possessive and Demonstrative Pronouns (**Grammar 20-22**)

1. To whom have you addressed the envelope?
2. Whose is that lovely car?
3. With what did you open the door?
4. What are you talking about?
5. What have you written here?
6. Whom did you see in town this morning?
7. What does bread consist of?
8. To whom have they sent this invitation?
9. I have lost my book, so I am using my sister's.
10. Your coat is very old; mine is quite new.
11. Is this your tent? Yes, it is mine, but it is not as big as yours.
12. That is my hat. Where is yours?
13. His bike looks new, but hers seems very old.
14. We are looking for our dog now. Have you found yours yet?
15. I can remember his face but I cannot remember his sister's.
16. That is the same man I saw with my uncle.
17. We do not seem to have visited the same buildings.
18. Those who do not play football have often no interest in it.
19. An artist frequently paints the same picture several times
20. The man who does not like trees is no friend of nature.

15. Translation of the English Present Participle (**Grammar 23**)

1. Charles was walking in the woods talking with the vicar.
2. Entering the room he sat down by the window.
3. The weather being so wet, we could not play on the sands.
4. The man carrying the rucksack was the tallest in the group.
5. On seeing the book in the window he rushed into the shop to buy it.
6. His father earns his living by selling vegetables in the market.

7. Do you remember seeing this view from the church tower?
8. The little boy continued asking questions.
9. He went into the house without taking off his hat.
10. Although it was getting cool they remained sitting in the open.
11. The sun had set without our realising it.
12. A ball came flying over the wall.
13. Coming into the room he saw his host sitting by the fire.
14. Can you hear that lark singing?
15. They have succeeded in passing their examinations.
16. He had been waiting an hour for her.
17. Talking is not allowed in the library.
18. My brother is very fond of reading.
19. After reading the letter, he began telling us about his travels.
20. Nothing interesting ever happens in our village.

16. *Numerals, dates, times* (**Grammar 24, 25**)

1. John will play his first game of football next Saturday.
2. He will be twelve on December 15th, 1959.
3. (At) what time will the theatre open? At half past six.
4. Can you come at a quarter to four on Friday afternoon?
5. The bus leaves at 7.35 A.M. every Sunday morning.
6. The postman comes twice a day, in the morning and in the afternoon.
7. The gardener has been working for two hours but he has done nothing.
8. Our whole family flew to Austria last year.
9. There are 94 rooms in this building and 182 in the next building; that makes 276 rooms.
10. Some boys arrived yesterday but the others will not arrive until to-morrow.
11. The sun is hot in summer but it does not shine for long in winter.
12. It was very cold during the second week in May.
13. Louis XIV was a king of France during the 17th century.

14. There are more than 3600 books in this library.
15. The traveller arrived on Friday, August 30th, 1956 and left early the following morning.
16. We bathe in the river almost every day in summer.
17. The gentleman asked the waiter to bring him half a bottle of wine.
18. Next week we are going to France for a month.
19. The shop had been open half an hour when I went in.
20. One-eighth and one-sixth make seven-twenty-fourths.

17. A. *Difficult translations* (**Grammar 28**)
    1. Why do you not ask your friend into the house?
    2. We are going to Spain next week.
    3. The prisoner begged for mercy.
    4. My father asked me to show him the letter I had written.
    5. He got on his feet as I spoke to him.
    6. Before beginning a journey you must know where you are going.
    7. As he was rather angry I remained downstairs in the dining-room.
    8. There are very few apples on the trees this year.
    9. If it does not stop raining we shall have to stay indoors.
    10. When did you get back from your voyage?
    11. I hope you enjoyed the drive.
    12. Only a few people applauded when the orchestra had finished.
    13. Will you please take these letters to the post?
    14. We could hear people talking in the room below.
    15. The Smiths tried to get there first but the Browns arrived before them.
    16. After dinner they decided to sing a few songs.
    17. There are one or two long rivers in the south of Europe.
    18. I have never enjoyed a meal so much in my life.
    19. All his friends have moved to other towns.
    20. That man has been begging at the same street corner for years.

B.
1. He has already told us all he knows.
2. Last year he stayed for a month with his uncle in France.
3. The boy went upstairs to wake his parents.
4. He put the lamp on the table when he was ready to work.
5. He knows French and German.
6. A slow train stops at almost every station on its route.
7. All the citizens took off their hats when they saw the mayor approaching.
8. The landlord put his hand in his pocket and pulled out his wallet.
9. I would like to leave early to-morrow.
10. Wake me immediately if you wake up before me.
11. Put your luggage in the hall when you are ready to leave the hotel.
12. Since your sister is ill you must not stay long.
13. My son hurt his leg playing football.
14. The shoes must be ready when I come to-morrow morning.
15. I have not seen you since your last birthday.
16. The policeman asked when we had last seen the stolen dog.
17. I first visited Germany when I was eight but I knew no German then.
18. The warden of the Youth Hostel took the boys to their dormitory.
19. He ran quickly up the stairs and then into the bathroom.
20. The hotel porter has taken your luggage upstairs.

Section 2B

SENTENCES FOR GENERAL REVISION

A.
1. She had not gone to bed but was sitting in a chair reading.
2. Yesterday we returned from Rome where we had been staying three weeks.

3. When I asked what time it was, he said he did not know.
4. The children have sometimes been allowed to go to the swimming-pool without their father.
5. Because of the storm he drove back to the nearest village.
6. Lend me your book please. Mine has been lost.
7. He would not believe me when I told him the story.
8. Here is the lady who wants to buy the house.
9. The professor has found something interesting in the hills.
10. It was thundering as we approached the first houses.

B. 1. The passenger would not have missed the plane if he had hurried.
2. I was walking along the road when I suddenly saw my cousin in her car.
3. It seems to me that he ought to go with you.
4. The warden said something that I could not hear.
5. We were told that you had gone away.
6. The boy had hidden his books in the long grass but they have now disappeared.
7. The longer we waited the colder the room became.
8. Will you please help me to find the right address?
9. I can find nothing good in his painting. Yours is much better.
10. Instead of working he only wanted to play the piano.

C. 1. The policeman who had stopped us directed us to the nearest petrol-station.
2. I imagine that his fall has hurt him.
3. Our friends have expressed their intention of coming to see us.
4. The lamps are lit at 9 P.M. every evening now.
5. Tell would not have saved his friend if he had been afraid of the storm.
6. You ought to have sent for the chimney-sweep.
7. The officer ordered the soldiers to fire.
8. Something very strange has happened in our town.
9. I left my bag at the station and went to have a look at the town.
10. The mother explained where she had found the coat.

EXERCISES ON GRAMMAR

D. 1. He continued reading without replying to my question.
2. We must buy you a dog that you will like.
3. Would you have gone to Rome if you had not known Italian?
4. They will at least reward the person who finds the lost purse.
5. The town has been spoilt by too many ugly buildings.
6. The guard demanded that the boy should leave the tram immediately.
7. There is nothing new under the sun.
8. The old dog served his master faithfully for many years.
9. Can you recognise those birds? These are larks, those are thrushes.
10. I hope I will be allowed to go to Germany.

E. 1. We were watching sparrows eating insects in the garden.
2. The Main is wider than the Neckar but the Rhine is the widest.
3. If you meet your brother in town tell him I have returned home.
4. The general threatened the inhabitants that his soldiers would burn the town.
5. The boy to whom they gave the prize is lazy.
6. The library is closed at Christmas.
7. His coat is lying on the stairs with mine.
8. The train could have arrived in time if it had not snowed.
9. It rained during the day so I do not think it will freeze to-night.
10. The monks saw something white walking in the moonlight.

F. 1. One works best in the afternoon after a light lunch.
2. It looks as if the sea might be very rough.
3. You have only succeeded by working hard.
4. Our dog is fiercer than yours; ours has bitten the butcher's boy.
5. Where is the axe with which you want to fell the tree?
6. The shopkeeper advised the customer to buy a new watch.
7. The Duke is reported to be very ill.
8. They undressed on the banks of the stream.

9. If he had eaten something bitter he would not be so thirsty now.
10. I have just remembered what the guard told me.

G. 1. The poor fellow has no money with which he can buy a meal.
2. He trod on the dog which made it bark suddenly.
3. If you go to that factory you will be shown all the machines.
4. He saved all his money so that he might go to America.
5. Which case would you rather carry? Yours or your brother's?
6. If he had stayed in bed he would have recovered from his illness.
7. The pilot had been flying the plane for twelve hours.
8. I have never heard her sing so well.
9. The Feldberg is the highest mountain in the Black Forest.
10. He hopes to earn a prize by swimming across the lake.

H. 1. The girl was given a reward for saving the child.
2. You must wash your hands and face before going to the theatre.
3. The chemist asked me if I had brought a bottle.
4. There are many people whose only interest is the wireless.
5. Can you please advise me what I ought to do?
6. A bottle of this wine should cost at most ten Marks.
7. My holidays are longer than his but yours are the longest.
8. On account of the rain we shall have to do something else.
9. "No soldiers have ridden through this area," the girl replied.
10. If he had bent down he would have seen the nail

I. 1. The soldier fell to the ground when he was struck by a bullet.
2. You look as if you were working too hard.
3. Will you allow Fred to go swimming this afternoon?
4. Your hat is the most beautiful one I have ever seen.
5. A child ran on to the street just as the bus stopped.

EXERCISES ON GRAMMAR

6. You must not drink too much when you are very thirsty.
7. Walking is easier than running.
8. Someone has opened the box that was on the table.
9. I have heard nothing new since last March.
10. One walks most comfortably if one has not eaten too much.

J.
1. Your luggage has been taken to the station.
2. I hope your friend will come to dinner.
3. He thanked me for having helped him.
4. As the farmer has no cart in which to carry his hay, he borrows ours.
5. It is usually the beautiful that attracts a poet or a painter.
6. "Help yourselves, please," our hostess said.
7. First of all he is too busy, secondly he does not want to go.
8. Crusoe was the king of all he could see.
9. You could attend the party if you wanted to do so.
10. The student was lying in bed learning his work.

K.
1. The baker was run over by a bicycle two days ago.
2. They spoke to each other for an hour at the most.
3. Can you pay me the money before starting on your journey?
4. The parents hope the postman will bring good news to-morrow.
5. A cousin of ours has a bigger house than yours.
6. I do not know the town of which you are speaking.
7. It happens that we have found nothing new on our walk.
8. To whom does this cap belong? It is John's.
9. He fell asleep while he was lying in the sun.
10. We woke up early because the children were excited.

L.
1. He must use his own bicycle, not hers.
2. Do not worry! Everything will be finished in time.
3. The thief admitted that he was ashamed of himself.
4. Is that all you have heard of the affair?
5. He lacks the courage to dive from the bank of the river.
6. Through a foolish mistake he has paid more than he owed.
7. It must have been ten o'clock when we left the cinema.

8. After he had closed the door he sat down in a chair near the window.
9. The king has died.   Long live the king!
10. They wished us all the best for Christmas.

M. 1. You ought not to swim across this swift river.
2. Our car is bigger than theirs but theirs is faster.
3. We enjoyed ourselves at the football match yesterday.
4. Did you thank the doctor for the advice he gave you?
5. There are very few people who do not like travelling.
6. The prisoner was compelled to fetch water from the well.
7. If the fire-brigade had arrived in time, the house would have been saved.
8. Have you heard anything that would interest me?
9. Our cat has disappeared.   Have you seen it?
10. Most people think they would be happier with more money.

N. 1. The butcher can never remember what has been ordered.
2. It would be a pity if he arrived too late, wouldn't it?
3. The friends with whom he has been living are moving to Cologne.
4. The mayor could tell us nothing new about the town.
5. Walking on the grass is forbidden.
6. Their prices are lower than ours.
7. A child ought to obey its parents.
8. I think he ought to light a fire, don't you?
9. This region is said to be rich in iron.
10. Their cook will prepare us a very good meal.

O. 1. Why were those boys fighting in the school playground?
2. That is my affair, not yours.
3. They were told to stop writing as soon as possible.
4. The more you fish the more you like it.
5. This girl resembles her father but not her mother.
6. The young man jumped up from the chair.
7. If that were my opinion I should tell him so.
8. She has received a letter in which her brother tells many strange things.
9. We hope that he will succeed.
10. Pleasant people can be met in every country.

SECTION 3

Prose Passages for Translation into German

The following plan for tackling passages for translation into German is recommended to you. Remember that it is just as important to be able to use words correctly as to know the German for the words.

1. Break down each long sentence into its clauses.
2. Study each clause and decide:
    (a) the tenses and parts of the verbs needed,
    (b) the position of the verbs,
    (c) the cases of the nouns, and
    (d) the position of pronouns and adverbs.
3. Write out a rough draft of each sentence until you have worked through at least a paragraph of the whole passage.
4. Examine and check your rough draft very carefully and critically.
5. Make a final, clear and legible version.

N.B. The necessary bare vocabulary for proses 1–45 will be found at the end of this part. For special constructions you must turn to the paragraphs referred to in the notes.

1. I remember very well the day when we made our first trip in our new car. My father said that he wanted to go to the seaside. We all got up early in the morning.

When I looked out of the window, it was raining a little. After breakfast, I asked my father if the weather was too bad. He said, "We must ask mother what we are to do." My mother said, "Perhaps the weather is better at the seaside. Let's try it."

She was right. Half an hour later the sun began to shine. We were just about to leave, when my father had to run back into the house. He had forgotten his wallet. He looked everywhere but could not find it in the house.

Suddenly I saw it. He had put it on the rear seat of the car, when he had fetched the car from the garage.

2. DEAR TOM,

Yesterday I received a letter from our friend Jack. He has been in Germany for two months. Now he wants to study there to become a doctor. When he first went abroad he was rather unhappy. Unfortunately he had not learnt much German at school.

Now he says he likes the country and people very much. Although he has only been there a few weeks, he has already learnt a lot. At first it was lonely but now he has many German friends. When he returns to England at Easter, he will visit us. If I give you his German address you will be able to write to him from time to time. I am sure that he looks forward to letters from England.

Your friend,
RUDOLF

3. The sun was shining brightly when we set out in the morning, but about midday it began to rain heavily. As we had not brought our coats we soon got wet. We had been walking half an hour in the shelter of the hedges and trees when we heard a car in the distance.

"Perhaps the driver will take us to the next town, if he sees us," I said. The next moment the car travelled quickly past us. It seemed as if nobody had seen us. Then the car stopped, and we hurried towards it. The driver asked if he could help us.

"It would be marvellous," said my friend, "if we could travel with you to the next village. We can spend the night there. In this weather we cannot walk farther." After a short ride we reached a village, where we got out. We thanked the man, and began to look for the Youth Hostel.

4. Yesterday evening my parents went to the cinema, which is not very far from our house. As they had said that they would come out at half past ten, I decided to go and meet them. After I had laid the table I left the house.

Before reaching the cinema I met an old friend, with whom I talked for a few minutes. As it was so dark, I did not notice that my parents had passed me. They had been on the other side of the street. When I at last reached the cinema not a soul was to be seen; everything was dark.

I immediately returned home. I knew that my parents

PASSAGES FOR TRANSLATION INTO GERMAN 85

were already back, because I could see a light in one of the rooms. My parents were about to eat something. During the meal they told me about the film they had seen.

5. I got up very early because I wanted to leave the inn before eight o'clock. When I set out a slight rain was falling. As the weather had become very cold I had to wear an overcoat.

I wanted to catch the early train, and walked to the station as quickly as possible. If I missed it I would have to wait two hours for the next express.

While I was standing on the platform, I heard a voice behind me. I turned round and recognised the man; it was the innkeeper. It was clear that he had followed me. I asked him what was the matter.

Without saying anything he put his hand into his pocket, and pulled out a gold wristlet-watch. I had left it in my room at the inn. I thanked him very much, and told him that the watch had belonged to my father, who had given it to me a few weeks previously.

6. My friend Peter, who lives in the country, made a trip one day to the nearest town to visit his old friend Charles. After a long, uninteresting journey, young Peter arrived. He had hoped to see his friend on the platform, but unfortunately he was not there.

When Peter got out of the train, he did not know at first what to do. He had never before seen so many people and he was rather frightened. Soon he found a porter, gave him his case and explained what had happened.

"If you have your friend's address, it will be quite easy to find him," the porter said. "If you follow me, we can get a taxi. There are always some near the station." They came out of the station and the porter soon found a taxi. Quickly Peter jumped in and showed the driver the address, which was on a piece of paper.

7. When I was very young, I lived in the north of England. Every day I had to walk across a bridge on the way to school. One day my friend and I were walking along the river bank when we saw a young man in the distance. He was climbing on to the high bridge. We saw him on the edge, high above the river.

"Perhaps he intends to throw himself into the water" said my friend. "What are we to do?" "Run as fast as possible," I replied, "fetch the policeman who always stands at the corner."

While my friend ran along the bank, I hurried to the place where I had last seen the man. Quickly I looked up but could see nothing, for the unfortunate man had disappeared!

A few minutes later my friend arrived with the policeman. I told him what I had seen. Without losing a moment we all ran to the river.

8. As John is now almost sixteen, he hopes to sit his leaving examination next summer. He has been at the Grammar School for five years. He tells me that he does not yet know what he wants to become.

Six years ago his parents were killed in a car accident. Until his death his father had worked in a bank. As John was the only child he was able to live with his grandparents.

His grandfather has always said that he ought to become a clerk like his father, but John has no interest in that work. As he is very fond of sport, he likes to be in the open air. It would perhaps be better if he told his grandparents this.

As soon as John has passed his examination, he will know better what he wants to do.

9. When we arrived in the little village it was already late. We had been travelling all day and were very tired. We walked slowly down the main street, hoping to find an inn where we could spend the night. It seemed as if the village possessed neither inn nor hotel.

We were about to go to the police-station to ask for help, when we saw a policeman. We asked him if there was an inn in the village. "Yes," he replied. "Go round the next corner, and you will see it on the left." When we reached the inn we had to knock several times. Then the door was opened by an old man. He was the innkeeper.

Fortunately he still had two rooms which we could have. After we had washed and changed, we came downstairs and had something to eat. At half past ten we wished him goodnight, and went up to bed. We were tired and soon fell asleep. About one o'clock in the morning a sound wakened us.

10. Last summer my friend and I worked for a week on a farm. We were trying to earn some money during the summer holidays. When we arrived in the evening we were greeted by a pleasant farmer, who explained what we were to do.

Next morning we got up at six o'clock. We had a good breakfast, and went out on to the field where we had to work. Our first task was to tie string round corn which still lay on the ground. Although I worked hard, my friend succeeded in working more quickly.

I was pleased when midday came. We went back to the house to have dinner. We now had two hours free. As I was so tired I lay down. My friend looked as if he were still quite fresh. He said that he preferred to sit outside.

After a rest we again returned to the field. Fortunately more people were there in the afternoon, and at half past five everything was finished. We had a large evening meal and then sat and talked until a quarter past nine. We then said we were tired. Having said good-night we went upstairs.

11. Yesterday my brother and I went for a trip into the country. We got up early, and were at the station before eight o'clock to catch the train. When we arrived at our destination we got out, and soon we were walking through a shady wood. We followed a little stream for about half an hour.

After we had walked for about one and a half hours, we sat down. As we were now very hungry, we opened our rucksacks. We wanted to see what sort of sandwiches our mother had given us. Everything tasted marvellous.

About twenty past four we left the wood, and walked through a pleasant valley where all sorts of pretty flowers were growing under the trees. At last we had to turn back. It was getting late. We were able to reach the station on a different path.

12. A little boy was playing on the river bank. Suddenly a dog appeared, seized the ball with which the boy was playing, and ran away with it. Naturally the child ran after the dog, which finally jumped into the water. The boy tried to reach the dog.

As the river bank was steep, he fell into the water. Although the river was not very deep, the boy was frightened and screamed for help.

A man who had been sitting on a bench had seen what had happened. He jumped up, and ran into the water. He soon succeeded in pulling the boy out of the river. Quickly he carried him up the bank, and laid him in the grass.

Many people now came running to see the child. A man stepped forward. He said he was a doctor. "The boy cannot walk; he must be carried home," he said. At that moment the child's mother appeared. When she heard what the man had done, she thanked him.

13. Last year we spent our holidays in the country. As the weather was so good we found it quite pleasant. This year we hope to go to the seaside. My parents say it will be something quite different for me.

Perhaps they are right. In any case I am looking forward to it. Two friends of ours who were on the south coast last August found it very difficult to get rooms there. When they visited us a few days ago, they advised us to write immediately to a good hotel in order to obtain accommodation.

It would be a pity if we had to stay at home the whole time. As my father has to work hard throughout the whole year he must have at least two weeks holiday. He can then lead a very lazy life.

14. It was quite early when John woke up. He had not slept very well because he was so excited. His uncle had invited him to spend a week in the country. He had to leave home early to catch the 8.20 A.M. train. Fortunately his mother had made everything ready the previous evening.

When he reached the station many people were already on the platform. All were waiting for the same train. As he had two suit-cases, John asked a porter to help him. In spite of the crowd John succeeded in finding a corner-seat.

After a pleasant journey he arrived in the little village near which his uncle lived. When the train stopped John jumped out with his luggage. His uncle came hurrying along the platform. "How are you, John?" he called. "I am glad you've come. Perhaps you will be able to help us during your stay."

15. DEAR MARGARET,

To-morrow we shall expect you here. During your stay we shall go for long walks across the hills and through the woods. Do not forget to bring your bathing-costume. I know that you are fond of swimming. I shall be delighted to bathe with you. I am glad that you are coming in June, for in August it is very hot here, and we have a lot of work to do.

I shall be at the station with father to meet you. If you are not too tired we can return on foot. You can leave your luggage at the station. As father often goes to town to do some shopping, he will be able to fetch it later.

Your friend,
ELSIE

16. Some years ago we lived in a small town in the south. We had a large house which my father had bought there. From the windows of the two rooms at the back we could see our garden which was very beautiful, although it was not very large.

This garden gave us great joy. My little sister found it especially pretty, and liked to play in it for hours. As I was older than she, I preferred to sit in the shade of the trees where I could read something interesting.

When my younger sister got tired, she often sat down near my chair and listened to me while I read her a story. Sometimes she was so tired that she fell asleep on the grass. I had to wake her up.

17. Before I fell asleep I prepared everything for the following day. I knew that I would have no time then. I slept well the whole night. When I looked out of the window the next morning, it was raining heavily.

I dressed, and then carried all my things downstairs as quietly as possible in order not to disturb the other people in the house. I put on my raincoat before I stepped out into the street. At that early hour the street was quite deserted.

Without looking round I hurried to the next corner. I was about to cross the road when a man appeared out of a shop. He ran quickly past me, and vanished round the corner. A moment later I heard the engine of a car. I was still wondering what to do when I heard a shout behind me.

18. A few days ago we took a trip to a small town which has a very old and interesting castle. This castle is visited by many people every year, although it is a ruin. As the castle stands on a high hill, the view is really marvellous.

We decided to rest before we entered the castle. Not far from us we saw some trees under which we could sit down. While we were sitting there we ate a few sandwiches.

About half past one we set off again. Slowly we climbed up the steep hill. When we reached the top we walked through the main entrance into the castle. Fortunately not many people had come that day. We were able to climb up the high tower without difficulty.

From here we had a splendid view. Below us lay the town, and in the distance the river gleamed like a piece of silver. After half an hour up here we visited other parts of the castle. We wanted, of course, to stay longer, but we had to hurry back into the town to catch the train at quarter to seven.

19. When I was a small child I was always ill. At last the doctor told my mother that I would never be healthy if I stayed in the smoke of a town. Therefore I was sent into the country to live with my grandfather, who had a large farm.

I shall never forget that long journey by train. I have no idea how long it lasted. I know that I gazed through the window, until I was so tired that I fell asleep.

When I woke up I had arrived. After I had waited a few minutes on the platform, a car appeared, out of which my grandfather slowly climbed. He looked as if he were pleased to see me. When he saw me he hurried across the road. I knew at once that I would be happy there.

20. We have now been in Germany for seven weeks. When we left Dover it was raining, and on the sea it was very cold. I was afraid that I would be seasick. Although I had never been on a steamer before, nothing happened to me during the crossing.

We spent all night in the train and at six o'clock in the morning we reached Cologne. After we had eaten something warm, we went on board the Rhine steamer. Here we were able to sleep a short while until we were wakened by the noise from the engine-room.

As the weather was bright and clear we were able to see the castles and towns on both banks. We spent the last week of the holidays in a small village in the mountains.

21. The doctor was tired. He had taken a long walk by the sea through the wind and rain. Now he wanted to read

for an hour. Suddenly he remembered the object which he had found on the beach. He drew it out of his pocket. It looked like an old whistle although it was quite different from anything he had seen before. He put it to his mouth, but no sound came. It seemed as if it were full of sand.

After he had knocked it against the table he tried it again. This time he succeeded. He held it in his hand and looked at it again. It was brighter than before and he could see something on it.

He went to the window in order to see better. There were three short words but he could not discover what they said. He put the whistle down and thought nothing more about it.

22. On Saturday our parents said to us, "We are going shopping. You must stay at home. Do not play in the street!" Little Hans replied, "We shall play the whole morning in the garden, until you come home."

Soon the parents were ready and left the house. As they had not much time they had to walk quickly down the street. They wanted to catch the bus that left at half past nine.

When they arrived in town they went from shop to shop. Sometimes they had to wait a long time, because so many people were there. At last they succeeded in getting everything. Before the departure of the bus they went into a restaurant to drink a cup of coffee.

At half past twelve they returned to the market-place. As the bus was already there they climbed in. A few minutes later the bus left. After travelling half an hour they reached the village where they lived. We two children were delighted to see our parents. We told them what we had done all morning.

23. Last Saturday my cousin returned from a German university. He has been studying there for six months. He visited me because he knew that I had lived in the same town many years ago.

He told me that everything was quite different now. When I was there it was still a small town, surrounded by woods and fields. All the trees have now been cut down, and in the fields stand many new houses.

There is only one piece of land which is still without houses. It is now a beautiful park with a large lake in the middle. Under the trees there are seats where one can sit for hours.

24. Peter woke up at half past six. Quickly he jumped out of bed and went to the window. He wanted to see if the day was fine. But the sky was dark and it was raining heavily. He hoped that the sun would soon come through the clouds, for to-day he wanted to visit his uncle and aunt who lived in the country.

After breakfast he walked to the station to catch the train. Before the train left the sky was much clearer. When he arrived at his uncle's the sky was cloudless, and Peter was able to spend the whole afternoon outside. He went for a walk with his cousin Hans. Then they bathed in a small lake near the house. Afterwards Peter sat in the garden in the shade of the trees, until it got dark. Then he had to return home.

25. On Saturday our uncle said to us: "Let's take a trip to the sea this afternoon. We have not been there for a long time and if the weather remains good it will be a marvellous day for us. You can bathe and climb up the steep rocks, whilst your aunt and I sit in the sunshine on the beach."

"It would be lovely," my brother said. Suddenly he remembered that he had promised to play tennis that afternoon. So he had to say "I'm sorry, but I cannot come with you." We therefore decided to stay at home.

At half past five it suddenly began to rain and it did not stop until it was quite dark. We were pleased that we had not gone to the seaside. If we had gone there it would have been very unpleasant.

26. Yesterday my eldest brother arrived early in the morning, although we had not expected him. He had travelled the whole night in order to see us as soon as possible. He looked tired and hungry. After he had eaten his breakfast he went to bed.

At half past five he got up and came downstairs. He then told us why he had come home. He had spent several weeks with friends in the country, where they have a house with a lovely garden. On the previous Sunday evening his friends told him that they wanted to sell this house. As our parents have always wanted a house with a large garden, he came home to ask them if he should buy it.

27. I have been learning German for five years. Now I want to travel abroad to visit countries where German is

spoken. My friend who was abroad last year advised me to visit Switzerland during the winter. He said that Basle was very interesting. I hope to spend a few days there, for there is much to see.

If I wish to visit Germany I can travel from Basle along the Rhine. It would be quite interesting to go by train to Bonn. The journey lasts about six hours, and on the way the scenery is really wonderful. If I had the time I could go by steamer to Koblenz and then travel on by train. By this means one has more time and opportunity to enjoy the beauties of nature.

28. The cinema was supposed to begin at half past seven. The two brothers set out at seven o'clock. If his brother had not held him tightly by the hand, little John would have fallen several times.

Many people were hurrying along the street. In the houses and shops and on the streets lights were burning. In the market-place a few men were standing reading the evening newspaper. The children hurried past them and at last they reached the cinema. They entered it through a large glass door. They had to wait almost half an hour until they were allowed to buy tickets.

As soon as they had bought the tickets they went upstairs to find a good seat. The film which they saw was very interesting.

29. Last summer I visited Germany for the first time. I spent the whole time with a German family in Hanover. The youngest son, who was just as old as I, had already visited England the previous year; he had stayed a month in our house.

I was rather frightened because I had to make the journey alone. I had never been abroad before. I remember the journey very well. I travelled across the North Sea during the night on a large steamer. I saw nothing until we arrived in Holland on the next morning.

After breakfast on the steamer I asked a porter where the train was. He helped me to find my seat and soon we were travelling through Holland.

I was very pleased to reach Hanover, where my German friend met me at the station. As he lived outside the town we had to take a taxi. At first I was afraid to speak German, but after a few days I discovered that people understood me quite well.

30. Once a stranger was visiting a small town. As he had missed the last train, he had to spend the night in the hotel. Because he was tired, he immediately went up to his room, undressed and went to bed. For a long time he could not get to sleep. At last he succeeded.

Suddenly he was awakened by a loud noise. Someone was knocking at the door. "What is the matter?" the gentleman called angrily. "Sir," came the reply, "you have left your umbrella downstairs." "It doesn't matter," he answered. "I can get it in the morning." Half an hour later the same voice wakened him again. "Sir, that umbrella did not belong to you. Another gentleman has taken it."

31. Last summer Peter decided to spend a few weeks abroad. He wished to visit Germany, as he had learnt a little German at school. Although it was the first time Peter had visited Germany, he enjoyed himself.

In the Youth Hostels he was able to meet all sorts of people from different countries. Every evening he listened, and soon was able to understand what was being said. He did not speak much himself, because his German was not very good.

In one hostel he was asked if he could sing an English song. He had a good voice, and another hiker accompanied him on the piano. After the song, he thanked the pianist in German.

To his surprise he found that the boy understood him very well. After they had talked for about an hour, Peter discovered that the boy wanted to visit the same towns as he. So they decided to continue their trip together.

32. When we got up it was a bright clear morning. It had rained heavily in the night but everything now looked fresh. Outside, the air was quite warm, although it was still so early. After we had had breakfast we walked along the main street of the village.

Although it was not yet eight o'clock, some shops were already open. A few children were playing in the street. People were hurrying to their work. I looked at the sky, which was cloudless and blue. Then I turned to my friend and said, "I like this village. Let's stay here a few days."

"Certainly," my friend replied. "I have nothing against it. I should also like to stay here. It would be interesting to climb that high church-tower. In good weather the view from the top must be marvellous. The inn is also very comfortable."

We returned to the inn and asked the innkeeper if we could stay a few days longer. He was very pleased. Not many strangers came to the village, and he was glad that we wanted to stay.

33. John and Henry were shopping in town for their mother. They had to visit a large number of shops and were therefore very tired when they were finished. As they were coming out of the last shop, John said, "Let's go home by taxi! We have so many parcels that we shall certainly lose some if we go by bus."

"That's a good idea!" Henry said. "If we wait at the corner of this street a taxi will soon pass." They waited on the pavement. There were crowds of people going home from their work, and the traffic was also very heavy.

At last a taxi came in sight. John waved to the driver who stopped near them. "Where d'you want to go?" he asked. "10 Frederick Street," Henry said, as he got in. Their parents were surprised to see them arrive in a taxi.

34. Dear Tom,

We have been at the sea-side since Tuesday. To-day is already Saturday and I have not yet written to you. How quickly the time has passed! We are leading a very lazy life here. I get up at half past nine, have breakfast, and then go for a walk through the town to buy something; later I go to the beach. If the weather is fine I undress and lie down. I am already quite brown.

Near us are little children who play for hours in the water with their little boats. Sometimes their parents help them to build harbours for these boats. When they come back again the next day, everything has been destroyed by the waves. In spite of this they are quite happy.

When a strong wind is blowing we sit in our deck-chairs near the pier. In the evening we sometimes go to the cinema, if there is a good film; otherwise we stay in the hotel and dance, or listen to the band whilst other people dance. Write soon,
Your old friend,
JOHN

35. My father bought me a bicycle for my birthday a few weeks ago. As all my friends had cycles I was very pleased. I should now be able to accompany them on their trips. My friends were also delighted, and we decided to go for a long trip on the first day of the holidays.

It was a hot day, and the roads were dusty. There was fortunately very little traffic, and the cars that passed us were travelling very fast. About midday we stopped for lunch. We had all brought sandwiches, so we only needed to buy lemonade in a village.

After we had been cycling for some hours, we knew that we were lost. However, we continued to the next village and looked for the policeman. He was standing by a shop talking to the butcher. He soon showed us the shortest way home.

36. Just as Fred was about to cross the bridge he heard someone call his name. Turning round, he saw his friend Albert. "Where are you going?" Albert asked. "Oh, I was only going for a walk," he replied. Suddenly the door of a shop near them was opened. A man rushed out, holding a parcel. He was seen immediately by the shopkeeper. "Stop thief!" the latter cried, as he ran after the man.

The thief was running towards the bridge. "Come on!" Fred cried. "We must catch him." They ran as fast as they could, but fortunately a policeman had seen the incident and arrested the man.

37. It was the first time that little Charles had travelled alone. His mother had gone to the station with him, and had waited until the train to Berlin had arrived. As soon as the train stopped, Charles got in and found an empty seat in the corner of a "non-smoker". Quickly he put his luggage on the rack above his seat, and then sat down. He looked out of the window until the train was about to leave.

Then he got up, ran to the window and called goodbye to his mother, who waved until the train had vanished in the distance. Half an hour after the departure, the ticket-collector entered the compartment. Charles looked everywhere, but could not find his ticket.

38. When I was in Germany last summer I spent two weeks with a German friend, whose parents live not far from Bonn.

Hannover: Brunnen am Holzmarkt

Hameln: zwei Bürgerhäuser am Rathausplatz

During my visit we were able to go on a cycling tour up the Rhine.

As the weather was so warm, we decided to sleep in the open whenever we could. We carried a tent with us, and were able to buy food and milk in the villages through which we travelled.

Every evening we cooked something warm before we went to sleep. Fortunately we had good weather the whole time, so that we looked quite brown when we returned home. If it had been cold, we would have had to spend the night in a Youth Hostel.

39. This morning I got up earlier than usual because I wanted to go to the market with my aunt. It was already a quarter past nine when we at last reached the market-place. There was so much to see—brightly-coloured flowers, and all sorts of vegetables and fruit.

After my aunt had bought everything she needed, we went into a small restaurant. Here we had a cup of coffee. As we still had half an hour before the departure of our train, we walked along the main street. We saw the town-hall, which is the oldest building in the town. We caught our train shortly after one o'clock, and arrived home tired but happy.

40. During our trip through the hills we had seen nobody. It seemed to us as if we were the only people here. After a warm morning it had begun to rain. We had come without raincoats, and were now cold. At last we saw a little farmhouse in the distance. We hurried across the fields to reach it.

When we were near enough, I noticed that the door was open, in spite of the cold weather. We knocked twice, but nobody appeared. We decided to go in, to see if anything was the matter. At first it seemed as if the whole house were empty.

We were about to leave the house when we heard a slight noise. It came from a room on the left. When we entered the room we saw a man on the floor. He was lying helpless in the middle of the room, which was in great disorder.

41. "Father, I'll fetch the doctor. You must stay at home with mother," Peter said. His father looked at him. "You might lose your way, and it will soon be very dark," he replied. "I know the path through the valley," the boy answered. "Mother needs you here."

"Then you must take Rex," his father answered. "Certainly. I wouldn't go without him." So the two set off, the boy and the dog. Peter's father had been quite right. Soon it became very dark in the valley, but Peter was not afraid because the dog remained with him the whole time.

Then the sky became darker still with heavy clouds. Rex trotted very near to his little master. Suddenly Peter felt something cold on his face. White flakes began to fall around him. It was snowing heavily. Peter knew that the snow would soon cover the path but he had to fetch the doctor.

42. DEAR FRED,

To-day I have received a long letter from my brother. As you know he has been very ill for several months. Have you already heard that he is now in France? He has been there since the beginning of June.

He says that the weather has been very warm. I hope that his visit will help him to get well again. As he learnt French at school, he ought to have no difficulty with the language.

In his last letter he told me that he bathed every day. There are many woods in the neighbourhood of the village where he is staying, so he frequently walks in them for hours. If you have the time, write to him; he is always glad to hear from his old friends.

With many greetings,
JOHN

43. A few years ago a gentleman was driving in his car in the country. Just as he drove past an old farmer, who was standing under a tree, a dog ran across the road. Before the man could stop, the animal had been killed by the car.

The driver, who had seen the farmer, got out of his car, went to him and said, "I am sorry that this accident has happened. As the animal is dead, I must pay for it." He then asked the man if twenty marks were enough for the dog.

For a moment the farmer said nothing. At last he said, "Yes." At once the man gave him the money, walked back to his car, and drove off. The old farmer waited until the car had vanished in the distance. Then he said to himself, "Now, I would like to find the man to whom the animal really belonged."

44. Little Joan often went shopping for her mother. One morning her mother said, "Joan, I want some coffee and butter from the grocer's. Would you like to fetch them?" "Certainly, mother," Joan replied, "and we also need some tea." "Good. You can buy that at Mr. Smith's, and you can also pay for the papers."

Joan felt very important as she set off with her little basket. She had to catch the bus into town. When she arrived, Joan first went to the grocer's shop. There she bought half a pound of coffee and a pound of butter.

Then Joan went to the bookshop. She had to wait a long time there, because there were so many people in the shop. Finally the shopkeeper came to her. She bought a bottle of ink and paid for the papers. Although she wanted to look at the shops, she went straight home.

45. After breakfast George climbed into his car and drove slowly through the village. A few children who were playing in the street looked at him as he drove past.

Soon the village lay far behind him, and he came nearer to the sea. At last he reached an old tower standing on the edge of a cliff. Here he got out of his car, sat down, and lit a cigarette, while he enjoyed the marvellous view. Below him lay the dark-blue sea. In the distance glittered the white houses of the little village.

Suddenly he heard a shout. He looked round. Four men jumped out of the bushes. George tried to run back to his car, but the men were standing between him and the road. Without losing a moment, he turned round and climbed down the cliff. Several shots whistled past him.

46. George and I have been good friends for many years. We are both in the same class, although he is six months older than I.

In the summer George hopes to go to Hanover, because his father is a soldier there. He is trying to learn as much German as possible. He wants to speak it well so that he can understand what people say when he speaks with them.

Naturally he is looking forward to his visit. It will be the first time that he has been abroad. He has promised to write to me frequently whilst he is there. I asked him to write in German. I shall then find out if he has learnt much.

47. After the ship left England, the sea became very rough. At first we stayed on deck to enjoy the fresh air. Soon, however, the wind became so strong that we could scarcely stand.

My father said we must go down below. We found our beds and lay down. Soon I fell asleep in spite of the noise.

When I woke up everything was quiet. I was very surprised until I went on deck. I then saw that we had already arrived in Ostend. The steamer lay at the quay opposite the station.

Soon afterwards we went ashore, showed our passports, and opened our cases for the customs. We had not much time to look round in Ostend, because we had to catch the Cologne train which departed at ten minutes to six.

48. Last Thursday I got up very early because I wanted to visit my uncle. As he lives in the country, I had to go by train. I walked to the station instead of going by bus. When I arrived I found a lot of people waiting for the train.

After I had waited on the platform more than half an hour, I asked a lady what was the matter. "I do not know," she replied. "I have been here since twenty past five, and the train on which I wanted to travel has not yet arrived."

At that moment a porter hurried past us. Quickly I followed him and asked him if he could tell me anything. He looked very serious.

49. A few days ago we were invited to visit some friends who had just bought a new house. We spent a very pleasant evening together, and it was nearly midnight when we said good-bye.

As it was so late we had to walk home. Fortunately the weather was fine, and it was quite pleasant to stroll through the empty streets. Most of the houses were quite dark, but at times we saw a light at a window as we went past. Sometimes we could hear voices in the distance, but we could not see anyone.

As we came round a corner a policeman appeared. He asked us politely who we were. He said, "Do not be alarmed. I have to ask on account of thieves who are often in this neighbourhood."

After he had wished us good-night, we hurried home. When we reached the house, we were surprised to see a light in one of the rooms. Then I remembered what the policeman had said. I quickly found him again, and asked him to come back with us.

50. It had been raining all morning, and a strong wind was blowing the leaves along the road. When we reached the river, the water was already high. We crossed the bridge, and arrived in the town.

Here we had something to eat, and then we did some shopping. It was about half past five when we set off home. It was still raining heavily, and the wind had become stronger. Suddenly I saw something which frightened me. A large branch had been broken off by the wind, and lay near the road.

It was quite dark when we again reached the river. I wanted to turn back, but my friend said we must go on. Suddenly we heard someone calling, "Help, help!"

51. It was late one stormy evening when the village policeman announced that two boys were lost in the mountains. He asked for help, because he had to find them. We all offered our assistance, for we knew the mountains well.

First we had to put on boots and heavy overcoats and we all brought torches with us. Then we met the policeman near the last house in the village. There were ten of us. Our families had also come so far with us to wish us good luck.

They waited until we had disappeared in the darkness and then went back home. We had not gone very far when we heard voices calling faintly. It was the two boys. They had seen our torches, and were very glad that we had found them so quickly.

52. When the day's work was finished, all the men went back home. In the fields and in the streets everything became silent. From time to time the barking of a dog was heard, or the call of a bird out of one of the tall oak-trees.

In the houses the women were cooking the evening meal. The men sat in the living-room, smoking and reading. They were looking forward to a pleasant evening by the fire.

While the older children were doing their homework, the youngest child played quietly with its toys on the floor. Soon the supper was brought in and put on the table.

When the meal was over the whole family sat round the fire. At half past nine the father said, "Put your toys away, children. You must go to bed now."

53. Last Saturday we wished to take a trip into the country. When we got up at half past seven the weather was marvellous. Quickly we got ourselves ready, and soon we were outside the town.

We left the road and wandered through the woods until we reached an inn near a small lake. Here we decided to drink a cup of coffee. Half an hour later we set off again. As the road was becoming steeper we had to walk more slowly. At last we reached the top of the mountain.

Here we had a marvellous view across the country. Below us lay a pretty valley through which a little stream was flowing. Not a cloud was to be seen in the sky.

As we were now hungry, we sat down and ate our sandwiches. For two hours we lay in the hot sunshine. The time passed all too quickly. The sinking sun reminded us of the time. Soon we were descending the slope.

54. DEAR MOTHER,

Have you received the postcard I sent a few days ago? I wrote as soon as I arrived in Aachen. After the long journey I was very tired so I did not write much.

Before I came to Germany I thought I could speak some German. Now I find that nobody seems to understand me. My German friends are trying to help me as much as possible. They speak slowly and clearly whenever I am with them. They say, "You must first understand before you can answer, so don't talk too much."

Father often said that I talked too much, didn't he? He would be very pleased if he saw me now. I hardly open my mouth. If I follow the advice of my friends, I shall perhaps succeed in learning the language.

With best wishes from your loving son,
TOM

55. Last year we spent our holidays in Switzerland. During our stay we visited several interesting towns. Once we decided to stay in one town for three days. Early on the first morning, we set out to visit the old castle which stands on a hill outside the town. When we reached the entrance, we

discovered that we could only visit it in the afternoon. So we had to return to the town.

As it was now getting warm we decided to walk to the river. Unfortunately the water was so cold that we could not bathe. It was a pity, because the sky was quite blue and cloudless. After a walk along the bank, we went to our hotel for lunch. In the afternoon we again left the hotel.

Vocabulary for Prose Passages 1–45

Note:
1. Vocabulary once given is not repeated.
2. Only irregular plurals of nouns are given.
3. Separable prefixes are shown thus: **an-sehen.**
4. Strong verbs are shown thus: **sehen** (*s*). A list of strong verbs and their changes will be found in § 5 of the grammar.

1.

trip	**der Ausflug**	to ask	**§ 28 B**
car	**das Auto (-s)**	to try	**versuchen**
sea	**die See, das Meer**	to be right	**recht haben**
		to begin	**beginnen** (*s*)
breakfast	**das Frühstück**	to leave	**§ 28 B**
weather	**das Wetter**	to forget	**vergessen** (*s*)
hour	**die Stunde**	to put	**§ 28 B**
wallet	**die Brieftasche**	early	**früh**
rear-seat	**der Rücksitz**	a little	**ein wenig**
garage	**die Garage**	bad	**schlecht**
to remember	**sich erinnern an** (*acc.*)	perhaps	**vielleicht**
		(just) about to	**(eben) im Begriff**
to get up	**auf-stehen** (*s*)		
to look (seek)	**suchen**	everywhere	**überall**

2.

letter	**der Brief**	to return	**zurück-kehren**
friend	**der Freund**	to visit	**besuchen**
month	**der Monat**	to look forward	**§ 26, see auf**
doctor	**der Arzt**	yesterday	**gestern**
country	**das Land**	rather	**ziemlich**
people	**die Leute** (*pl.*)	unhappy	**unglücklich**
week	**die Woche**	unfortunately	**leider, unglücklicherweise**
address	**die Adresse**		
to receive	**bekommen** (*s*)	at first	**zuerst**
to study	**studieren**	lonely	**einsam**
to go abroad	**ins Ausland fahren** (*s*)	at Easter	**zu Ostern**
to learn	**lerne**	sure	**sicher**

3.

coat	**der Mantel**	to rain	**regnen**
shelter	**der Schutz**	to stop	**§ 28 B**
hedge	**die Hecke**	to hurry	**eilen**
distance	**die Ferne**	to spend (time)	**verbringen** (*s*)
driver	**der Fahrer**	to reach	**erreichen**

104

moment	der Augenblick	to get out	aus-steigen (s)
ride	die Fahrt	to thank	danken (dat.)
village	das Dorf	bright	hell
Youth Hostel	die Jugendherberge	heavily	schwer
		wet	naß
to set out	sich auf den Weg machen	nobody	niemand
		marvellous	herrlich

4.

parents	die Eltern (pl.)	to lay (a table)	decken
cinema	das Kino (-s)	to talk, chat	plaudern
table	der Tisch	to notice	bemerken
side	die Seite	to tell	erzählen
soul	der Mensch (-en)	yesterday evening	gestern abend
light	das Licht	far	weit
film	der Film	dark	dunkel
to decide	beschließen (s)	at last	endlich
to go (and meet)	ab-holen	immediately	(so)gleich

5.

train	der Zug	to miss (a train)	verpassen
station	der Bahnhof	to wait	warten
platform	der Bahnsteig	to turn	sich um-wenden (s)
voice	die Stimme		
innkeeper	der Wirt	to recognise	erkennen (s)
hand	die Hand	to put	§ 28 B
pocket	die Tasche	to belong (to)	gehören (dat.)
wristlet-watch	die Armbanduhr	gentle	leicht
to fall	fallen (s)	possible	möglich
to wear	tragen (s)	what is the matter?	was ist los?
to catch (train)	erreichen		

6.

to live	wohnen	to explain	erklären
nearest	nächst	to happen	geschehen (s)
town	die Stadt	quite	ganz
old	alt	easy	leicht
uninteresting	uninteressant	to find	finden (s)
journey	die Reise	to follow	folgen (dat.)
to hope	hoffen	taxi	das Taxi
to see	sehen (s)	quick	schnell
to know	wissen (s)	to jump in	hinein-springen (s)
to do	tun (s)		
frightened	erschrocken	to show	zeigen
porter	der Gepäckträger	driver	der Fahrer
		piece	das Stück
case	der Koffer	paper	das Papier

7.

bridge	die Brücke	to climb	steigen (s)
bank (river)	das Ufer	to throw	werfen (s)
river	der Fluß	to fetch	holen

7.

edge	der Rand	to disappear	verschwinden (s)
policeman	der Schutzmann (-leute)	to lose	verlieren (s)
corner	die Ecke	unfortunate	unglücklich
place	die Stelle		

8.

leaving examination	das Abitur	interest (in)	das Interesse (für)
grammar school	das Gymnasium	to sit (an exam)	machen
accident	der Unfall	to be killed	um-kommen (s)
death	der Tod	to pass (an exam)	bestehen (s)
bank	die Bank	almost	fast
clerk, employee	der Angestellte (adj. noun)	only (adj.)	einzig
		in the open air	im Freien

9.

hotel	das Hotel (-s)	to change (clothes)	sich um-ziehen (s)
police-station	die Polizeiwache	to wish	wünschen
help	die Hilfe	to fall asleep	ein-schlafen
time (occasion)	das Mal	to waken	§ 28 B
sound	das Geräusch	tired	müde
to possess	besitzen (s)	slowly	langsam
to knock	klopfen	on the left	links
to wash	waschen (s)	fortunately	glücklicherweise
		still	noch

10.

farm	der Bauernhof	to tie	binden (s)
holidays	die Ferien (pl.)	to lie	liegen (s)
farmer	der Bauer (-n, -n)	to be pleased	sich freuen
task	die Aufgabe	to lie down	sich hin-legen
string	der Bindfaden	to look (seem)	scheinen (s)
corn	das Korn	to prefer	vor-ziehen (s)
ground	die Erde	hard	schwer
rest	die Pause	fresh	frisch
to earn	verdienen	outside	draußen
to greet	begrüßen	finished	fertig

11.

destination	das Ziel	to sit down	sich hin-setzen
stream	der Bach	to open	öffnen
rucksack	der Rucksack	to taste	schmecken
sandwich	das Butterbrot	to grow	wachsen (s)
valley	das Tal	shady	schattig
one and a half	anderthalb	different (adj.)	ander

12.

ball	der Ball	to step forward	hervor-treten (s)
to appear	erscheinen (s)		

to seize	**ergreifen** (s)	suddenly	**plötzlich**
to scream	**schreien** (s)	naturally	**natürlich**
deep	**tief**	steep	**steil**

13.
coast	**die Küste**	in any case	**jedenfalls**
accommodation	**die Unterkunft**	difficult	**schwer**
life	**das Leben**	at least	**wenigstens**
to advise	**raten** (s) (dat.)	lazy	**faul**
to obtain	**erhalten** (s)	a pity	**schade**

14.
crowd	**die Menge Leute**	to invite	**ein-laden** (s)
corner-seat	**der Eckplatz**	excited	**aufgeregt**
luggage	**das Gepäck**	previous	**vorig**
stay	**der Aufenthalt**	pleasant	**angenehm**

15.
bathing-costume	**der Badeanzug**	to meet	**abholen**
hill	**der Hügel**	to go shopping	**Einkäufe machen**
to expect	**erwarten**		
to bathe	**schwimmen** (s)	glad	**froh**

16.
south	**der Süden**	to listen	**zu-hören**
joy	**die Freude**	at the back	**hinten**
shade	**der Schatten**	especially	**besonders**
story	**die Geschichte**	interesting	**interessant**
grass	**das Gras**		

17.
thing	**die Sache**	to disturb	**stören**
shop	**der Laden**	to look round	**sich um-sehen** (s)
shout	**der Ruf**		
engine	**der Motor** (-en)	to wonder	**überlegen**
to prepare	**vor-bereiten**	deserted	**verlassen**

18.
castle	**das Schloß**	difficulty	**die Schwierigkeit**
ruin	**die Ruine**		
view	**die Aussicht**	part	**der Teil**
top (mountain)	**der Gipfel**	to rest	**sich aus-ruhen**
main entrance	**der Haupteingang**	to gleam	**glänzen**
tower	**der Turm**	really	**wirklich**

19.
smoke	**der Rauch**	to gaze	**blicken**
idea	**die Ahnung**	never	**nie**
to send	**schicken**	at once	**sofort**
to last	**dauern**	healthy	**gesund**

20.

steamer	der Dampfer	engine room	der Maschinen-raum (⸚e)
crossing	die Überfahrt	to be afraid	sich fürchten
while	die Weile	seasick	seekrank
noise	der Lärm	bright	hell

21.

wind	der Wind	sound	der Ton
rain	der Regen	sand	der Sand
object	der Gegenstand	to try	versuchen
beach	der Strand	to discover	entdecken
whistle	die Pfeife	different (from)	anders (als)
mouth	der Mund	bright, clean	blank

22.

bus	der Autobus	market-place	der Marktplatz
departure	die Abfahrt		
restaurant	das Restaurant	a long time	lange
cup	die Tasse	delighted	erfreut

23.

cousin (m)	der Vetter (-s, -n)	seat, bench	die Bank (⸚e)
university	die Universität	to surround	umgeben (s)
park	der Park (-s)	to cut down	fällen
lake	der See (-s, -n)	for hours	stundenlang

24.

sky	der Himmel	cloudless	wolkenlos
cloud	die Wolke	afterwards	nachher

25.

rock	der Felsen (-)	marvellous	herrlich
sunshine	der Sonnenschein	lovely	wunderbar
to climb	hinauf-klettern	pleased	froh
to promise	versprechen (s)	unpleasant	unangenehm

26.

several	mehrere	previous	vorig
		to expect	erwarten

27.

Switzerland	die Schweiz	nature	die Natur
scenery	die Landschaft	beauty	die Schönheit
opportunity	die Gelegenheit	to enjoy	genießen (s)
		by this means	auf diese Weise

28.

paper	die Zeitung	to burn	brennen (s)
ticket	die Eintrittskarte	tightly	fest
seat	der Platz	almost	fast, beinahe

29.

to understand	verstehen (s)	alone	allein
rather	ziemlich	in our house	bei uns

30.

stranger	der Fremde (*adj. noun*)	reply	die Antwort
gentleman	der Herr (-n, -en)	to spend (night)	übernachten
umbrella	der Regenschirm	angrily	zornig
		it doesn't matter	es macht nichts

31.

hiker	der Wanderer	to enjoy oneself	sich amüsieren
song	das Lied	to accompany	begleiten
surprise	die Überraschung	all sorts of	allerlei
piano	das Klavier	to continue	weiter-machen

32.

main street	die Hauptstraße	to turn to	sich wenden an (*s*) (*acc.*)
to have nothing against it	nichts dagegen haben	certainly	gerne, jawohl
		to have breakfast	frühstücken

33.

number	die Anzahl	pavement	der Bürgersteig
parcel	das Paket (-e)	traffic	der Verkehr
idea	der Einfall	heavy (of traffic)	stark, rege

34.

life	das Leben	to lead	führen
boat	das Boot	to build	bauen
harbour	der Hafen	to destroy	zerstören
deck-chair	der Liegestuhl	to blow	wehen
pier	die Landungsbrücke	to dance	tanzen
		otherwise	sonst
band	die Kapelle	to cross	überqueren

35.

birthday	der Geburtstag	to need	brauchen
lemonade	die Limonade	to cycle	radeln
butcher	der Metzger	dusty	staubig

36.

name	der Name (-ns, -n)	to rush	stürzen
		to catch	fangen (*s*)
incident	der Vorfall	to arrest	verhaften
thief	der Dieb	to cross	überqueren

37.

non-smoker	der Nichtraucher	ticket	die Fahrkarte
rack	das Gepäcknetz	to wave	winken
ticket-collector	der Schaffner	empty	leer
compartment	das Abteil	departure	die Abfahrt

38.

Rhine	der Rhein	milk	die Milch
tent	das Zelt	to cook	kochen
food, provisions	die Lebensmittel (*pl.*)	in the open	im Freien

39.
vegetables	**das Gemüse**	building	**das Gebäude**
fruit	**das Obst**	usual	**gewöhnlich**
town-hall	**das Rathaus**	brightly coloured	**bunt**

40.
farmhouse	**das Bauernhaus**	disorder	**die Unordnung**
floor	**der Boden**	helpless	**hilflos**

41.
master	**der Herr (-n, -en)**	to look at	**an-sehen** (s)
flake	**die Flocke**	to feel	**spüren**
to cover	**bedecken**	to touch	**berühren**

42.
language	**die Sprache**	to get well	**genesen** (s)
neighbourhood	**die Nachbarschaft**	frequently	**oft, häufig**

43.
to drive	**fahren** (s)	dead	**tot**
to pay	**zahlen**	six marks	**sechs Mark**

44.
butter	**die Butter**	pound	**das Pfund**
bus	**der Autobus**	bookshop	**die Buchhandlung**
grocer	**der Lebensmittelkaufmann**		
basket	**der Korb**	shopkeeper	**der (Buch-)händler**
grocer's shop	**das Lebensmittelgeschäft**	bottle	**die Flasche**
		important	**wichtig**

45.
cliff	**der Felsabhang**	to light	**an-zünden**
cigarette	**die Zigarette**	to glitter	**glänzen**
bushes	**das Gebüsch**	to whistle	**pfeifen** (s)
shot	**der Schuß**	shout, call	**der Ruf**

In order to provide practice in unseen translation, no vocabularies are given for proses 46–55

SECTION 4

German Prose Extracts for Translation into English

The following hints on translation into English should be carefully studied and followed.

1. Always aim at an accurate translation which contains every idea in the passage.
2. Never make blind guesses at words or parts of sentences; proceed from what you do know to what is doubtful.
3. Do not twist what you know to be correct to fit something you know little about. Be sure that what you write makes sense; read your version to yourself, and if it does not sound sensible, then it is inaccurate. So many translations lose marks because they are not written in English.
4. Always revise your translation carefully to ensure that you have used correct tenses and correct singulars or plurals.
5. Your final version must be neatly written, grammatical and in accurate English.

1.   SOUNDS IN THE NIGHT

Als Hans in der Mitte der Nacht aufwachte, war sein Freund schon fort. Sogleich stand er auf und ging an die Tür, die offen stand. Nichts war zu sehen oder zu hören. Hans fing an sich zu fürchten; er kehrte ins Zimmer zurück und eilte ans Fenster. Ein Streifen Mondlicht fiel durch die Scheibe. Das Zimmer war so hell, daß er alles auf dem Fußboden erkennen konnte. Draußen blies der Wind; die großen Bäume in der Allee beugten sich, und die welken Blätter raschelten in der Veranda. Durch all den Lärm hörte Hans eine Stimme. Er wußte nicht, ob diese von einem Tier oder von einem Menschen kam. Jedenfalls war der Ton so traurig, daß es ihm weh tat. Leise ging er die Treppe hinab und trat in den mondhellen Garten. Er spähte überall hin. Endlich erblickte er jemand, der auf der Erde lag und ächzte.

2. A RESTLESS EVENING

Reinhard setzte sich hin, um zu arbeiten, aber es gelang ihm nicht. Nachdem er es eine Stunde lang vergebens versucht hatte, ging er ins Wohnzimmer hinab. Es war aber niemand da. Auf Elisabeths Nähtisch lag ein rotes Band, das sie am Nachmittag um den Hals getragen hatte. Er nahm es in die Hand, sah es an und legte es wieder hin.

Er hatte keine Ruhe; er ging an den See hinab und band den Kahn los; er ruderte hinüber und ging noch einmal alle Wege, die er kurz vorher mit Elisabeth gegangen war. Als er nach Hause kam, war es dunkel. Auf dem Hofe begegnete ihm der Kutscher, der die Pferde auf die Wiese bringen wollte. Die Reisenden waren eben zurückgekehrt. Bei seinem Eintritt in den Hausflur hörte er Erich im Wohnzimmer auf und ab schreiten. Er ging nicht zu ihm hinein; er stand einen Augenblick still und stieg dann leise die Treppe hinauf nach seinem Zimmer. Hier setzte er sich in den Lehnstuhl ans Fenster. So saß er stundenlang.

Nach T. STORM, *Immensee*

3. A FAITHFUL DOG

Vorigen Winter ging ich in der Abenddämmerung am Kanal entlang, als ich plötzlich etwas winseln hörte. Ich stieg hinab und griff nach der Stelle, wo ich die Stimme hörte, denn ich glaubte, ein Kind zu retten. Statt dessen aber zog ich einen Pudel aus dem Wasser.

Der Pudel folgte mir nach, aber ich bin kein Liebhaber von Pudeln, also jagte ich ihn fort — aber umsonst, denn er kam mir immer noch nach. Ich prügelte ihn von mir — auch umsonst. Wenn er mir zu nahe kam, stieß ich ihn mit dem Fuß; er schrie, sah mich an, wedelte mit dem Schwanz und begleitete mich nach Hause. Noch hat er keinen Bissen Brot aus meiner Hand bekommen, und doch bin ich der einzige, dem er gehorcht und der ihn anrühren darf. Er ist ein häßlicher Pudel aber ein treuer Hund. Wenn er es länger treibt, werde ich aufhören, auf ihn zornig zu sein.

Nach G. LESSING, *Minna von Barnhelm*

PASSAGES FOR TRANSLATION INTO ENGLISH

4. VIEW FROM A TOWER

Langsam stieg Anton die steile Treppe des Turms hinauf. Oben trat er auf eine Plattform hinaus. Jetzt sah er über den Mauerrand in die Tiefe und hinaus über die ganze Landschaft. Zur Linken sank die Sonne hinter grauen Wolkenmassen in den dunklen Schatten der Wälder hinab; zur Rechten lagen ein großer Bauernhof und dahinter an der Landstraße die strohgedeckten Häuser eines Dorfes. Hinter ihm lag der Bach, der nach dem Dorfe zu floß und an seinen Ufern einen Streifen Wiesenland zeigte. Aus dem Boden erhoben sich hier und da wilde Apfelbäume mit ihren starken Stämmen und mächtigen Kronen. Unter jedem Baum war eine Insel aus Gras und Pflanzen, bunt gefärbt durch die abgefallenen Blätter.

Nach G. FREYTAG, *Soll und Haben*

5. THE MYSTERIOUS RIDER

Jetzt aber kam auf dem Deich etwas gegen mich heran; ich hörte nichts; aber immer deutlicher, wenn der halbe Mond ein schwaches Licht herabließ, glaubte ich eine dunkle Gestalt zu erkennen, und bald, da sie näher kam, sah ich es, sie saß auf einem Pferd, einem hageren Schimmel; ein dunkler Mantel flatterte um ihre Schultern und im Vorbeifliegen sahen mich zwei brennende Augen aus einem bleichen Gesicht an.

Es fiel mir jetzt ein, daß ich keinen Hufschlag gehört hatte; und Pferd und Reiter waren doch nahe an mir vorbeigeflogen. In Gedanken darüber ritt ich weiter, aber ich hatte nicht lange Zeit zum Denken, denn schon fuhr es von rückwärts wieder an mir vorbei. Dann sah ich es immer ferner vor mir; dann war es, als ob ich plötzlich seinen Schatten an der Binnenseite des Deiches hinuntergehen sähe. Als ich jene Stelle erreichte, sah ich neben dem Deich einen kleinen Teich, dessen Wasser trotz des Deiches bewegt war. Von dem Reiter sah ich nichts mehr.

Nach T. STORM, *Der Schimmelreiter*

6. FRITZ HAS A BIRTHDAY

Seit Wochen freute sich der kleine Fritz auf seinen Geburtstag, denn an jenem Tag sollte er ein schönes Geschenk von seinem Vater bekommen. Endlich war der Tag gekommen.

Die ganze Nacht vorher hatte Fritz vor Erwartung kaum schlafen können.

Beim Frühstück überreichte ihm der Vater ein großes Paket. Als er es öffnete, fand er einen schönen Drachen aus leichtem Papier darin. Am selben Nachmittag begleitete ihn der Vater auf die Wiese hinter dem Hause. Nachdem er eine lange Schnur an den Drachen gebunden hatte, lief Fritz gegen den Wind, während sein Vater den Drachen hielt. Sobald Fritz „Jetzt" rief, ließ der Vater den Drachen los; sofort stieg er gerade in die Luft hinauf. Fritz lachte vor Freude.

Aus seinem Lachen wurde aber bald Weinen, denn ein Gegenwind stürzte den Drachen in einen hohen Baum, wo er zwischen den Ästen hängenblieb. Der Vater mußte den Drachen herunterholen. Das Papier war zerrissen, eine Holzrippe war gebrochen. Weil Fritz so unglücklich aussah, versprach ihm der Vater einen neuen Drachen.

7. PAULINE TELLS OF THE CROSS AND THE OLD CUPBOARD

Der alte Herr hielt das Kreuz noch immer in seiner Hand. Nun sagte er zu Pauline: „Das Kreuz gehört dir. Sei mir nicht böse, wenn ich frage, wie es in deinen Besitz gekommen ist."

Pauline erzählte, unter welcher Bedingung und mit welchen Worten ihre Mutter es ihr gegeben hatte.

„Glück könne es dir bringen?" sagte der alte Herr. „Ach, es könnte noch jemand Glück bringen, ein unbeschreiblich herrliches Glück, wenn wir nur mehr wüßten. Hast du sonst nichts mehr von deiner Mutter?"

Pauline erzählte von dem alten Schrank, wo außer dem Kreuz noch mancherlei von ihr liege, freilich nur kleine Schmucksachen aus einer früheren Zeit, von der die Mutter nie etwas erzählt hatte.

„Die müssen wir sehen", sagte der alte Herr. An der Raschheit, mit der er von seinem Stuhle aufstand, sah man, wieviel ihm daran gelegen sei. So machten sich denn die drei auf den Weg; der alte Herr ging, in seine Gedanken vertieft, voran.

Nach O. LUDWIG, *Die Buschnovelle*

8. ON TOP OF A MOUNTAIN

Endlich waren wir auf einem Berggipfel angekommen, der uns eine herrliche Aussicht ins Tal offenbarte. Wir beschloßen, hier abzusteigen und ein bißchen zu Fuß zu gehen, um den Anblick zu genießen, der sich vor unseren Augen ausbreitete. Von waldbedeckten Hügeln umringt, lag vor uns eine weite Ebene, wodurch ein großer Fluß sich schlängelte. Zur Rechten befand sich eine Hügelkette, zur Linken waren in weiter Ferne die schneebedeckten Höhen der Alpen. Im freundlichen Blau spannte sich der Himmel über uns und seine lichte Farbe kontrastierte stark mit den schwarzen Dächern der Häuser, die um einen dunkelgrauen Kirchturm standen. Gerade in diesem Augenblick begannen die Glocken der alten Kirche den Mittag einzuläuten.

Nach W. HAUFF, *Lichtenstein*

9. THE LONE RIDER

Der Weg wurde immer steiler und der junge Reiter ließ sein Pferd jetzt langsamer gehen. Nachdem er etwa eine Stunde hinaufgestiegen war, beschloß er, unter dem Schatten einer am Wege wachsenden Eiche auszuruhen. Er stieg ab, löste den Sattelgurt und ließ das ermüdete Tier das kurze Gras aufsuchen. Er streckte sich unter der Eiche nieder und im Nu schlief er ein. Er mochte wohl eine Stunde geschlafen haben, als ihn das Wiehern des Pferdes aufschreckte. Er sah sich um und erblickte einen Mann, der sich mit dem Tier beschäftigte. Sein erster Gedanke war, daß man seine Unachtsamkeit benutzen und das Pferd entführen wolle. Er sprang auf, zog sein Schwert und war in drei Sprüngen dort. „Halt! Was hast du da mit dem Pferde zu schaffen!" rief er, indem er seine Hand etwas unsanft auf die Schulter des Mannes legte.

Nach W. HAUFF, *Lichtenstein*

10. A DOG THAT DISLIKES STRANGERS

Pauline hörte den Meerschaum; sie wußte, daß er ihr entgegenlaufen würde. Sie sagte besorgt: „Daß dich nur Meerschaum nicht beißt, wenn er sieht, daß du mich angefaßt hast."

„Der Meerschaum?" sagte der alte Herr, indem er sich hastig nach Pauline umwendete. „Heißt der alte Hund Meerschaum, der sich so fröhlich bezeigte, wie ich neulich hier war?"

Pauline bejahte und sagte: „Er ist sonst gegen Unbekannte

nicht so. Es war das erstemal, daß ich ihn freundlich gegen einen andern sah, als uns, um die er täglich ist. Besonders kann er Herrn Rebbel nicht leiden, und der Mann muß sich vor ihm fürchten, so lang und stark er auch ist."

„Rebbel, Rebbel", sagte der alte Herr vor sich hin. „Rebbel, so lang und stark. Hat der Rebbel, wie du ihn nennst, etwas im Gesicht, an dem man ihn erkennen könnte?"

„Er muß etwas", sagte Pauline, „an der Stirn haben, denke ich, über dem rechten Auge, so wie eine Narbe."

Nach O. LUDWIG, *Die Buschnovelle*

11. AN OLD MAN RETURNS HOME

An einem Herbstnachmittag ging ein alter, wohlgekleideter Mann langsam die Straße entlang. Unter dem linken Arm trug er einen Spazierstock mit goldenem Knopfe. Mit seinen dunkeln Augen sah er ruhig umher oder in die Stadt hinab, welche im Abendsonnenschein vor ihm lag. Nur wenige Leute grüßten ihn, aber viele sahen ihm mit neugierigen Blicken nach.

Endlich blieb er vor einem hohen Hause stehen, sah noch einmal in die Stadt hinaus und trat dann durch die Haustür. Langsam stieg er die schmale Treppe hinauf und öffnete oben eine Tür, die in ein großes, helles Zimmer führte. Hier war es bequem und still. Die eine Wand war fast mit Bücherschränken bedeckt; an der andern hingen Bilder von Menschen und Gegenden. Vor einem Tische mit grüner Decke, worauf einige offene Bücher lagen, stand ein Lehnstuhl mit roten Kissen. Nachdem der Alte Hut und Stock in die Ecke gestellt hatte, setzte er sich und ruhte mit gefalteten Händen von seinem Spaziergang aus.

Nach T. STORM, *Immensee*

12. A DANGEROUS SWIM

Reinhard ging am Seeufer entlang. Einen Steinwurf vom Lande konnte er eine weiße Wasserlilie erkennen. Plötzlich hatte er den Wunsch, die Blume näher anzusehen; schnell warf er seine Kleider ab und stieg ins Wasser. Scharfe Pflanzen und Steine schnitten ihn an den Füßen, und er kam immer nicht in die zum Schwimmen nötige Tiefe. Dann war es plötzlich unter ihm weg, die Wasser quirlten über ihm zusammen, und es dauerte eine Zeitlang, ehe er wieder an die Oberfläche kam.

Bald sah er die Lilie wieder. Sie lag einsam zwischen den großen blanken Blättern. Er schwamm langsam hinaus. Endlich war er der Blume so nahe, daß er die silbernen Blätter unterscheiden konnte. Zugleich aber fühlte er sich wie in einem Netze verstrickt; die glatten Stengel langten vom Grunde herauf und rankten sich um seine Glieder. Es wurde ihm unheimlich im Wasser. In atemloser Hast schwamm er dem Ufer zu. Hier angekommen, kleidete er sich an und ging langsam nach Hause zurück.

Nach T. STORM, *Immensee*

13. A MYSTERIOUS LAKE

Vor einigen Jahren wurde ein unbekannter See auf einem hohen Berg von deutschen Wanderern entdeckt. Viele Versuche sind gemacht worden, den Boden dieses Sees zu erreichen, aber es gelang keinem. Der See, dessen Wasser klar und dunkelblau war, enthielt viele seltene Fische und war nur den Bewohnern des kleinen Dorfs am südlichen Abhang des Berges bekannt. Zu gewissen Zeiten des Jahres war das Wasser so warm, daß ein Dampf zu sehen war, der langsam in die Höhe stieg wie Nebel über dem Fluß an einem Herbstabend.

Niemand wußte, wie der See genährt wurde und man glaubte, daß eine Quelle am Boden des Sees sei. Sogar beim kältesten Wetter fror das Wasser nie. Die Wanderer waren hoch erfreut über die Entdeckung und faßten den Plan, im nächsten Sommer diesen See zu besuchen. Die Berichte, die man später über diese Entdeckung in den Zeitungen las, bewogen viele Leute, in die Berge zu fahren, um diesen See zu besuchen.

14. A CUNNING DOG

Während ihre Familie die Ferien am Meer verbrachte, blieb eine alte Dame zu Hause. Der Hund wurde auch im Haus zurückgelassen. In dem Wohnzimmer war ein sehr bequemer Lehnstuhl, worauf die Dame sehr gern saß. Oft aber fand sie den Hund im Besitz des Stuhls. Da sie sich vor dem Hund fürchtete, hatte sie nicht den Mut, ihn von dem Stuhl zu treiben.

Eines Tages kam sie auf eine gute Idee. Während sie am Fenster stand, rief sie laut: „Katze, Katze!" Sofort sprang der Hund von dem Stuhl, lief ans Fenster und begann laut zu bellen. Die Dame ging ebensoschnell zu dem Stuhl und setzte sich darauf.

Einige Tage später kam der Hund ins Wohnzimmer und als er die alte Dame auf dem Lehnstuhl sah, lief er ans Fenster und bellte laut. Die Dame dachte, daß ein Dieb in der Nähe des Hauses sei, stand auf und eilte ans Fenster. Sofort rannte der schlaue Hund vom Fenster und setzte sich bequem auf den Lehnstuhl der alten Dame.

15. SIGNALMAN THIEL PREPARES FOR THE NIGHT

Die beiden Männer reichten sich die Hände, machten sich einige kurze Mitteilungen und trennten sich. Der eine verschwand im Innern der Bude, der andere ging quer über die Strecke. Thiel begann, wie immer, die enge, viereckige Wärterbude auf seine Art für die Nacht herzurichten. Er tat es mechanisch, während sein Geist mit dem Eindruck der letzten Stunden beschäftigt war. Er legte sein Abendbrot auf den schmalen, braunen Tisch an einem der beiden Seitenfenster, von denen aus man die Strecke bequem übersehen konnte. Hierauf entzündete er in dem kleinen, rostigen Ofen ein Feuer und stellte einen Topf kalten Wassers darauf. Nachdem er noch in die Schaufeln, Spaten usw. einige Ordnung gebracht hatte, begab er sich ans Putzen seiner Laterne, die er zugleich mit frischem Petroleum versorgte.

Als dies geschehen war, meldete die Glocke mit drei schrillen Schlägen, daß ein Zug in der Richtung von Breslau her aus der nächstliegenden Station abgelassen sei.

Nach G. HAUPTMANN, *Bahnwärter Thiel*

16. A LATE RETURN HOME

Es war inzwischen völlig dunkel geworden. Das Haus lag im schwarzen Schatten von zwei großen Walnußbäumen, die sich zu beiden Seiten der Haustür hochreckten. Die Eltern saßen noch in der Wohnstube. Heinrich trat vorsichtig an das Fenster; er stieg auf die darunterliegende Holzbank, spähte durch die Vorhänge in die Stube und sah, wie der Vater im Lehnstuhl an der einen Seite des Tisches saß, den Rücken dem Fenster zu. Er las in der Zeitung. Das Licht der von der Decke herabhängenden Lampe fiel voll auf das Blatt. Er wußte, daß der Vater langsam las, Artikel für Artikel, Wort für Wort; besondere und wichtige Stellen pflegte er der Mutter laut vorzulesen. Jetzt wandte er den Kopf etwas zur Seite. Wahrscheinlich wollte er der Mutter etwas zeigen. Diese saß an der anderen Seite des Tisches und stopfte Strümpfe. Sie war aber zu tief in die Arbeit versunken und merkte die Absicht des Vaters nicht. Also bog er den Kopf zurück. An der Schmalseite des Tisches las sein drei Jahre älterer Bruder eine Abenteuergeschichte.

17. AN ACCIDENT ON THE RAILWAY

Der schlesische Schnellzug war gemeldet, und Thiel mußte auf seinen Posten. Kaum stand er dienstfertig an der Barriere, so hörte er ihn auch schon heranbrausen.

Der Zug wurde sichtbar — er kam näher — und gleich darauf brachte die Luft den Pfiff der Maschine getragen. Dreimal hintereinander, kurz, grell, beängstigend. Sie bremsen, dachte Thiel, warum nur? Und wieder schrieen die Notpfiffe, diesmal in langer, ununterbrochener Reihe.

Thiel trat vor, um die Strecke überschauen zu können. Mechanisch zog er die rote Fahne aus dem Futteral und hielt sie gerade vor sich hin über die Geleise. Was war das dort zwischen den Schienen? „Halt!" schrie der Wärter aus Leibeskräften. Zu spät. Eine dunkle Masse war unter den Zug geraten und wurde zwischen den Rädern wie ein Gummiball hin- und hergeworfen. Noch einige Augenblicke, und man hörte das Knarren der Bremsen. Der Zug stand. Zugführer und Schaffner rannten über den Kies nach dem Ende des Zuges. Aus jedem Fenster blickten neugierige Gesichter.

Nach G. HAUPTMANN, *Bahnwärter Thiel*

18. SHIPWRECK AND RESCUE

Der Sturm brauste immer heftiger, und ehe eine Stunde verging, wurde das Schiff auf eine Sandbank geworfen, wo es hilflos lag. Schnell wurden die Boote hinabgelassen, und kaum hatten sich die letzten Matrosen gerettet, als das Schiff vor unseren Augen verschwand. Unsere Lage wurde immer gefährlicher, denn der Sturm wurde noch heftiger, so daß das Boot nicht mehr zu lenken war. Ich hatte meinen alten Diener fest umschlungen, und wir versprachen uns, uns nie von einander zu trennen.

Endlich wurde es Tag. Aber mit dem ersten Anblick der

Morgenröte ergriff der Wind das Boot, worin wir saßen, und stürzte es um. Von den anderen Schiffsleuten habe ich keinen wieder gesehen. Der Sturz hatte mich betäubt. Als ich wieder zu Sinnen kam, befand ich mich in den Armen meines treuen Dieners, der sich auf das umgestürzte Boot gerettet hatte und mich nachgezogen hatte.

Der Sturm hatte sich gelegt.| Als das Wetter sich aufklärte, erblickten wir nicht weit von uns ein anderes Schiff, auf das der Wind und die Wellen uns hintrieben. Als wir näher kamen, erkannte ich das Schiff als dasselbe, das in der Nacht an uns vorbeigefahren war.

Nach W. HAUFF, *Die Karawane*

19.   THE TREASURE

In Süddeutschland wohnte einmal ein Bauer, der träumte, im Stall eines benachbarten Bauernhofs liege ein wertvoller Schatz, der nur um Mitternacht gefunden werden könne. Als er am folgenden Morgen erwachte, hatte er Schatz und Traum völlig vergessen. Doch träumte er dasselbe zweimal hintereinander. Als er zum dritten Mal den Traum hatte, sprang er sofort aus dem Bett, zog sich schnell an und ging eiligst in den Stall.

Nach kurzem Suchen entdeckte er unter dem Boden einen hölzernen Kasten voll Goldstücke und glitzernder Juwelen. Als er sich über den Kasten bückte, um den Schatz genauer anzusehen, bemerkte er plötzlich, daß ein großer Stein an einem dünnen Faden über ihm hing. Im selben Augenblick flüsterte eine hohle Stimme: ,,Was suchst du hier?" Da er sich umsah, erblickte er eine große Gestalt, die den Faden mit einem Messer durchschneiden wollte. Bei diesem Anblick ließ der Bauer alles fallen und lief zur Stalltür hinaus. Nachdem er sich erholt hatte, dachte er wieder an den Schatz und kehrte vorsichtig nach dem Stall zurück. Es war aber umsonst, denn alles war spurlos verschwunden.

20.   ARRIVING AT AN HOTEL

Herr Aschenbach betrat das Hotel von hinten und begab sich durch die große Halle in die Vorhalle. Hier wurde er freundlich empfangen. Ein Gepäckträger begleitete ihn im Lift zum zweiten Stockwerk hinauf und führte ihn in ein helles, bequemes Zimmer, dessen hohe Fenster die Aussicht aufs offene Meer gewährten.

Er trat an eins davon, nachdem der Gepäckträger sich zurückgezogen hatte. Er blickte auf den Strand und die dunkelblaue See hinaus, die kleine Wellen gegen das Ufer sandte. Er wandte sich endlich, badete sein Gesicht und ließ sich von einem grüngekleideten Diener, der den Lift bediente, hinunterfahren.

Er nahm seinen Tee auf der Terrasse, stieg dann hinab und verfolgte den Promenadenquai eine gute Strecke in der Richtung auf das Hotel Excelsior. Als er zurückkehrte, schien es schon an der Zeit, sich zur Abendmahlzeit umzukleiden. Er tat es langsam und genau. Trotzdem fand er sich ein wenig früh in dem Speisesaal ein.

Nach T. MANN, *Der Tod in Venedig*

21.   I SEE A GHOST

An jenem Abend habe ich zum ersten und letzten Mal in meinem Leben einen Geist gesehen. Es war gegen elf Uhr, als ich über den Kirchhof ging, um für meine Mutter, die ein leichtes Fieber hatte, etwas bei der Apotheke zu holen. Man muß nämlich über diesen Kirchhof gehen, wenn man zur Apotheke will.

Ich dachte nicht an Geister noch Gespenster, sondern nur daran, wie angenehm es sein würde, wenn ich wieder zu Hause wäre; ich lief, als ob meine Mutter todeskrank wäre. Plötzlich erblickte ich etwas Weißes, was lang und sonderbar in die Höhe ragte.

Ich wurde zu Eis und blieb stehen. Hätte der Geist mir gewinkt, so wäre ich zu ihm hingegangen. Aber er bekümmerte sich gar nicht um mich, sondern schwebte langsam über die Gräber fort, ohne ein Zeichen von sich zu geben. Erst, als er verschwunden war, kam mir die eigentliche Angst. Wie ich von der Apotheke zurückkehrte, vermied ich natürlich den unheimlichen Kirchhof und machte einen Umweg, der mich an einem tiefen Teich vorbeiführte.

Nach F. HEBBEL, *Schnock*

22.   CELEBRATING THE BIRTHDAY OF A DUCHESS

In meinem väterlichen Hause lebte man gut und reichlich. Wir Kinder genossen eine vielleicht nur allzu liberale

Erziehung, und es gab keine Freude, kein fröhliches Fest, woran wir nicht teilnehmen durften. Besonders lebhaft tauchte jetzt wieder ein glänzendes Fest vor mir auf, welches zu Ehren der Herzogin veranstaltet wurde. Sie hatte eine Vorliebe für unsere Stadt, und da sie eine große Kinderfreundin war, so war in diesem Sinne ihr jährlicher kurzer Aufenthalt immer durch neue Wohltaten gesegnet. Diesmal feierte sie ihr Geburtstagsfest in unsern Mauern. Am Abend sollte durch eine Anzahl von Kindern vor ihrer Hoheit ein Schauspiel aufgeführt werden, und zwar auf einem kleinen natürlichen Theater. Wir hatten unter der Leitung eines erfahrenen Mannes verschiedene Proben gehalten, und endlich schien zu einer erfolgreichen Aufführung nichts mehr zu fehlen. Mein Vater hatte mir einen vollständigen türkischen Anzug machen lassen, meiner Rolle gemäß, welche auch einen berittenen Mann verlangte. Dieses wurde durch die Gunst des Stallmeisters erreicht.

Nach E. MÖRIKE, *Lucie Gelmeroth*

23. THE FIRE (I)

Als junger Student wohnte ich drei Treppen hoch in einem alten Haus. In dem Hause mir gegenüber wohnte ein junger Gelehrter, aber wir kannten uns damals nicht. Mitten in der Nacht weckte mich ein ungewöhnlicher Lärm. Meine Stube war hell erleuchtet. Ich sprang an das Fenster; da schlug eine helle Flamme aus dem Stockwerk unter mir bis zu mir herauf. Meine Fensterscheiben sprangen um meinen Kopf herum und ein Qualm drang auf mich ein. Weil es unter diesen Umständen unmöglich wurde, mich zum Fenster hinauszulehnen, so lief ich an die Tür und öffnete sie. Auch die Treppe brannte in heller Flamme. Drei Treppen hoch und kein Ausweg — ich gab mich für verloren! Halb besinnungslos stürzte ich zum Fenster zurück. Ich hörte, daß man auf der Straße rief: ,,Ein Mensch, ein Mensch! Die Leiter her!" Eine Leiter wurde angelegt, sie fing im Nu an zu rauchen und zu brennen. Sie wurde weggerissen. Da rauschten die Wasserstrahlen aller Spritzen in die Flamme unter mir. Eine neue Leiter wurde angelegt. Es war unten totenstill. Auf einmal rief jemand: ,,Es geht nicht!"

Nach G. FREYTAG, *Die Journalisten*

24. THE FIRE (II)

Da klang eine Stimme: „Höher die Leiter!" Ich wußte auf der Stelle, daß dies die Stimme meines Retters war. „Schnell!" riefen die Leute unten. Da drang eine neue Rauchwolke in die Stube. Ich hatte genug von dem dicken Rauch verschluckt und legte mich am Fenster auf den Fußboden.

Da faßte mich eine Menschenhand am Hals. Ein Seil wurde mir unter die Arme geschlungen und ein kräftiger Arm hob mich vom Boden. Einen Augenblick später war ich auf der Leiter, halb gezogen, halb getragen. Mit brennendem Hemd und bewußtlos kam ich auf dem Straßenpflaster an. Ich erwachte im Zimmer des jungen Gelehrten. Außer einigen kleinen Brandwunden hatte ich nichts in die neue Wohnung herübergebracht.

Meine ganze Habe war verbrannt. Der fremde Mann pflegte mich und sorgte für mich, wie ein Bruder für den anderen. Erst als ich wieder ausgehen konnte, erfuhr ich, daß dieser Gelehrte derselbe Mann war, der mir in jener Nacht auf der Leiter seinen Besuch gemacht hatte.

Nach G. FREYTAG, *Die Journalisten*

25. CLIMBING THE BROCKEN

Je höher man den Berg hinaufsteigt, desto kürzer und seltener werden die Tannen, denn sie scheinen immer mehr zusammen zu schrumpfen. Dabei wird es auch fühlbar kälter. Die wunderlichen Gruppen der Granitblöcke werden erst jetzt sichtbar und diese sind oft von erstaunlicher Größe. Es ist ein äußerst ermüdender Aufstieg, und ich war froh, als endlich das langerwünschte Brockenhaus in Sicht kam. Dieses Haus, das auf der Spitze des Berges liegt, wurde vor einigen Jahren wieder erbaut.

Nach einem langen Aufstieg zwischen Tannen und Felsen wird man in eine Art Wolkenhaus versetzt. Städte, Berge und Wälder bleiben unten liegen, doch oben findet man eine wunderlich zusammengesetzte, fremde Gesellschaft, die einen wie einen erwarteten Bekannten halb neugierig, halb glücklich begrüßt. Ich fand das Haus voller Gäste. Sofort dachte ich an die Nacht und die Unbequemlichkeit eines Strohlagers. Mit leiser Stimme bestellte ich Kaffee. Der Wirt sah bald ein, daß ich als müder Mann ein ordentliches Bett haben müsse. Dieses zeigte er mir in einem schmalen Zimmerchen, wo ein junger Student schon eingezogen war.

Nach H. HEINE, *Die Harzreise*

26. A FATHER AND MOTHER DISCUSS THEIR CHILDREN

Marie Salander wurde noch viel ernster, als sie schon gewesen war, sagte aber nur:

„Ich weiß nicht, was es ist, es fällt mir auch auf. Aus ihren knappen Briefchen ist schon lange nichts mehr zu entnehmen, was sie näher angeht. Ich dachte, du wüßtest mehr von ihnen, weil du ja mit den Schwiegersöhnen verkehrst, die sich noch weniger hier sehen lassen."

„Es hat auch aufgehört bei mir! Als ich wahrnahm, wie sie sich betrugen, hielt ich als Schwiegerpapa es für meine Pflicht, diese Art Verkehr einzustellen."

„Seit einem halben Jahre ist weder Setti noch Netti mehr hier gewesen; von guter Hand habe ich jedoch vernommen, daß sie untereinander sich seit länger als einem Jahre nicht mehr sehen, daß sie sich sogar zu vermeiden scheinen, so gut sie können. In den ersten Zeiten ihrer Verheiratung besuchten sie einander jede Woche einmal. Was ist nun das? Was ist geschehen? Ich weiß es nicht, und niemand will es wissen."

„In diesem Falle müßte man doch suchen, dahinterzukommen und ihnen zu helfen."

„Das habe ich schon gedacht; aber wie, ohne mehr zu schaden als zu nützen?"

Nach G. KELLER, *Martin Salander*

27. WATCHING A TRAIN GO PAST

Ohne die mindeste Hast zu zeigen, blieb Thiel noch eine gute Weile im Innern der Bude, trat endlich, Fahne in der Hand, langsam ins Freie und bewegte sich trägen Ganges über den schmalen Sandpfad, dem etwa zwanzig Schritt entfernten Bahnübergang zu. Seine Barrieren schloß und öffnete Thiel vor und nach jedem Zuge, obgleich der Weg nur selten von jemand benutzt wurde.

Er hatte seine Arbeit beendet und lehnte jetzt wartend an der schwarzweißen Sperrstange. Endlich trat er einen Schritt vor. Ein dunkler Punkt am Horizonte, da wo die Geleise sich trafen, vergrößerte sich. Von Sekunde zu Sekunde wachsend, schien er doch auf einer Stelle zu stehen. Plötzlich bekam er Bewegung und näherte sich. Durch die Geleise ging ein Summen, das, lauter und lauter werdend, zuletzt den Hufschlägen eines Reitergeschwaders nicht unähnlich war.

Dann plötzlich zerriß die Stille. Ein rasendes Toben erfüllte den Raum, die Geleise bogen sich, die Erde zitterte — eine Wolke von Staub und Dampf, und das schwarze Ungetüm war vorüber. Zum Punkt eingeschrumpft, schwand der Zug in die Ferne.

Nach G. HAUPTMANN, *Bahnwärter Thiel*

28. AN UNWORTHY NEWSPAPER ARTICLE

BOLZ, *mit Haltung*. Herr Oberst, ich komme, Ihnen eine Mitteilung zu machen, welche für die Ehre eines Dritten notwendig ist.

OBERST. Ich bin darauf gefaßt, und bitte Sie, dieselbe nicht zu lang auszudehnen.

BOLZ. Nur so lang, als nötig ist. Der Artikel in dem heutigen Abendblatt der Union, welche Ihre Persönlichkeit bespricht, ist von mir geschrieben und von mir ohne Oldendorfs Wissen in die Zeitung gesetzt.

OBERST. Es ist mir kaum von Interesse zu wissen, wer den Artikel geschrieben hat.

BOLZ, *artig*. Aber es ist mir von Wichtigkeit, Ihnen zu sagen, daß er nicht von Oldendorf ist und daß Oldendorf nichts davon gewußt hat. Mein Freund war in den letzten Wochen so sehr in Anspruch genommen, daß er die Leitung des Blattes mir allein überließ. Für alles, was in dieser letzten Zeit darin stand, bin ich allein verantwortlich.

OBERST. Und wozu machen Sie diese Erklärung?

BOLZ. Es wird Ihrem Scharfblick nicht entgehen, Herr Oberst, daß nach der Szene, welche heute zwischen Ihnen und meinem Freunde vorgefallen ist, Oldendorf als Mann von Ehre einen solchen Artikel weder schreiben noch in seine Zeitung aufnehmen konnte.

Nach G. FREYTAG, *Die Journalisten*

29. WINTER LANDSCAPE

Wie schön war der Wald an diesem ersten Morgen unserer Ferien! Über dem ganzen Gebirge lag dicker, weißer Nebel, kein Wind wehte und eine leichte Schneedecke hatte sich während der Nacht über alles gelegt. Nur ein paar steile Felsen und einige Steinmassen erhoben sich dunkel aus der sonst weißen Landschaft. Alle Zweige der Bäume und Gebüsche sahen aus, als ob sie mit Zucker bestreut wären. Es war ein Bild, das sich weder malen noch beschreiben ließ. Eben in dem Augenblick, als es seine größte Herrlichkeit entfaltete, verschwand das wunderbare Bild, denn die Sonne durchdrang den Nebel. Bald danach erhob sich ein Wind und schüttelte den Schnee von den Zweigen. Aber für einen Freund der Jagd hatte der Wald immer noch Anreiz, denn der frische Schnee zeigte noch die Spuren der Tiere.

30.   COLUMBUS

Es war am dritten August, an einem Freitag, als Kolumbus mit drei kleinen Schiffen aus dem Hafen segelte. Am neunten August erreichte man eine Insel, wo Kolumbus drei Wochen lang auf einen günstigen Wind warten mußte; endlich konnte er seine Reise fortsetzen. Bis gegen Mitte Oktober fuhren die Schiffe auf unbekanntem Meer, ohne Land zu erblicken.

Als die Tage vergingen, sank den Seeleuten der Mut. Einige wollten Kolumbus über Bord werfen, um nach Hause zurückkehren zu können. Aber er beruhigte sie und erweckte in ihnen neuen Mut. Am elften Oktober, um halb elf am Abend, erblickte Kolumbus ein Licht in der Ferne, das sich hin und her bewegte. Zwei Stunden nach Mitternacht rief ein Seemann: „Land, Land!" und gab noch andere Zeichen der Freude. Sie hatten die Küste entdeckt und waren nur noch zwei Meilen davon entfernt. Bei Tagesanbruch sah man eine schöne, flache Insel. Kolumbus befahl, die Anker zu werfen und ein Boot zu bemannen. Als er als der erste ans Land stieg, nahm er von dem neuentdeckten Land Besitz.

31.   A STRANGE HORSE

Alles ging sehr gut, bis ich nach Rußland kam, wo ich einen kleinen Rennschlitten mit einem einzelnen Pferd nahm und auf Sankt Petersburg losfuhr. Ich besinne mich noch wohl, es war mitten in einem fürchterlichen Walde, als ich einen entsetzlichen Wolf mit aller Schnelligkeit hinter mir hersetzen sah.

Er holte mich bald ein und es war unmöglich, ihm zu entkommen. Mechanisch legte ich mich in dem Schlitten nieder und ließ mein Pferd ganz allein laufen. Der Wolf bekümmerte sich aber nicht im mindesten um meine Wenigkeit, sondern sprang über mich hinweg, fiel wütend auf das Pferd und verschlang auf einmal den ganzen Hinterteil des armen Tieres, welches vor Schrecken und Schmerz nur desto schneller lief. Ich erhob mich ganz verstohlen und nahm wahr, daß der Wolf sich beinahe in das Pferd hineingefressen hatte.

Kaum aber hatte er sich so hübsch hineingefressen, so nahm ich meine Gelegenheit wahr und fiel ihm mit meiner Peitsche auf das Fell. Solch ein unerwarteter Überfall erschreckte den Wolf und er strebte mit aller Macht vorwärts. Der Leichnam des Pferdes fiel zu Boden und an seiner Statt lief mein Wolf in dem Geschirr. Ich hörte nicht auf zu peitschen und so langten wir in vollem Galopp in Sankt Petersburg an, ganz gegen unsere beiderseitigen respektiven Erwartungen.

Nach MÜNCHHAUSEN, *Reisen und Abenteuer*

32. A CONFESSION

Seitdem hab ich keine Nacht geschlafen; die ganzen Nächte hab ich aufgesessen im Bett und bin voll Todesangst gewesen. Ich hab dich in Gefahr gesehen und durft es dir nicht sagen und durfte dich nicht retten. Und er hat die Seile zerschnitten mit der Axt in der Nacht, eh' du nach Brambach gingst. Der Valentin hat mir's gesagt, der Nachbar hat ihn in den Schuppen schleichen sehen. Ich hab dich tot gemeint und wollte auch sterben. Denn ich wär schuld gewesen an deinem Tod und stürbe tausendmal um dich. Und nun lebst du noch und ich kann's nicht begreifen. Und es ist alles noch, wie es war; die Bäume da, der Schuppen, der Himmel, und du bist doch nicht tot. Und ich wollte auch sterben, weil du tot warst. Sag du mir's doch: ist's wahr? Dir glaub ich alles, was du sagst. Und sagst du, ich soll sterben, so will ich's, wenn du's nur weißt. Aber er kann kommen. Vielleicht hat er gelauscht, daß ich dir's sagte, was er will. Schick den Valentin in die Gerichte, daß sie ihn fortführen und er dir nichts mehr tun kann.

Nach O. LUDWIG, *Zwischen Himmel und Erde*

33. BISMARCK AND HIS DOCTOR

Als Bismarck einmal krank war, sandte er nach einem jungen Arzt, den er nie gesehen hatte, aber der ihm sehr empfohlen worden war. Der junge Arzt kam sofort, untersuchte

Bismarck und fing an, allerlei Fragen zu stellen. Er fragte unter anderem: „Wie lange schlafen Sie während der Nacht? Wie lange gehen Sie jeden Tag spazieren? Wieviel Wein oder Bier trinken Sie täglich?" Zuerst beantwortete Bismarck die Fragen sehr höflich, aber endlich verlor er die Geduld und rief: „Ich habe Sie kommen lassen, damit Sie mich kurieren, und nicht damit Sie mich ausfragen!" „Gut", sagte der junge Arzt kaltblütig, „wenn Sie kuriert sein wollen, ohne ausgefragt zu werden, so schicken Sie nach einem Tierarzt." Diese Antwort gefiel dem berühmten Staatsmann so gut, daß er den jungen Arzt zu seinem persönlichen Arzt machte.

34. PREPARATIONS FOR DEFENCE

Jetzt mit einem Male scholl aus dem Dorfe ein gellendes Geschrei, und jetzt dröhnte es über ihm — die Kirchenglocke schlug an und läutete in hastigen Schwüngen Sturm. Alexanders Blick fiel auf den wieder ins Dunkel hinausleuchtenden Schein der verräterischen Lampe, er schlug die dicken Läden des Erdgeschosses zu und schritt ins Haus zurück, in der Absicht, es mit den Freunden wie eine Festung bis auf den letzten Mann zu verteidigen; denn schon knallten Schüsse von der Gasse her und Schläge fielen gegen die vordere Haustür. Fausch hatte sie eben verriegelt und stürzte die Bodentreppe hinauf, um durch die Dachluken auszuschauen. Der Prädikant aber lud seine Flinte wieder und stellte sich an das schmale vergitterte Küchenfenster, das nach der Gasse ging, wie hinter eine Schießscharte.

„Die Schurken!" rief er dem Schweizer zu, der eben hastig aus seiner Kammer trat, wo er seinen Ranzen geholt und seinen leichten Degen umgeschnallt hatte, „wir wollen unser Leben teuer verkaufen!"

„Um Gottes willen, Herr Blasius", warnte dieser, „gedenkt denn Ihr, ein Diener am Wort, auf die Leute zu schießen?"

„Wer nicht hören will, muß fühlen", war die kaltblütige Antwort.

Nach C. F. MEYER, *Jürg Jenatsch*

35. BAD NEWS

Margret saß am Herde; sie spann und dachte wenig Erfreuliches. Im Dorfe schlug es halb zwölf; die Tür klinkte, und der Gerichtsschreiber Trapp trat herein.

„Guten Tag", sagte er, „könnt Ihr mir einen Trunk Milch geben?" Er trank zögernd und in kurzen Absätzen. „Wißt Ihr wohl", sagte er dann, „daß die Blaukittel in dieser Nacht wieder im Walde eine ganze Strecke so kahl gefegt haben wie meine Hand?"

„So?" versetzte sie gleichgültig.

Der Schreiber hatte getrunken und ging noch immer nicht. Er schien etwas auf dem Herzen zu haben.

„Habt Ihr nichts von Brandes gehört?" sagte er plötzlich.

„Nichts; er kommt niemals hier ins Haus."

„So wißt Ihr nicht, was ihm begegnet ist?"

„Was denn?" fragte Margret gespannt.

„Er ist tot!"

„Tot!" rief sie, „was, tot? Er ging ja noch heute morgen ganz gesund hier vorüber mit der Flinte auf dem Rücken!"

„Von den Blaukitteln erschlagen", sagte der Schreiber, sie scharf fixierend. „Vor einer Viertelstunde wurde die Leiche ins Dorf gebracht!"

Nach A. von Droste-Hülshoff, *Die Judenbuche*

36. A FRIEND ON THE MOUNTAINS

Wir bogen in eine andere Straße ein und begannen, bergauf zu steigen. Wir gingen an vielen steilen Felsen vorbei, von denen kleine Bäche herunterstürzten. Nachdem wir eine halbe Stunde gegangen waren, wurde der Pfad breiter. Die Sonne brannte auf uns herab, obgleich es kaum sieben Uhr war. An den Abhängen der Berge war kein Mensch zu sehen. Alles war ganz einsam. In der Ferne wuchsen einige dünne Tannen zwischen großen Steinblöcken. Als wir den Höhepunkt des Weges erreichten, machten wir Halt.

Weit unter uns lag die Landschaft in einem weißen Nebel, durch den ein Fluß wie eine silberne Schlange schimmerte. Den ganzen Tag gingen wir weiter. Als es Abend wurde, kamen wir zu einem einsamen Haus, dessen Bewohner uns freundlich grüßte. Schnell holte er uns etwas Warmes zu essen und er lud uns ein, bei ihm zu übernachten. Seine Einladung nahmen wir dankbar an. Wegen unsrer Müdigkeit schliefen wir sogleich ein. Am nächsten Morgen standen wir früh auf und machten uns um halb acht auf den Weg der in der Morgensonne viel freundlicher aussah, als bei der Dunkelheit des vorigen Abends.

Nach W. Hauff, *Lichtenstein*

37. A MYSTERIOUS VISITOR

Ich trat auf den dunklen Flur hinaus und schloß die Tür des Zimmers hinter mir zu. Es war etwas nach halb zehn. Während ich die Treppe hinabstieg, hörte ich jemand heraufkommen. Ich blieb stehen, um zu warten, bis die Tür unter mir geöffnet würde, und die Schritte dahinten verschwänden. Die Schritte hörten auf, ein Schlüsselbund klirrte, und ein Schlüssel wurde ins Türschloß gesteckt. Ich wartete auf das Öffnen und Zuschlagen der Tür. Es dauerte lange, der Schlüssel wurde mehrere Male herumgedreht, dabei wurde an der Tür gerüttelt. Vorsichtig stieg ich die Treppe hinab. Vor der Tür stand ein Mann und versuchte, sie aufzuschließen. Er war breitschultrig und kräftig und über Mittelgröße. Plötzlich sah er sich um. Als er mich erblickte, stürzte er die Treppe hinab und verschwand in der Dunkelheit.

38. AN EARLY SWIM

Als Karl aufwachte, war es noch ganz früh. Rasch suchte er seinen Badeanzug, wickelte ihn mit einem Kamm zusammen in ein Handtuch, ging hinunter, trat auf die Straße hinaus und eilte zum Strand hinab. Die Flut war im Abnehmen. Schnell ging er in eine Badekabine, zog sich aus, zog den Badeanzug an und lief über den glatten Sand zum Meer. Trotz der frühen Stunde war eine ganze Menge Leute schon am Strand oder im Wasser. Weit weg sah er eine weiße Linie von Wellen und dahinter das offene Meer. Er watete hinaus. Trotz des kalten Wassers tauchte er, als eine Welle heranrollte, und schwamm einige Augenblicke unter dem Wasser.

Als er wieder an die Oberfläche kam, war es ihm ganz warm. Jetzt versuchte er verschiedene Taucharten, bis er müde wurde. Schließlich schwamm er an den Strand zurück. Dort lag er auf dem Sand, bis er trocken war. Bevor er den Strand verließ, ging er in die Badekabine, um sich noch einmal abzutrocknen und anzuziehen.

39. A VISIT TO THE NATIVES

Endlich erreichten wir den Gipfel. Vor unseren Augen entfaltete sich ein herrliches Bild. Der Pfad führte in ein kleines Tal hinab, das von hohen Felsen umgeben war. Von einer der steilen Wände stürzte ein kleiner Wasserfall herunter, der in einem schmalen Bachbett dann die ganze Breite des Tals durchfloß. An seinen Ufern wuchs ein Streifen Gras, auf dem ein paar Schafe weideten. Überall waren kleine Steinhütten verstreut, ohne Fenster und mit Türen, die kaum mehr als ein Loch waren. Die Dächer waren mit Stroh bedeckt. Nicht viele Menschen waren zu sehen. Es war die heißeste Stunde des Tages, und wahrscheinlich schliefen sie in den Hütten. Nur um einen Mühlstein, der von zwei Eseln gedreht wurde, saßen einige Frauen. Sie waren barfuß und in bunten Röcken. Ihr langes, schwarzes Haar hing ihnen über den Rücken. So schnell wie möglich stiegen wir den Abhang hinab und eilten zu den Hütten, wobei die Frauen uns neugierig ansahen, doch rührten sie sich nicht.

Nach H.-J. LATURNER, *Capitano Terrore*

40.   MAKING AMENDS

Die Frau hatte aber noch kaum die Zeit gehabt, ihr Erstaunen durch einen Laut auszudrücken, als an die Tür gepocht wurde.

„Riegel vor!" rief Herr Haidvogel, und als er sah, daß die Tür bereits aufging, griff er nach seinem Stock, der zu Häupten des Bettes stand.

Der Kellner trat mit seiner Last herein; die Gesichter der Kinder, die sich schon verfinstert hatten, klärten sich wieder auf, denn der leckere Duft, der sich im Zimmer verbreitete, und das fröhliche Klappern der Schüsseln verkündeten ihnen den Inhalt des Korbes.

„Reue? Gewissensbisse?" fragte Herr Haidvogel den Menschen, der den Korb stillschweigend auf den Tisch stellte. „Ich hätte es kaum erwartet."

„Mich schickt der Viehhändler", entgegnete dieser, „er hat alles bezahlt!"

„Der!" rief Herr Haidvogel. „Was untersteht der Kerl sich. Nun wohl! Aber wohl gemerkt, nur für die Kinder. Ich berühre nichts davon!"

Der Kellner wollte sich wieder entfernen, die Frau trug ihm einen herzlichen Dank auf.

„Kein Wort von Dank!" schrie Herr Haidvogel. „Er hat seine Schuldigkeit getan. Aber Deinem Herrn kannst Du melden, daß ich ihm mit den Schüsseln, wenn er sie zurückverlangt, die Fenster einwerfen werde."

Nach F. HEBBEL, *Herr Haidvogel und seine Familie*

41.   IN A SUBTERRANEAN CAVERN (I)

Das Licht des Tages schien durch das Wasser und gab den Wänden der Höhle eine eigenartige blaue Färbung. Überall war alles blau, die Felsen, das Wasser und ein kleiner, schmaler Strand in der linken Ecke der Höhle. Dieser kleine, unterirdische See war doppelt so lang wie das Boot und dreimal so breit. Als ich auf eine der Ruderbänke kletterte, konnte ich mit ausgestreckten Armen fast die Decke erreichen. Während ich es noch versuchte, kam ein Schreckensschrei von meinem Freund. Dann zeigte er stumm auf den Grund des Meeres. Ich blickte schnell hin. Was wir dort entdeckten, war schrecklich anzusehen. Durch das klare Wasser konnte man alles deutlich erkennen. Der ganze Meeresboden war mit großen Pflanzen bedeckt, die sich hin und her bewegten wie ein Wald von Totenarmen, die um Hilfe baten.

42.   IN A SUBTERRANEAN CAVERN (II)

Mit einigen kräftigen Schlägen ruderten die beiden Freunde das Boot über den kleinen, unterirdischen See. Als sie an der gegenüberliegenden Felswand ankamen, ergriff der zwei Jahre ältere Hans eine Pflanze, die sechs Fuß über dem Wasserspiegel stand, um das Boot näher an den Felsen heranzuziehen. Dabei ergriff er etwas Hartes und Rundes. Als er genauer hinsah, wurde es ihm klar, daß er einen eisernen Ring in der Hand hielt, der hinter der Pflanze versteckt in die Felswand eingelassen war. Triumphierend rief er Toni seine Entdeckung zu. Seine Stimme hallte von den Felsen wider. Schnell machte er die Bugleine des Bootes an dem Ring fest. Dann suchten sie nach einem gleichen Ring für die Heckleine. Aber es war nirgendwo etwas zu entdecken. Vielleicht war er im Laufe der Zeit aus der Wand gefallen, oder es war niemals einer da gewesen, denn es war keine Spur davon zu finden.

Nach H.-J. LATURNER, *Capitano Terrore*

43.   THE SON'S RETURN

Am nächsten Abend saß die Frau schon seit einer Stunde bei der Arbeit vor der Tür und wartete auf ihren Sohn. Es war die erste Nacht, die sie zugebracht hatte, ohne den Atem ihres Kindes neben sich zu hören. Friedrich kam noch immer nicht. Sie wurde ärgerlich und ängstlich, und wußte, daß sie beides ohne Grund war.

Die Uhr im Turm schlug sieben, das Vieh kehrte heim; er war noch immer nicht da, und sie mußte aufstehen, um nach den Kühen zu sehen. Als sie wieder in die dunkle Küche trat, stand Friedrich am Herde; er hatte sich vornübergebeugt und wärmte sich die Hände an den Kohlen. Der Schein spielte auf seinen Zügen. Die Frau blieb in der Tür stehen, so seltsam verändert kam ihr das Kind vor.

„Friedrich, wie geht's dem Onkel?"

Der Junge murmelte einige unverständliche Worte und drängte sich dicht an die Mauer. Das Kind sah zu ihr auf mit dem Jammerblick eines halbwüchsigen Hundes, der Schildwacht stehen lernt, und begann in seiner Angst mit den Füßen zu stampfen.

Nach A. VON DROSTE-HÜLSHOFF, *Die Judenbuche*

44. TREASURE-TROVE

Über eine Stunde arbeiteten die drei. Der Schweiß lief ihnen in Strömen über das Gesicht. Sie wollten die vollen Kisten so schnell wie möglich leeren. Es folgte Korb auf Korb mit Gold- und Silberstücken. Endlich hatten sie den Boden der letzten Kiste erreicht. Als Emil seinem Freund den letzten Korb herunterreichte, riß ein Henkel des Korbes entzwei und der ganze Inhalt ergoß sich wie ein goldener Regen über das Boot. Die Goldstücke rollten überall hin, einige schlugen auf die Bänke des Boots, andere verschwanden, kleine Spritzer aufwerfend, in dem See. Traurig sahen die Freunde zu, wie sie langsam auf den Grund sanken. Unten glänzten und glitzerten sie zwischen den Steinen.

Nach H.-J. LATURNER, *Capitano Terrore*

45. A SHOT IN THE NIGHT

Das Mädchen stellte die schwere Lampe auf den Tisch und die helle Flamme warf einen roten Widerschein auf ihr liebliches Gesicht. Das Mädchen lächelte und setzte sich. Da stürzte plötzlich die Lampe auf den Boden. Es wurde dunkel im Zimmer. Ein Schuß war durch das Fenster gefallen. Die Männer sprangen alle auf und zugleich sank das junge

Mädchen ohne Laut zusammen. Eine tödliche Kugel hatte sie ins Herz getroffen.

Während einer sich bemühte, die Lampe wieder anzuzünden, ergriff Alexander sein Gewehr und schritt ruhig in den mondhellen Garten hinaus. Es dauerte nicht lange, bis er den Mörder fand.

Da kauerte zwischen den Stämmen der Bäume ein langer Mensch, dessen Gesicht in der Dunkelheit nicht zu erkennen war. Neben ihm lag eine noch rauchende Pistole. Durch die Stille der Nacht drang auf einmal ein ungewisser Lärm an Alexanders Ohr.

„Zwei Vögelchen haben gepfiffen", sagte er vor sich hin, „bald fliegt uns der ganze Schwarm aufs Dach."

Nach C. F. Meyer, *Jürg Jenatsch*

46. AUNT FRIEDA THREATENS A VISIT

Meine Mutter sagte: „Ach Gott ja, übermorgen kommt die Schwägerin." Und da tat sie einen tiefen Seufzer, als wenn der Lehrer da wäre und von meinem Talent redete.

Und Ännchen hat ihre Kaffeetasse weggeschoben und hat gesagt, es schmeckt ihr nicht mehr, und wir werden schon sehen, daß die Tante den Amtsrichter beleidigt und daß alles schlecht geht.

„Warum hast du sie eingeladen?" sagte sie.

„Ich hab sie doch gar nicht eingeladen", sagte meine Mutter, „sie kommt doch immer ganz von selber."

„Man muß sie hinausschmeißen", sagte ich.

„Du sollst nicht so unanständig reden", sagte meine Mutter, „du mußt denken, daß sie Schwester von deinem verstorbenen Papa ist. Und überhaupt bist du zu jung."

„Aber wenn ihr sie doch gar nicht mögt", habe ich gesagt, „und wenn sie den Amtsrichter beleidigt, daß er Ännchen nicht heiratet. Vielleicht sagt sie ihm, daß er schielt."

Da hat Ännchen mich angeschrieen: „Er schielt doch gar nicht, du frecher Lausbub!"

Nach L. Thoma, *Tante Frieda*

47. A STREET SCENE IN NOVEMBER

Es war ein finsterer Novemberabend; der Nebel lag auf der Stadt, er füllte die alten Straßen und Plätze und drang durch die offenen Türen in die Häuser; er ballte sich um die

Straßenlaternen, deren Licht die Erde kaum drei Schritt weit erhellte. Der Nebel hing über dem Fluß und wälzte sich dort in dichten Massen über den Schiffen.

Die Straßen waren ganz leer; hier and da sah man eine Gestalt in der Nähe einer Laterne auftauchen und schnell wieder in der Finsternis verschwinden. Unter diesen dämmerigen Menschen war auch ein kleiner Mann, der unter den Laternen fortschlüpfte, so schnell ihm dies die unsicheren Füße erlaubten. Plötzlich blieb er vor einem Hause stehen. Er sah nach den Fenstern hinauf.

Die Vorhänge waren heruntergelassen, aber aus den Ritzen drang ein Lichtschimmer. Der kleine Mann versuchte fest zu stehen, starrte nach dem Licht, streckte die geballte Faust in die Höhe und schüttelte sie drohend; dann stieg er die Treppe hinauf und klingelte heftig, zwei-, dreimal.

Nach G. FREYTAG, *Soll und Haben*

48.   A BUG TOURS THE NEAR EAST

Während ich nun auf die große Wandkarte hinstarrte, fiel es mir allmählich auf, daß in der Gegend von Palästina was krabbelte. Ich trat näher und sah mit Jauchzen, es war die Wanze. Sie saß ganz nahe beim Toten Meere. Ich nahm meine Feder hinter dem Ohre hervor und zielte mit der Spitze sorgfältig auf das stattliche Tier. Da aber erkannte es die Gefahr, stürzte sich eilend in das Jordantal und floh mit großer Geschwindigkeit gen Norden. Ich mit der Feder immer hinterher. Beim See Genezareth schien es, sie wolle auf Damaskus zu und in Syrien ihr Heil versuchen, allein sie änderte ihren Plan, rannte um den See herum und dann hindurch bis zur Küste und an dieser entlang, bis sich ihr das Taurusgebirge in den Weg stellte.

Aber das findige Tier nahm den Kurs wieder nach Norden, bis sie in der Gegend von Hissarlyk wieder die See erreichte. Die Verzweiflung gab ihr Riesenkräfte, sie setzte an und in gewaltigem Sprunge erreichte sie das europäische Ufer. Von diesem Erfolg scheinbar frisch gestärkt, rannte sie in genau westlicher Richtung.

Doch meine Geduld war nun zu Ende. Ich setzte ihr schärfer nach und endlich in Makedonien, sieben geographische Meilen von Salonichi, kriegte ich sie gefaßt. Ich sage

Ihnen, meine Herrschaften, ihr Blut — es war eigentlich mein Blut — spritzte über den Balkan hinweg bis nach Bukarest.

Nach H. Seidel, *Das Hochzeitsfest*

49. THE ATTACK ON THE CASTLE

Wohl eine Stunde dauerte der Kampf um die Mauern des Schlosses. Finster lag der große Bau in dem schwachen Licht der Sterne; kein Licht, kein Mensch war zu sehen. Nur der Feuerstrahl, der zuweilen aus einer Ecke der Fensteröffnungen herunterfuhr, zeigte den Leuten draußen, daß Leben im Schlosse war.

Wenn man durch die Zimmer ging, konnte man hier und da eine dunkle Gestalt im Schatten erkennen. Man sah das Auge glänzen und den Kopf sich vorbeugen, um den Feind zu erspähen. Keiner der Männer, die jetzt Kriegsdienst taten, war an diese Arbeit gewöhnt. Aus jeder Art friedlicher Tätigkeit waren sie zusammengekommen und fieberhafte Erwartung war den ganzen Tag über auch im Gesicht der Stärksten sichtbar gewesen.

Underdes stiegen die Sterne auf, immer höher; auf beiden Seiten wurden die Schüsse spärlich; wie eine Ermüdung kam es über beide Teile.

„Unsere Leute haben die bessere Kraft", sagte Anton zu dem Freunde, „die im Hofe sind nicht mehr zu halten."

„Das Ganze ist nicht viel mehr als blindes Schießen", erwiderte Fink. „Außer einigen Verwundeten ist uns kein Schaden geschehen."

Nach G. Freytag, *Soll und Haben*

50. A CHEAP EVENING

„Famos", sagte er, „also dreißig Pfennig hast du noch? Wenn wir beide zusammenlegen, haben wir auch nicht mehr. Ich habe soeben alles fortgegeben an unseren Landsmann Braun, der das Geld notwendig braucht. Also dreißig Pfennig hast du noch? Dafür wollen wir einen schönen Abend machen!"

Ich sah ihn verwundert an.

„Gib mir das Geld", sagte er, „ich will einkaufen — zu Hause habe ich auch noch allerlei."

Wir gingen durch einige enge Gassen der Vorstadt zu seiner Wohnung. Unterwegs verschwand er in einem kleinen

Laden und kam nach kurzer Zeit mit zwei Tüten wieder zum Vorschein.

Er wohnte in dem Giebel eines lächerlich kleinen und niedrigen Häuschens, das in einem ebenso winzigen Garten stand. In seinem Wohnzimmer war eben so viel Platz, daß zwei anspruchslose Menschen die Beine ausstrecken konnten. Nebenan befand sich eine Dachkammer, die fast vollständig von seinem Bette ausgefüllt wurde, so daß Hühnchen, wenn er auf dem Bette sitzend die Stiefel anziehen wollte, zuvor die Tür öffnen mußte. Dieser kleine Vogelkäfig hatte aber etwas Behagliches; etwas von dem sonnigen Wesen seines Bewohners war auf ihn übergegangen.

Nach H. SEIDEL, Leberecht Hühnchen

SECTION 5

GERMAN PROSE EXTRACTS FOR DICTATION, ORAL AND AURAL PRACTICE

Dictation
(a) The passage should be read once through before the pupils begin to write.
(b) It should then be dictated slowly a few words or a phrase at a time, while the pupils write.
(c) The passage should then be read once more completely and at normal speed.
(d) A few minutes should be allowed in order that the pupils may check what they have written.

Oral practice
(a) The pupils should be allowed about 5 minutes to study the passage set, after which time they will be expected to be able to read it at normal reading speed and with reasonable accuracy of pronunciation.
(b) When the pupils have closed their books, the teacher may ask questions on the passage.
(*Note:* The normal practice of adding the questions to be asked has not been followed. Firstly, because the pupils should not see the questions; secondly, because it was accepted that the teacher would be capable of inventing his or her own questions.)

Free composition
For the use of these passages in teaching free composition, outlines have been added at the end of the section. The passage should be read through twice while the pupils study the outline. After the final reading, and with the outline before them, they should recapitulate the story in their own words.

1. AN UNDERSTANDABLE MISTAKE

In der guten alten Zeit, als wenige Leute das Rauchen kannten, saß ein Engländer in seinem Arbeitszimmer und schrieb Briefe. Weil er durstig wurde, ließ er einen Diener kommen und befahl ihm, eine Flasche Wein aus dem Keller zu holen.

Nachdem der Diener das Zimmer verlassen hatte, steckte der Herr seine Pfeife an und begann zu rauchen. Nach einigen Minuten erschien der Diener wieder. Als er eine große Wolke Rauch über dem Kopf seines Herrn sah, eilte er durch das Zimmer und leerte die Flasche über den Kopf des Mannes. Dann stürzte er zur Tür hinaus, rannte die Treppe hinunter und schrie: „Feuer! Hilfe! Mein Herr brennt!" Was der Herr wirklich gesagt hat, läßt sich hier nicht wiedererzählen.

2.   A BRAVE DAUGHTER

An der Küste von Nordamerika stand ein Leuchtturm, dessen Wächter nur eine Tochter hatte. Der Name des Mädchens war Ida. Eines Tages mußte der Wächter ans Land rudern, um Brot und Lampenöl zu holen. Während er in der Stadt war, erhob sich ein unerwarteter Sturm. Der Himmel wurde ganz schwarz und die Wellen warfen sich gegen den Leuchtturm. Am Strand lief der Wächter hilflos auf und ab, denn es war ganz unmöglich, auf dem stürmischen Meer zu fahren. Er dachte immer an seine Tochter und an die Gefahr für die Schiffe, wenn das Licht sie vor den gefährlichen Riffen nicht warnte. Plötzlich traf ein heller Schein das Auge des Vaters. Das Licht des Leuchtturms brannte und schien hell über das Meer. Seine kleine Tochter hatte das Licht angezündet.

3.   THE CUNNING BEGGAR IS CAUGHT

Ein Mann saß jeden Tag auf der Straße. Er hielt ein Bein vor sich ausgestreckt und sah so unglücklich aus, daß jeder Fußgänger ihm etwas Geld in die Mütze warf. Wenn man ihn fragte, wie er das andere Bein verloren habe, sagte er: „Ich bin vor vielen Jahren von einem Auto überfahren worden; seit der Zeit bin ich hilflos."

Eines Tages ging eine Dame mit ihrem Hund vorbei. Sie blieb vor dem Mann stehen, um mit ihm zu sprechen. Der Mann wollte den Hund streicheln. Plötzlich wurde der Hund zornig und biß ihn in das Bein. Sofort sprang der Mann auf und lief heulend weg. Es war jetzt klar, daß er zwei starke Beine hatte.

4. A CLEVER DOG SAVES HIS MASTER

Einmal machte ein Arbeiter einen Spaziergang mit seinem Hund im Walde. Weil er weit umhersehen wollte, kletterte er auf einen hohen Baum. Unglücklicherweise machte er einen Fehltritt und fiel herunter. Dabei blieb er mit dem Fuß zwischen zwei Ästen hängen. Jetzt hing er hilflos zwischen Himmel und Erde und konnte sich gar nicht helfen. Zuerst lief der Hund hin und her und heulte, um seine Angst zu zeigen. Endlich lief er nach Hause, wo er noch lange heulte. Dadurch wollte er zeigen, daß man ihm folgen sollte.

Endlich verstand man, was er wollte. Schnell führte er die Leute in den Wald. Wenn sie nicht schnell genug gingen, lief er immer zu ihnen zurück. Auf diese Weise brachte er sie an die Stelle, wo sein Herr bewußtlos hing. Bald hatte man den unglücklichen Mann aus seiner peinlichen Lage gerettet.

5. THE ELEPHANT NEVER FORGETS

Die folgende Geschichte zeigt die Dankbarkeit eines Elefanten. Eines Tages machten einige Soldaten einen Marsch durch den dichten Dschungel. Plötzlich hörten sie ein lautes Brüllen und ein großer Elefant erschien zwischen den Bäumen. Es sah aus, als ob er die Soldaten zerstampfen würde. Als das Tier die Menschen erblickte, blieb es ganz still und hob das rechte Vorderbein. Ein Offizier trat vorsichtig zu dem Tier. Im Fuß des Elefanten konnte er einen langen, scharfen Dorn sehen. Es war klar, daß der Elefant in großen Schmerzen war. Langsam ergriff der Offizier den Fuß und zog den Dorn heraus. Dadurch wurden die Schmerzen des Tieres gelindert. Im nächsten Augenblick verschwand das Tier im Wald.

Einige Jahre später besuchte derselbe Offizier einen Zirkus in seiner Heimatstadt. Weil er jetzt außer Dienst war, mußte er die billigste Platzkarte kaufen und er saß ganz unten. Als die Elefanten eine Runde machten, kam einer von ihnen zu ihm, faßte ihn um den Körper, hob ihn in die Luft und setzte ihn auf den teuersten Platz im Zirkus. Dadurch zeigte der Elefant seine Dankbarkeit.

6. THE PIPER OF HAMELIN

Im dreizehnten Jahrhundert waren sehr viele Ratten in einer Stadt an der Weser. Diese Stadt hieß Hameln. Obgleich die Einwohner alles versuchten, konnten sie die Ratten nicht töten. Endlich fraßen diese Tiere alles auf. Eines Tages erschien ein Fremder, der versprach, alle Ratten zu vernichten, wenn man ihm eine gewisse Summe Geld schenkte. Nachdem die Bürger ihm diese Summe versprochen hatten, holte er eine Pfeife aus der Tasche und begann eine Melodie zu spielen. Sofort sprangen die Ratten aus ihren Löchern und folgten ihm an die Weser, wo sie alle ins Wasser sprangen und ertranken. Als der Rattenfänger in die Stadt zurückkehrte, um sein Geld zu holen, wollten die Einwohner ihm nichts geben. Er wurde sehr zornig und beschloß, die Stadt zu bestrafen.

Wieder trat er auf die Straße hinaus, holte seine Pfeife hervor und spielte eine andere Melodie. Diesmal liefen die Kinder aus den Häusern und folgten ihm in die Berge, wo sie verschwanden. So wurden die treulosen Bürger bestraft.

7. TELL SHOOTS AN APPLE FROM HIS SON'S HEAD

Wilhelm Tell war ein kühner Schweizer. Er konnte besser schießen als alle anderen Leute. Eines Tages machten Tell und sein kleiner Sohn einen Besuch nach einem Dorf, in dessen Nähe sie wohnten. Als sie es erreichten, sahen sie auf dem Marktplatz eine große Stange mit einem Hut darauf. Geßler, der österreichische Vogt, hatte befohlen, daß jeder den Hut grüßen müsse, wenn er vorbeiging. Als Tell vorbeiging, ohne den Hut zu grüßen, nahmen die Soldaten ihn gefangen. Er wurde vor Geßler gebracht, und dieser befahl Tell, einen Apfel von dem Kopf seines Sohnes zu schießen. Tell war sehr unglücklich, aber der Junge hatte keine Angst. Er stellte sich an einen Baum und stand ganz still. Tell durchbohrte den Apfel und dadurch rettete er sich und seinen Sohn. Später wurde Geßler von Tell getötet. Der Dichter Schiller erzählt diese Geschichte in einem seiner Dramen.

8. SIEGFRIED IS KILLED BY TREACHERY

Eine berühmte Sage aus dem zwölften Jahrhundert erzählt, wie der Held Siegfried in der Nähe der Stadt Worms getötet wurde.

Acht Jahre lang warteten seine Feinde auf den Augenblick, wo sie ihren bösen Plan, Siegfried zu ermorden, ausführen konnten. Es geschah endlich, daß Siegfried und sein Freund Hagen an einem Sommertag in einem dichten Wald waren, der nicht weit von Worms lag. Die beiden Freunde waren auf der Jagd gewesen und suchten jetzt einen Fluß, um ihren Durst zu stillen. Nachdem Hagen getrunken hatte, bückte sich Siegfried, um sein Gesicht mit dem Wasser zu kühlen. Sofort faßte der Freund seinen Speer und durchbohrte Siegfried an der Stelle auf dem Rücken, wo man ihn am besten verwunden konnte. Siegfried sank bewußtlos auf die Erde. Bevor er starb aber, erkannte er, daß sein treuloser Freund ihn ermordet hatte. Einige Augenblicke später starb er an seiner schweren Wunde.

9. FAUST SELLS HIS SOUL TO THE DEVIL

Die Geschichte von Faust ist überall bekannt. Faust, der im Mittelalter lebte, wollte alles wissen. Endlich bat er den Teufel um Hilfe. Der Teufel versprach, ihm vierundzwanzig Jahre lang alles zu geben, was er haben wollte. Dafür mußte Faust ihm am Ende dieser Zeit seine Seele versprechen. Vierundzwanzig Jahre lang diente der Teufel dem Faust und gab ihm alles, was er sich nur wünschte. Am Ende der Zeit wurde Faust trotz seines fröhlichen Lebens traurig, denn er begann, die Nähe des Todes zu merken.

Am letzten Abend lud Faust seine Freunde zu einem Fest ein, um seine letzten Stunden mit ihnen zu verbringen. Als es Mitternacht schlug, schickte er alle aus dem Zimmer. Als sie das Haus verließen, heulte ein furchtbarer Sturmwind um das Haus; aus Fausts Zimmer hörten sie lautes Geschrei und dann herrschte Totenstille. Als sie das Zimmer am nächsten Morgen betraten, entdeckten sie eine Leiche mit blassem Gesicht in einer dunklen Ecke des Zimmers. Der Teufel hatte seine Belohnung geholt.

10. LATE FOR THE TRAIN

Der Schnellzug sollte im nächsten Augenblick abfahren. Die letzten Reisenden waren schon eingestiegen. Die Lokomotive pfiff ein paarmal. Auf dem Bahnsteig standen Freunde der Reisenden und winkten mit den Taschentüchern. Plötzlich hörte man einen lauten Ruf und ein Mann lief atemlos den Bahnsteig entlang. Als er den letzten Wagen erreichte, konnte er kein einziges Wort sprechen. Schnell ergriff ein Gepäckträger den Arm des Mannes, half ihm in den Wagen und schlug die Tür hinter ihm zu. Als der Mann wieder Atem holte, war der Zug schon aus dem Bahnhof. Eine alte Dame, die in der Ecke saß, sah den Mann freundlich an und sagte:

„Sie haben Glück gehabt, den Zug zu erreichen."

„Vielleicht", sagte der Mann, „aber ich wollte gar nicht mitfahren; ich bin nur gekommen, um einem Freund gute Reise zu wünschen."

11. STRANDED IN SWITZERLAND

Edith kam erst wieder richtig zu sich, als sie vor dem Bahnhof stand. Und dann saß sie im Wartesaal und wußte nicht weiter. In der kleinen Handtasche, die an ihrem Arm baumelte, waren ungefähr achtzehn Mark, und ihren Koffer hatte sie verloren. Sie preßte die Lippen aufeinander, um nicht zu weinen.

Wie weit werde ich mit den achtzehn Mark kommen...? dachte sie. Das reicht doch nicht bis nach Hause. Aber vielleicht bis an die Grenze? Sie hatte plötzlich das Gefühl, daß alles viel einfacher sein würde, wenn sie nur erst wieder in Deutschland wäre.

Sie stand auf und ging zum Fahrkartenschalter.

„Bitte", sagte sie zu dem Beamten, und ihr Herz klopfte so stark, daß sie kaum sprechen konnte, „komme ich mit achtzehn Mark bis nach Deutschland?"

Der Beamte streifte sie mit einem raschen Blick durch seine funkelnden Brillengläser und sagte: „Sie können dafür eine Fahrkarte nach Rottweil haben oder nach Freiburg im Breisgau. Aber heute abend fährt kein Zug mehr nach Deutschland."

„Aber", sagte Edith verzweifelt, „ich muß so schnell wie möglich nach Deutschland."

Der Beamte sah auf seinen Fahrplan. „Morgen früh um sechs Uhr zwei, Bahnsteig fünf."

Edith antwortet nicht. Eine ganze Nacht in diesem gräßlichen Wartesaal... Sie setzte sich wieder in eine Ecke. Andere Mädchen an ihrer Stelle hätten geweint. Aber Edith war zäh.

Nach MARION KELLERMANN, *Liebe hinterm Ladentisch*
Neue Illustrierte, Köln, 15.2.58

12. A SCHOOLBOY IS PUNISHED

In meiner Jugend war ich sehr faul. In der Schule wollte ich weder fleißig noch ernst arbeiten, und am Ende des Schuljahres war ich immer der letzte in der Klasse. Niemals konnte ich eine Aufgabe schreiben, ohne viele grobe Fehler zu machen. Obwohl ich mehrmals von den Lehrern bestraft wurde, half es nichts.

Obgleich ich erst sechzehn Jahre alt war, war ich sehr stark und groß. Meine Schultern waren so breit, daß man mich oft Goliath nannte. Wegen dieser großen Kraft wurde ich eines Tages nach Hause geschickt und durfte nie wieder in die Schule zurückkommen. Jetzt will ich erzählen, wie das geschehen ist.

Es war der letzte Schultag vor den Sommerferien. Natürlich waren wir alle sehr lustig in der Klasse. Während der Pause hatten wir einen heftigen Kampf im Klassenzimmer. Endlich warf die Gruppe, zu der ich gehörte, die andere zur Tür hinaus.

Da rief jemand mir zu: „Du bist der stärkste von uns allen hier im Zimmer. Also mußt du die Tür zuhalten, damit unsere Gegner nicht wieder hereinkommen." Sofort stemmte ich meine beiden Schultern gegen die Tür und hielt sie fest zu.

Nach ein paar Minuten wurde der Druck gegen die Tür zu stark, und ich mußte zurücktreten. Als die Tür aufsprang, fielen der Schuldiener, der Direktor und fast ein halbes Dutzend Lehrer herein. Auf der Stelle wurde ich bestraft und nach Hause geschickt. Nach jenem Tag durfte ich die Schule nie wieder betreten.

13. AN OLD LADY SAVES HER FRIENDS

An einem frostklaren Winterabend beschlossen die Einwohner einer Stadt an der Nordseeküste, ein großes Fest auf dem Eis zu halten. Die ganze Stadt war da; einige liefen Schlittschuh, andere fuhren in Schlitten über das Eis. Als der Mond aufging, wurde ihre Freude noch größer.

Nur eine alte Frau war von allen Leuten in der Stadt zurückgeblieben. Sie war krank und schwach und konnte ihr Bett nicht mehr verlassen. Da ihr Häuschen hoch auf dem Deich stand, konnte sie von ihrem Bett aufs Eis hinuntersehen und die Freude der Leute betrachten. Als es Abend wurde, merkte sie ein kleines, weißes Wölkchen im Westen, das eben über dem Horizont aufstieg.

Sofort hatte sie große Angst, denn sie wußte, daß das einen Sturm bedeutete. In kurzer Zeit würde die Flut da sein, dann würde ein Sturm losbrechen, und alle würden im Wasser sterben.

Sie rief so laut, wie sie nur konnte. Aber niemand war im Hause, denn alle Nachbarn waren auf dem Eis. Die Wolke wurde immer größer und schwärzer. Bald mußte die Flut da sein, und der Sturm losbrechen.

Da raffte sie ihre Kraft zusammen und kroch auf Händen und Füßen aus dem Bett zum Ofen. Hier fand sie ein brennendes Stück Holz. Sie ergriff es und warf es auf ihr Bett, das bald in Flammen stand. Dann kroch sie aus dem Zimmer.

Als der Feuerschein vom Eise gesehen wurde, stürzten alle in wilder Hast dem Strande zu. Schon sprang der Wind auf und der Himmel wurde dunkel. Das Eis begann zu zersplittern und der Wind wuchs zum Sturm. Als die letzten Menschen den Fuß aufs feste Land setzten, trieb sich die Flut an den Strand.

Die arme Frau hatte die ganze Stadt auf diese Weise gerettet.

Nach K. MÜLLENHOFF, *Sagen und Märchen aus Schleswig-Holstein*

14. AN ACCIDENT IN THE AIR

Vor einigen Tagen war ein junger Pilot bei uns zu Besuch. Wir baten ihn, uns etwas aus seinem Leben zu erzählen. Nach einigen Augenblicken erzählte er uns die folgende Geschichte.

Einmal flog ich mit einem Freund nach der Schweiz. Zuerst ging alles gut. Nach zweistündigem Flug aber begannen die Motoren unregelmäßig zu arbeiten, und bald mußte ich ohne Motorkraft fliegen.

Als ich hinausblickte, sah ich nichts als undurchdringlichen Wald unter mir; kein freier Platz zur Landung war sichtbar. Immer wieder versuchte ich die Motoren in Gang zu bringen, aber es war nutzlos. In langsamem Flug senkte sich das Flugzeug. Ich machte mich zum Absprung bereit und schrie meinem Freunde zu, daß er dasselbe machen sollte.

Als er aber in die Tiefe hinausblickte, wurde er ängstlich, schüttelte den Kopf und trat zurück. Die Maschine glitt langsam tiefer. Da ich meinen Freund in solcher Gefahr nicht verlassen konnte, kehrte ich auch an meinen Platz zurück und steuerte das Flugzeug auf die dichten Bäume. Jetzt gab ich alle Hoffnung auf, denn das Unglück mußte bald geschehen. Es wurde vor meinen Augen schwarz und ich konnte nicht mehr klar denken.

Plötzlich kam ein heftiger Krach. Die Motoren rissen sich los und fielen zur Erde, während der Rumpf der Maschine in den hohen Zweigen hängenblieb. Ich wurde durch die Luft geschleudert und landete glücklicherweise auf einem Haufen trockener Blätter. Ich verlor das Bewußtsein.

Als ich wieder zu Sinnen kam, lag ich in einem bequemen Bett im Krankenhaus. Im Nebenbett lag mein Freund. Wir hatten wirklich Glück gehabt, denn wir waren alle beide kaum verletzt, und nach ein paar Tagen durften wir das Krankenhaus wieder verlassen.

15. A LONG-SOUGHT FRIEND IS FOUND—DEAD

Jan Mertens ging schnell die Straße entlang. Diesmal kannte er seinen Weg. In der Telefonzelle wählte er Ellens Nummer.

Das Mädchen meldete sich mit leiser Stimme.

„Hören Sie, Ellen", sagte er. „Ich muß Sie noch einmal sehen. Und Sie müssen mir noch einmal helfen. In ein paar Stunden geht mein Schiff. Ich habe eine Entdeckung gemacht. Sie hängt mit dem Mann zusammen, den ich die ganze Zeit suche. Ich erwarte Sie auf der Straße. In der Nähe vom 'Blauen Bock' an der Telefonzelle. Bitte, kommen Sie gleich!"

„Ich komme..." das war alles, was Ellen antwortete.

Jan Mertens verließ die Zelle und wanderte auf der Straße hin und her. Jetzt schien alles klar zu sein. Er hatte nicht einen Betrunkenen aus der Ruine weggeschleppt, sondern einen Toten. Und die beiden Kerle aus dem ‚Blauen Bock' wußten es.

Darum hatten sie die ganze Zeit versucht herauszubekommen, ob er sich an irgend etwas erinnerte. So muß es gewesen sein... dachte er. Ellen würde ihm helfen, die Kerle zu finden.

Mit einem Ruck drehte er sich um.

Ein Taxi war in die Straße eingebogen. Sein Herz schlug höher. Langsam näherte sich der Wagen der Telefonzelle.

Ellen stieg aus. Sie bezahlte den Fahrer, und dann kam sie mit einem Lächeln auf Jan Mertens zu.

„Ich danke Ihnen", sagte der Seemann. Er nahm ihren Arm, und während sie weitergingen, erzählte er ihr, daß man seinen unbekannten Freund gefunden hatte.

Weder er noch Ellen merkten, daß ihnen zwei Schatten folgten.

Nach IAN STUART BLACK, *Spuk in St. Pauli*
Neue Illustrierte, Köln, 8.2.58

16. A GIRL RETURNS HOME LATE

Myrna nahm den Schlüssel aus ihrer Abendtasche und öffnete die Haustür. Dann stand sie in der Halle, und plötzlich empfand sie eine tiefe Stille. Völlige Ruhe umfing sie.

Sie schritt nach der Treppe und griff links nach dem Lichtschalter. Sie schloß ein wenig die Augen in Erwartung des hellen Lichtes. Aber der Raum blieb dunkel. Eine sonderbare Unsicherheit umfing sie.

Sie lauschte. Nichts rührte sich. Sie stand einen Augenblick still. Dann eilte sie hastig die Treppe hinauf. Schon im Laufen rief sie laut nach ihrer Freundin: „Tatjana!" und, da keine Antwort kam, nochmals lauter.

Ihre Stimme hallte in der Dunkelheit des Hauses, doch keine Antwort kam.

Sie riß atemlos die Tür zu ihrem Boudoir auf, rief in die Finsternis den Namen der Freundin—und hielt inne. Sie fühlte das Hämmern ihres Pulses. Mechanisch, ohne Hoffnung, daß es einen Erfolg haben könne, drückte sie den Lichtschalter nieder. Im selben Augenblick war der Raum hell erleuchtet. „Sonderbar", dachte sie, aber da sie auf ihren Ruf wieder keine Antwort bekam, suchte sie, eine Erklärung für die Abwesenheit der Freundin zu finden.

Die Uhr zeigte halb vier. Wo konnte Tatjana sein—zu dieser Stunde?

Sie ging langsam zu ihrem Schlafzimmer, durchquerte es und betrat das Wohnzimmer. Sie drehte das Licht an. Plötzlich blieb sie stehen und blickte nach dem Lehnstuhl. Sie lächelte. Die Freundin saß schlummernd im Stuhle. Sie ging hinter den Stuhl und strich ihr sanft über das Haar.

Sie sagte wieder: „Tatjana." Sie ging um den Stuhl herum und stand nun der Schlafenden gegenüber.

Und dann stieß sie einen hellen Schrei aus.

Nach FRANK ARNAU, *Mordkommission Hollywood*

17. ARRESTED AT THE PETROL-STATION

Am Nachmittag stand ein Spaziergänger an der Tankstelle. Oft sah er der Arbeit des Tankwarts zu, manchmal zog er eine Zeitung aus der Tasche und las, manchmal ging er auch ein paar Schritte auf und ab, oder plauderte mit dem Tankwart.

Die Sonne schien noch immer und es war viel zu tun, denn viele Autofahrer benutzten das schöne Herbstwetter, um noch einmal hinauszufahren auf das Land.

Es war viel Interessantes da zu sehen, aber der Spaziergänger, der immer in der Nähe der Tankstelle herumwanderte, schien keine Lust dazu zu verspüren. Er wurde erst aufmerksam, als ein zweisitziger Wagen vorfuhr. Ein gutgekleideter, junger Mann stieg aus dem Wagen und sprach mit dem Tankwart. Eine große Ungeduld war in seinem Benehmen. Er sah sich öfters um, als erwarte er eine unangenehme Begegnung. Den Spaziergänger, der jetzt langsam herankam, beachtete er nicht.

„Stellen Sie den Wagen hier ab...", hörte der Spaziergänger den Autofahrer zu dem Tankwart sagen. „Das Fräulein wird den Wagen wohl durch ihren Fahrer abholen lassen. Wo ist hier die nächste Taxistelle?"

Ehe der Tankwart antworten konnte, war der Spaziergänger heran. Er lüftete den Hut, während er sich an den Autofahrer wandte.

„Herr von Galan, wenn ich nicht irre?"

Ein erstaunter Ausdruck erschien in Galans Gesicht. „Was wünschen Sie?" fragte er.

„Ich hätte Sie gern für einen Augenblick allein gesprochen..."

„Es tut mir leid", antwortete von Galan. „Ich muß zum Bahnhof. Der Zug nach Hamburg fährt in einer halben Stunde ab...!"

„Sie werden den Zug nicht benutzen können, Herr von Galan!" sagte der Fremde. „Ich bin Kommissar Kramer."

Nach CARL OTTO WINDECKER, *Nebel über den Straßen*

18. INTERVIEWING A SUSPECT

Ich fuhr in das Hotel Excelsior, um den Architekten zu besuchen.

Der Portier kannte mich natürlich, und so nahm ich ihn

etwas beiseite, um ihm einige Fragen zu stellen. Dann ging er in seine Loge, nahm den Hörer ab und meldete mich bei Dublas an. „Er wird in zehn Minuten herunterkommen!" berichtete er. Aber das paßte mir nicht. Ich fragte nach der Zimmernummer.

„Ich werde hinaufgehen und warten", sagte ich, „bis er sein Appartement verläßt. Und dann mit ihm in sein Zimmer gehen."

Der Portier nickte.

Ich ging im Korridor des ersten Stockwerkes auf und ab, doch stets mit einem Blick nach der Tür zu seinem Zimmer. Als sie schließlich geöffnet wurde und ein Herr an der Schwelle erschien, trat ich an ihn heran.

„Herr Dublas?" fragte ich. Er nickte bejahend. „Ich würde vorziehen, Sie privat zu sprechen", sagte ich. „Ich bin Kriminalkommissar Lamont."

Ich öffnete die Tür, bat ihn voranzugehen und sah mich dann in dem Raum um. Ein Doppelbett stand an der rechten Wand. Auf einem Tisch stand eine Schreibmaschine. Auf dem Schrank bemerkte ich zwei große Koffer. Auf einem Stuhl stand ein Radio mit Antenne.

„Sie sind Architekt, Herr Dublas?" fragte ich. Er ging zu seinem Schreibtisch, suchte und fand einige Briefe, die er mir überreichte. Die Namen der Schreiber kannte ich.

Was mich wunderte, war, daß Dublas mich nicht fragte, weshalb ich ihn besuchte. Ich gab ihm die Briefe zurück. Er warf sie auf den Schreibtisch.

„Ich habe noch andere Papiere—falls diese nicht genug sein sollten", sagte er.

Er nahm seinen Paß aus der Tasche und überreichte ihn mir. Der Paß war in Marseille ausgestellt und alles war in bester Ordnung. Ich wäre sicher gegangen, hätte der Mann sich „normal" benommen. Aber irgend etwas wollte mir nicht gefallen.

Nach FRANK ARNAU, *Tanger- nach Mitternacht*

19. TRAPPED IN A RUINED HOUSE (1)

Es roch nach verfaultem Holz, als sie den Eingang des Hauses betraten. Ellen verspürte ein starkes Herzklopfen, als sie die Stelle erreichten, an der sie in der ersten Nacht gestanden hatte.

Sie hielt sich am Ärmel des Seemanns fest. „Warten Sie", flüsterte sie.

Jan Mertens blieb bewegungslos stehen.

Es dauerte eine Weile, ehe sie sich beruhigt hatte.

„Hier stand ich", sagte sie leise. „Ich sah, wie die beiden Männer an mir vorbeigingen, als sie das Haus verließen."

Ohne zu antworten ging Jan weiter. Sie folgte ihm. Durch das Loch in der hinteren Hauswand fiel Licht von der Straße.

„Hier habe ich den Mann gefunden und aufgehoben", murmelte Jan. „Ich schleppte ihn durch das Loch nach draußen, ohne zu wissen, was mit ihm los war..."

Ellen blieb plötzlich wie erstarrt stehen. Sie hatte von der Tür her Atmen gehört.

„Was ist los?" fragte Jan.

„Die Mörder sind im Hause...", keuchte sie.

Jan drehte sich um. Und da sah er die beiden Schatten.

„Stellen Sie sich hinter mich", befahl er dem jungen Mädchen leise.

Der größere der beiden Schatten war jetzt keine zwei Meter von ihm entfernt.

Jan ließ den Mann herankommen. Dann holte er zum Schlag aus. Aber der Mann vor ihm wich zurück.

Der Seemann machte einen Schritt nach vorn, um ihn zu packen. Da sauste die Stahlrute auf seinen Kopf.

Ellen hörte es. Sie schrie und rannte auf den Seemann zu, der am Boden lag. Sie wollte sich über ihn beugen, als sie zurückgerissen wurde.

„Sei ruhig, oder es geht dir wie ihm!" zischte eine Stimme.

Nach Ian Stuart Black, *Spuk in St. Pauli*
Neue Illustrierte, Köln, 8.2.58

20. TRAPPED IN A RUINED HOUSE (2)

Ellen tastete sich mit zitternden Händen weiter. Im ersten Stock ging sie in eines der Zimmer. Es hatte keinen Fußboden mehr, nur ein paar Balken waren noch geblieben.

Schwer atmend preßte sie sich an die Wand.

Die Schritte der Mörder kamen näher. Vorsichtig glitt Ellen an der Wand entlang in den nächsten Raum. Sie wußte, es ging um ihr Leben, denn unten lag Jan Mertens hilflos.

Durch die Tür gegenüber konnte sie einen großen leeren Fensterrahmen erkennen. Vielleicht konnte sie sich hinausschwingen. Aber auch hier war der Fußboden beinahe ganz eingestürzt. Ein einziger falscher Schritt konnte den Tod bedeuten.

Ellen konnte jetzt das Atmen der Verfolger hören. Eine Stimme zischte: „Du wirst mir nicht entkommen!"

Das Mädchen lief zum Fenster. Sie wollte sich hinausschwingen, doch sah sie die Tiefe unter sich und schreckte zurück. Da merkte sie, wie die Verfolger das Zimmer betraten.

Da begann sie laut zu schreien.

Unten war Jan Mertens wieder zu sich gekommen. Der Schrei durchfuhr ihn. Er taumelte die Treppe hinauf. Als er im Zimmer stand, sah er im Mondlicht Ellen, die sich am Fensterkreuz festhielt. Dicht hinter ihr standen Olsen und sein Freund.

„Hab keine Angst, Ellen", rief Jan laut.

Die beiden Männer drehten sich entsetzt zur Tür um.

„Halt dich am Fenster fest", schrie Jan.

Dann rannte er und sprang Olsen an. Dieser brüllte wie ein wütendes Tier. Als die Planke unter ihnen zerbrach, griff er mit beiden Händen nach seinem Freund.

Die drei Männer stürzten in die Tiefe, während Ellen sich noch immer am Fenster anklammerte.

Eine entsetzliche Stille trat ein.

Dann hörte sie laute Stimmen von der Straße. „Hilfe!", rief sie, „Hilfe!"

Nach IAN STUART BLACK, *Spuk in St. Pauli*
Neue Illustrierte, Köln, 8.2.58

OUTLINES OF PASSAGES FOR REPRODUCTION

Instructions

Listen carefully to the passage as it is read to you, and study the outline during the reading. The passage will be read twice, after which you will rewrite the story in your own words, using the outline as a basis. Your composition should be about 130 to 150 words.

Suggestions

1. During the reading try to make a mental note of any words you do not know, *e.g.* gender of nouns, form of verbs.
2. You may know some very useful German words and phrases, but do not force them into the framework of a story in which they do not fit. The result might be very bad German; it will almost certainly sound nonsense.
3. Your aim should be a reproduction of the story in simple but accurate German; therefore, check every word you have written.
4. Remember the general rules for composition as given in the introduction to the section on Free Composition.

1. Die Zeit — das Rauchen — der Engländer — der Brief — durstig — der Diener — die Flasche Wein — hinausgehen — die Pfeife — rauchen — zurückkommen — die Wolke — der Rauch — eilen — leeren — hinausstürzen — hinunter — „Hilfe" — der Herr — sagen — nicht erzählen.

2. Nordamerika — der Leuchtturm — Ida — rudern — Brot holen — der Sturm — der Himmel — die Wellen — hilflos — denken — die Riffe — die Schiffe — plötzlich — der Schein — brennen — hell — anzünden.

3. Auf der Straße — das Bein ausgestreckt — unglücklich — das Geld — das andere Bein — überfahren — die Dame — der Hund — stehen bleiben — streicheln — zornig — beißen — weglaufen — zwei Beine.

4. Der Arbeiter — der Spaziergang im Wald — klettern — der Fehltritt — hängen bleiben — hilflos — hin und her laufen — die Angst — nach Hause — folgen — verstehen — in den Wald führen — an die Stelle — retten.

5. Die Geschichte — die Dankbarkeit — die Soldaten — der Dschungel — Elefant erscheinen — zerstampfen — still bleiben — das Vorderbein — vorsichtig treten — der Dorn — die Schmerzen — herausziehen — verschwinden — später — der Zirkus — außer Dienst — unten sitzen — eine Runde machen — fassen — setzen — Dankbarkeit zeigen.

6. Viele Ratten — Hameln — die Weser — allerlei Versuche — töten — auffressen — der Fremde — Geld schenken —

versprechen — die Pfeife — Ratten springen — folgen — ertrinken — zurückkehren — nichts geben — zornig — bestrafen — hinaustreten — Kinder laufen — verschwinden — treulos.

7. Tell — kühn — schießen — der Besuch — das Dorf — wohnen — der Marktplatz — der Hut — Geßler — befehlen — grüßen — vorbeigehen — die Soldaten — vor Geßler — Apfel schießen — der Junge — die Angst — still stehen — retten — später — Schiller — das Drama.

8. Die Sage — der Held Siegfried — töten — acht Jahre lang — der Feind — der Plan — durchführen — Hagen — die Jagd — der Fluß — trinken — kühlen — der Speer — durchbohren — der Rücken — verwunden — sinken — erkennen — ermorden — sterben — die Wunde.

9. Faust — bekannt — das Mittelalter — alles wissen — der Teufel — die Hilfe — vierundzwanzig — die Seele geben — dienen — traurig — die Nähe des Todes — am letzten Abend — das Fest — die Mitternacht — verlassen — der Sturmwind — das Geschrei — am nächsten Morgen — die Leiche — die Ecke — die Belohnung.

10. Der Schnellzug — einsteigen — auf dem Bahnsteig — winken — der Ruf — atemlos — erreichen — der Gepäckträger — helfen — die Tür — Atem holen — die Dame — ansehen — den Zug erreichen — nicht mitfahren — wünschen.

11. Der Bahnhof — der Wartesaal — achtzehn Mark — nach Hause — die Grenze — der Fahrkartenschalter — der Beamte (-n, -n) — die Fahrkarte — heute abend — der Fahrplan — die Nacht — zäh.

12. Faul — ernst arbeiten — grobe Fehler — mehrmals bestraft — Goliath — nach Hause geschickt — der Kampf — zur Tür hinaus — die Tür zuhalten — zurücktreten — der Direktor — auf der Stelle — betreten.

13. Der Winterabend — das Fest — das Eis — eine alte Frau — krank — betrachten — das Wölkchen — die Angst — — der Sturm — rufen — die Kraft zusammenraffen — kriechen — das Stück Holz — stürzen — retten.

14. Der Pilot — die Geschichte — fliegen — gut gehen — unregelmäßig arbeiten — der Wald — der Absprung —

ängstlich werden — nicht verlassen — der Krach — die Blätter — das Krankenhaus — Glück haben.

15. Jan Mertens — die Straße entlang — die Telefonzelle — Ellen — helfen — der Mann — der „Blaue Bock" — der Tote — versuchen — der Kerl (-e) — das Taxi — bezahlen — erzählen — folgen.

16. Myrna — der Schlüssel — die Stille — der Lichtschalter — dunkel — die Unsicherheit — die Freundin Tatjana — keine Antwort — hell — die Erklärung suchen — das Wohnzimmer — das Licht andrehen — der Lehnstuhl — schlafen — der Schrei.

17. Der Spaziergänger — die Tankstelle — der Tankwart — viel Interessantes — keine Lust — der zweisitzige Wagen — die Ungeduld — abholen lassen — die Taxistelle — Herr von Galan — erstaunt — der Zug — Kommissar Kramer.

18. Das Hotel Excelsior — der Architekt (-en, -en) — der Portier — Dublas — zehn Minuten — hinaufgehen — der Korridor — öffnen — privat sprechen — fragen — der Brief — der Paß — Marseille — nicht gefallen.

19. Riechen — Ellen — das Herzklopfen — die erste Nacht — sich beruhigen — die Männer — das Loch — das Atmen — die Mörder — die beiden Schatten — der Schlag — die Stahlrute — schreien — die Stimme.

20. Ellen — der erste Stock — kein Fußboden — die Schritte — Jan Mertens hilflos — der Fensterrahmen — der Verfolger — sich hinausschwingen — schreien — zu sich kommen — sich am Fensterkreuz festhalten — keine Angst — anspringen — stürzen — die Stille.

SECTION 6

FREE COMPOSITION

The subjects suggested for free composition are divided into the following categories
A. A series of ten pictures. It is suggested that these should be used in the beginning stages so that the work may be prepared in class by the question and answer method. Only when the pupil has mastered the necessary vocabulary of a picture, should he be asked to write out the story.
B. Twenty-five outlines or suggestions of an incident, given in German.
C. Twelve suggestions, given in German, continuing one of the English prose passages. The number of the prose passage is given in brackets.

SOME HINTS ON THE FREE COMPOSITION

The free composition is your opportunity to show what German words, constructions and phrases you already know. The scope is not limited to certain words and phrases that you are expected to know, as in a translation. If you do not know the German for a certain word or idea, then you need not write about it; bring in something connected with the subject that you do know. It is foolish, for example, to try to describe a cricket match in German, when you do not know the words for stumps, bails, bowler, etc. Similarly, if the construction of a sentence is becoming complicated, forget that sentence; you are not compelled to write it; begin a simpler one. The main thing to keep in mind is that you are going to use only what you already know. It is even better to do without a dictionary for this type of exercise; dictionaries can be so misleading. They will often lead you to use words you have never met before, and whose real meaning you do not understand.

The writing of free compositions should be developed in the following stages.

First stage

From the outset your free composition should be thought out in German. This may sound difficult, but in actual fact it is easier than thinking it out in English and then translating that into German. With any picture in front of you, ask yourself questions in German; the answers to these questions will provide the story you are expected to write. Imagine, for example, that you are looking at a picture of a garden with an apple-tree in it. A family is looking up into the tree. Here are your questions and answers:

Wo wohnten die Brauns?	Die Brauns wohnten in Berlin.
Was war hinter ihrem Hause?	Hinter ihrem Hause lag ein Garten.
Was stand in dem Garten?	In dem Garten stand ein Apfelbaum.
Wie war der Baum?	Der Baum war voll Äpfel.
Wer wollte einige Äpfel?	Frau Braun wollte einige Äpfel.
Warum wollte sie die Äpfel?	Ihre kleine Tochter Ilse wollte die Äpfel essen.
Wer mußte die Äpfel pflücken?	Herr Braun mußte die Äpfel pflücken.

The answers written out in essay form give the following:

Die Brauns wohnten in Berlin. Hinter ihrem Hause lag ein Garten. In dem Garten stand ein Apfelbaum. Der Baum war voll Äpfel. Frau Braun wollte einige Äpfel. Ihre kleine Tochter Ilse wollte die Äpfel essen. Herr Braun mußte sie pflücken.

Second stage

When you have attained tolerable accuracy and fluency with such simple statements, you should begin to join the sentences together with the co-ordinating conjunctions (*und, aber, allein, denn, sondern, oder*) that do not alter the order of words in a sentence. Add also an occasional adjective, making sure that it is correctly declined. Here is the same passage as above, taken just one small step further.

Die Brauns wohnten in Berlin. Hinter ihrem Hause lag ein schöner Garten, und in dem Garten stand ein großer

Apfelbaum voll reifer Äpfel. Frau Braun wollte einige Äpfel, denn ihre kleine Tochter Ilse wollte die roten Äpfel essen. Aber Herr Braun mußte sie pflücken.

Third stage

Once the co-ordinating conjunctions have been thoroughly mastered, and in order to give further variety to your style, you should now develop the use of subordinating conjunctions. An essay, or even a paragraph, composed entirely of main clauses sounds very tedious, so you must vary the sentence construction. This does not mean that every sentence has to be compound or complicated; there must still be a number of simple sentences. Remember also such helps as beginning your sentence with an adverb (*Hinter ihrem Hause lag ein Garten*) and the use of the relative pronoun. Here again is the same German paragraph, taken another step further.

Die Brauns wohnten einmal in Berlin. Hinter ihrem Hause lag ein schöner Garten, worin ein großer Apfelbaum voll reifer Äpfel stand. Da ihre kleine Tochter Ilse einige der roten Äpfel essen wollte, wünschte Frau Braun die Äpfel zu pflücken. Herr Braun aber mußte sie pflücken.

Fourth stage

To help your style further, you should now be ready to add a few adverbs and some phrases. A glance through Sections 25–27 of the grammar in this book will reveal many phrases suitable for use in compositions. A cautionary word is, however, very necessary. Firstly, vary the phrases you use; *eines Tages* and *er ging ins Bett* become very boring when they appear repeatedly in your essays. Secondly, choose phrases that fit exactly into the sentence; however wonderful a phrase may be, it will be wrongly used, if its meaning is out of place in that sentence in which you wish to use it. Therefore, it will be counted a mistake. Thirdly, do not make your composition a string of phrases; a few, well-placed idioms are much more effective than a large number of unco-ordinated phrases. Here then is the suggested final version.

Vor vielen Jahren wohnten die Brauns in Berlin. Hinter ihrem Hause lag ein großer Garten worin ein Apfelbaum voll reifer Äpfel stand. Da ihre kleine Tochter Ilse eines

Tages die roten Äpfel essen wollte, wünschte Frau Braun die Äpfel zu holen, Herr Braun aber mußte sie natürlich pflücken.

One last word of general advice on the writing of free compositions. Since you will, in all probability, only be asked to write short stories or describe short incidents, you must remember that a story has three parts, a beginning, a middle and an end. In other words, your final version must have three paragraphs of about equal length.

Section 6a

Free Composition from Pictures

1. Auf frischer Tat ertappt
2. Das zerbrochene Fenster
3. Unglück auf dem Eis
4. Morgenbesuch im Lager
5. Der Diebstahl
6. Schiffbruch
7. Die Feuerwehr kommt
8. Angeln verboten
9. Gerettet
10. Der fahrlässige Autofahrer

1

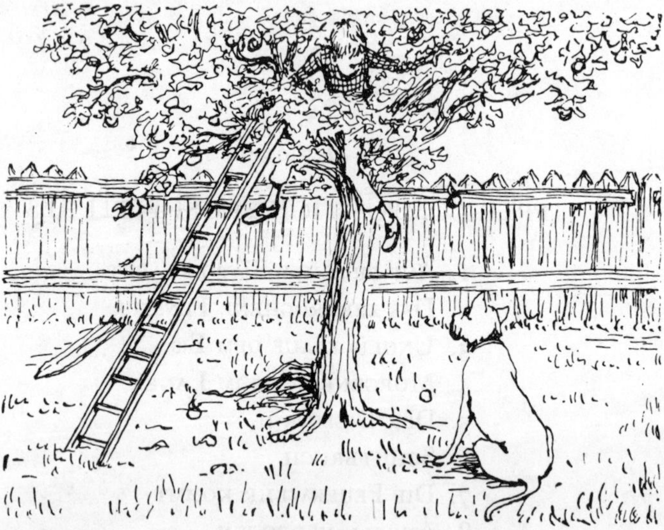

2

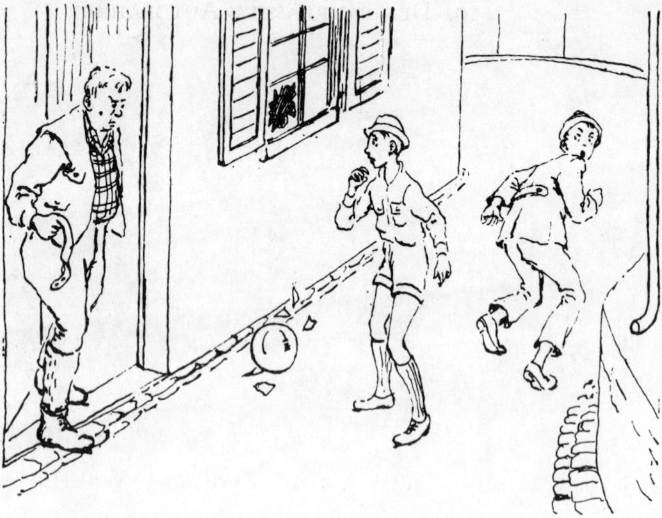

3

4

5

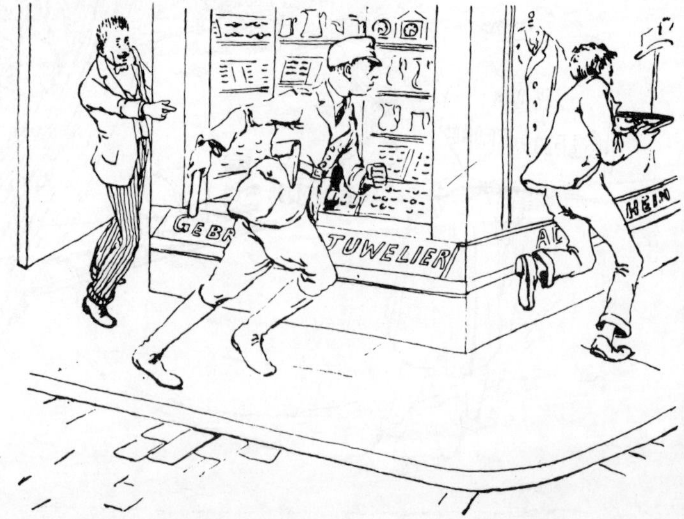

6

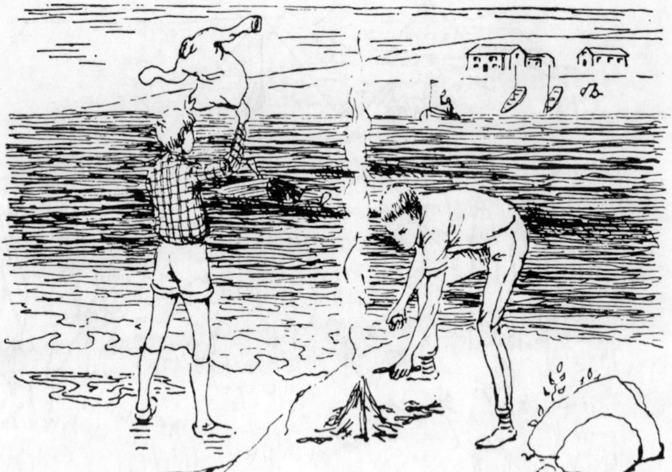

7

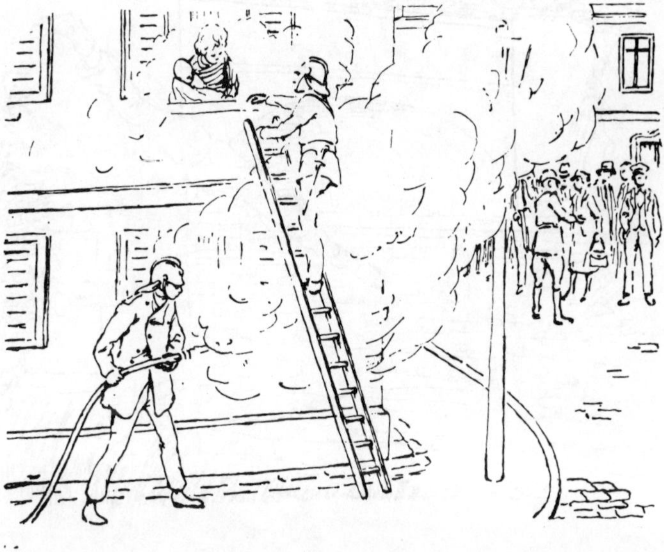

8

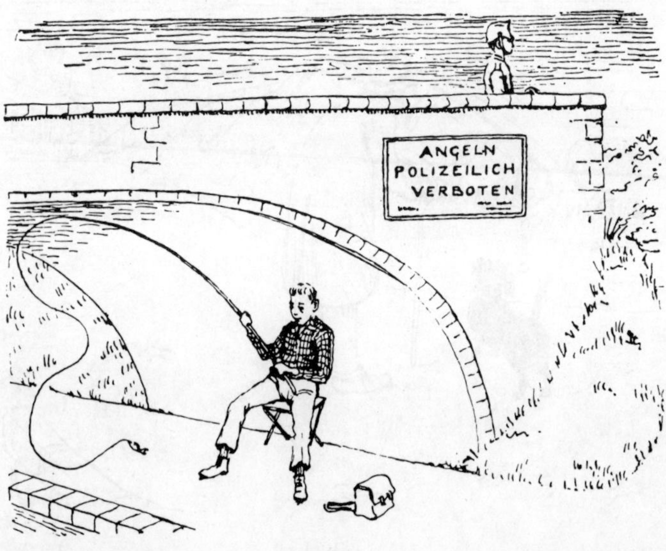

9

10

Section 6b
SUGGESTED SUBJECTS FOR FREE COMPOSITION

1. Sie kommen spät nach Hause und finden die Küche Ihres Hauses in Flammen. Ihre Eltern schlafen schon. Was tun Sie?
2. Ein Kind verliert den Weg in einem großen Wald. Es wird dunkel. Plötzlich hört es ein leises Geräusch, als ob jemand stöhne (*groan*). Was tut das Kind?
3. Während der Ferien am Meer klettern Sie auf einige Felsen am Strande. Plötzlich bemerken Sie, daß die Flut Sie abgeschnitten hat. Was geschieht?
4. Während Sie im Lager sind, frißt ein Hund das Mittagessen. Das nächste Dorf ist zehn Kilometer entfernt. Was tun Sie, um ein Mittagessen zu bekommen?
5. Sie fuhren mit einem Freund rad, als Sie plötzlich einen Verkehrsunfall sahen. Beschreiben Sie einem Schutzmann alles, was Sie gesehen haben.
6. Während einer Seereise fiel ein Kind über Bord. Erzählen Sie, wie das Kind gerettet wurde.
7. Ihr Vater hat einige Hennen gekauft, aber am ersten Tag fliegen die Hennen in den Garten des Nachbars. Beschreiben Sie, wie Sie die Hennen fangen.
8. Hans fuhr in die Ferien. Als er ankam, entdeckte er, daß man sein ganzes Gepäck auf dem Bahnhof zu Hause gelassen hatte. Was machte er?
9. Sie wollen eine Eisenbahnfahrt nach Schottland machen und entdecken, daß Sie in den D-Zug nach London eingestiegen sind. Sie fahren also in der falschen Richtung. Was tun Sie, wenn Sie London erreichen?
10. Zwei Kinder ruderten auf einem Fluß. Plötzlich fielen die Ruder ins Wasser. Was machten die Kinder?
11. Sie fuhren mit dem Zug. Plötzlich hielt der Zug. Erzählen Sie, was geschehen war.

12. Sie waren in den Bergen, als Sie einen Ruf um Hilfe hörten. Was machten Sie?
13. In der Mitte der Nacht hörten Sie etwas unten im Eßzimmer. Was machten Sie?
14. Ein Junge fuhr allein im Zug. Unterwegs konnte er seine Fahrkarte nicht finden. Was machte er?
15. Ihre Klasse machte einen Ausflug nach einer großen Stadt. Beschreiben Sie, was Sie sahen und taten.
16. Schreiben Sie einen Brief, worin Sie jemand aus Deutschland einladen, ein paar Wochen im Sommer bei Ihnen zu verbringen.
17. Die Großmutter hat Ihnen DM 20 zum Geburtstag geschickt. Was machen Sie damit?
18. Eines dunklen Abends sahen Sie, wie ein Mann durch ein Fenster stieg. Erzählen Sie, was Sie machten.
19. Sie erwachten in der Nacht voll Angst, denn Sie hatten eben geträumt. Erzählen Sie, was Sie geträumt hatten.
20. Zwei Kinder fanden ein Paket auf der Straße. Was machten sie damit?
21. Zwei Freunde schliefen im Zelt. Plötzlich kam ein furchtbarer Sturm, so daß das Zelt zerriß. Was machten sie?
22. „Der Mann wurde vom Schupo gefangen." Erzählen Sie, warum dies geschehen war.
23. Das Bellen des Hundes weckte Sie während der Nacht auf. Erzählen Sie, was Sie entdeckten, als Sie nach unten gingen.
24. Im Zoo sehen Sie einen Taschendieb. Was machen Sie?
25. Zwei Freunde übernachteten in einer Jugendherberge. Erzählen Sie, was sie am Abend machten, bevor sie ins Bett gingen.

Section 6c

CONTINUATION OF AN ENGLISH PROSE PASSAGE

1. (*Prose* 3)   Erzählen Sie, wie Sie die Jugendherberge gefunden haben und was dort geschehen ist.
2. (*Prose* 4)   Erzählen Sie die Geschichte von dem Film, den Ihre Eltern gesehen haben.
3. (*Prose* 7)   Erzählen Sie diese Geschichte weiter.
4. (*Prose* 9)   Beschreiben Sie, was Sie in der Nacht geweckt hat und was Sie getan haben.
5. (*Prose* 17)   Erzählen Sie diese Geschichte weiter.
6. (*Prose* 29)   Beschreiben Sie, was Sie in der ersten Woche in der fremden Stadt getan und gesehen haben.
7. (*Prose* 40)   Erzählen Sie, was Sie weiter gemacht haben.
8. (*Prose* 41)   Beschreiben Sie, wie Peter glücklich durch den Schnee zum Arzt kam.
9. (*Prose* 45)   Erzählen Sie diese Geschichte weiter.
10. (*Prose* 48)   Was war geschehen? Warum hatte der Zug Verspätung?
11. (*Prose* 49)   Was geschah und was haben Sie gefunden, als Sie mit dem Schutzmann nach Hause kamen?
12. (*Prose* 50)   Was machten Sie, als Sie den Hilferuf hörten?

SECTION 7

A. Passages for comprehension.
B. Multiple-choice exercises.

SECTION 7A

PASSAGES FOR COMPREHENSION

Lesen Sie den Text und beantworten Sie die Fragen.

1. Während der Nacht vom Dienstag zum Mittwoch ist etwa gegen 23.00 Uhr in der Hauptstraße ein dunkelgrüner Mercedes gestohlen worden. Dieser Wagen gehört einer bekannten Filmschauspielerin, die, an dem in Frage kommenden Abend, Bekannte besuchte, deren Wohnung in der Nähe des Tatortes liegt.
Den Wagen hatte sie auf der rechten Straßenseite am Bürgersteig geparkt. Zu dieser Zeit haben mehrere Fußgänger einen jungen Mann beobachtet, der sich etwa eine halbe Stunde lang in der Nähe des Wagens aufhielt. Er ist des Diebstahls verdächtig.
Dieser junge Mann hatte einen Schnurrbart und eine dunkle Hornbrille. Er trug eine braunkarierte Jacke und blaue Jeans. Der verschwundene Wagen trägt das Frankfurter Kennzeichen F TB 304 und hat eine dunkelgrüne Karosserie mit einem schwarzen Verdeck. Im Wagen lagen auf dem Rücksitz ein Kofferradio (Marke: *Blaupunkt*) und eine braune Lederaktentasche. Außerdem lag auf dem linken Vordersitz ein Damenpelzmantel.
Hinweise über die oben beschriebene Person oder den entwendeten Wagen nimmt jede Polizeidienststelle entgegen. Fernruf: (06 11) 02 13 25.

1. Was besitzt die Filmschauspielerin?
2. Wo war sie gegen 23.00 Uhr?
3. Von wem wurde der junge Mann beobachtet?

4. Was hat der junge Mann eine Zeitlang getan?
5. Was vermutet die Polizei?
6. Warum ist der junge Mann leicht zu erkennen?
7. Woher weiß man, daß der Wagen aus Frankfurt stammt?
8. Was bedeutet *Blaupunkt*?
9. Wessen Mantel ist gestohlen worden?
10. Was für Wertsachen sucht die Polizei?
11. Was soll man tun, wenn man etwas über den Mann oder den Wagen weiß?
12. Schreiben Sie die Zahlen 02 13 25 in Worten aus.

2. Als ich eines Abends von einem Spaziergang ins Hotel zurückkehrte, wurde ich vom Geschäftsführer gebeten, ihn in sein Büro zu begleiten. Da erzählte er mir, daß mein Handkoffer gestohlen worden sei. Zum Glück hatte man den Dieb erwischt, ehe er das Hotel verlassen konnte. Ich sollte sofort auf die Polizeiwache kommen, wo man den Dieb festhielt.

Als ich da ankam, führte man mich ins Büro des Polizeichefs, der an einem Schreibtisch saß, auf dem ich meinen Koffer erblickte. Der Chef bat mich höflich, Platz zu nehmen. Nachdem er geklingelt hatte, öffnete sich eine Tür, und ein Mann wurde von zwei Polizeibeamten hereingeführt. Ich hatte erwartet, einen kräftigen, stämmigen Kerl zu sehen aber der Mann, der jetzt vor mir stand, sah blaß, mager und entmutigt aus. Er stand mit gesenktem Blick und schien Angst zu haben.

Man fragte mich, ob der Mann bestraft werden solle. Weil mir der Mann leid tat, schüttelte ich den Kopf. Darauf blickte er auf und sah mich dankbar an. Einen Augenblick lang überlegte der Chef, dann befahl er den beiden Polizisten, den Mann freizulassen.

Ich war im Begriff, den Dienstraum der Polizeiwache zu verlassen, um ins Hotel zurückzukehren, als der Dieb auf mich zutrat und sagte: „Darf ich Ihnen aus Dankbarkeit, Ihren Koffer tragen helfen?" Ich nickte und von dem Mann begleitet, machte ich mich auf den Weg ins Hotel zurück.

1. Warum hatte ich das Hotel verlassen?
2. Was tat der Geschäftsführer, als ich zurückkehrte?

3. Was war im Hotel passiert?
4. Welche Person sah ich am Schreibtisch?
5. Was taten zwei Polizeibeamte?
6. Was für ein Mann war der Dieb?
7. Wann sah mich der Dieb dankbar an?
8. Warum ließen die Polizisten den Mann frei?
9. Wann trat der Mann auf mich zu?
10. Auf welche Weise wollte er seine Dankbarkeit zeigen?

3. Vorigen Sonnabend ging ich die Hauptstraße entlang. Dabei sah ich ein Portemonnaie auf dem Gehsteig liegen. Ich bückte mich, hob das Portemonnaie auf und machte es auf: vielleicht würde ich die Adresse des Besitzers darin finden. Außer einem ziemlich alten Foto einer Dame mit einem etwa elfjährigen Mädchen fand ich nur etwas Kleingeld darin.

Ich steckte das Foto wieder in das Portemonnaie und begab mich auf die Polizeiwache, wo ich meinen Fund überreichte. Ehe ich nach Hause ging, notierte sich der Beamte meinen Namen und meine Adresse, falls der Besitzer mir schreiben und danken wollte.

Am nächsten Abend aß ich bei meiner Tante zu Abend. Sie hatte auch eine Bekannte eingeladen. Mir kam das Gesicht des Gastes irgendwie bekannt vor, jedoch konnte ich mich nicht erinnern, wo ich die Dame schon mal gesehen hatte. Im Verlauf des Gesprächs fiel mir ein, warum mir ihr Gesicht so bekannt vorkam. Obgleich sie jetzt viel älter aussah, war die Dame bestimmt das junge Mädchen auf dem Foto.

Natürlich war sie sehr erstaunt, als ich ihr ihr eignes Portemonnaie beschreiben konnte. Ich erklärte ihr auch, daß ich ihr Gesicht vom Foto erkannt hätte, das im Portemonnaie gewesen wäre.

Meine Tante bestand darauf, daß wir sofort alles bei der Polizei abholen sollten. Beim Überreichen des Fundes bemerkte der Beamte: „Es ist ja merkwürdig, daß Sie sowohl das Portemonnaie als auch seine Besitzerin gefunden haben."

1. Wann fand ich am vorigen Sonnabend das Portemonnaie?
2. Warum bückte ich mich?
3. Warum machte ich das Portemonnaie auf?

4. Was für Sachen waren darin?
5. Wie alt war das Mädchen auf dem Foto?
6. Warum begab ich mich auf die Polizeiwache?
7. Welche drei Personen saßen am Abend am Tisch?
8. Woher wußte ich, daß das Portemonnaie der Dame gehörte?
9. Warum gingen wir auf die Polzeiwache?
10. Was hielt der Beamte für sehr merkwürdig?
11. Aus dem Text suchen Sie Synonyme für:
    (a) Samstag
    (b) Bürgersteig
    (c) bevor
    (d) Freundin
    (e) sicherlich
    (f) überrascht
    (g) ohne weiteres.

4. (a) Bei Wind und Regen trat ich aus dem Haus. Während ich die Straße entlang eilte, dachte ich immer noch an mein gemütliches Zimmer und fragte mich, warum ich es verlassen hatte. Jetzt war es aber zu spät zurückzukehren: ich hatte den festen Entschluß gefaßt, mein Heimatland für immer zu verlassen und anderswo ein neues Leben zu beginnen.

Sobald ich den Bahnhof erreicht hatte, löste ich eine Fahrkarte nach der Grenzstadt Aachen. Von da aus plante ich, zu Fuß über die Grenze zu kommen.

Als ich erfuhr, daß der nächste Zug erst gegen Mitternacht eintreffen sollte, trat ich wieder auf die Straße hinaus, um in der Stadt ein bißchen spazieren zu gehen. Während ich durch die fast menschenleeren Straßen wanderte, regnete es in Strömen. Trotz meines Mantels war ich bald bis auf die Haut durchnäßt.

Zum Bahnhof zurückgekehrt, mußte ich doch noch eine Zeitlang warten, bis der Aachener Zug einfuhr. Glücklicherweise war im Zug genug Platz; einige Abteile waren ganz leer. Ich wählte mir eines davon und stieg ein. Sofort legte ich mich hin, benutzte meinen Rucksack als Kopfkissen und deckte mich mit meinem Mantel zu. Obwohl mein Liegeplatz nicht besonders bequem war, machte mir das nichts aus. Ich war todmüde und schon vor der Abfahrt des Zuges war ich fest eingeschlafen.

1. Wie war das Wetter?
2. Wohin konnte ich nicht zurückkehren?
3. Warum löste ich eine Fahrkarte?
4. Was ist Aachen?
5. Warum war es nicht möglich, sofort in den Zug einzusteigen?
6. Weswegen war ich bald durchnäßt?
7. Warum mußte ich noch eine Zeitlang warten?
8. Warum hatte ich mit dem Zug Glück?
9. Was für ein Abteil wählte ich?
10. Warum suchte ich mir solch ein Abteil aus?
11. Wo lag mein Rucksack?
12. Warum schlief ich sofort ein?

4. (b) Ein paar Stunden später wachte ich auf, denn ein Bahnbeamter mit einer Taschenlampe in der Hand schüttelte mich am Arm. Er verlangte meine Fahrkarte, sah sie und mich genau an und sagte schließlich: „Sie sind schon in Aachen. Hier ist Endstation—Sie müssen aussteigen." Ich packte meine Sachen zusammen und eilte den Bahnsteig entlang. Außerhalb des Bahnhofs betrat ich eine Schnellimbißstube, wo ich ein paar Käsebrote und eine Tüte Milch kaufte.

Nachdem ich die mitgebrachte Landkarte studiert hatte, machte ich mich auf den Weg. Dabei merkte ich, daß der Regen aufgehört hatte und die Sonne jetzt von einem fast wolkenlosen Himmel schien.

Etwa zwei Stunden später spürte ich wieder Hunger und Durst. Am Straßenrand setzte ich mich hin. Gegen einen Baumstamm gelehnt, packte ich meinen Reiseproviant aus und aß und trank etwas. Einigermaßen erfrischt, brach ich wieder auf.

Am frühen Nachmittag erreichte ich die deutsch-belgische Grenze und kam ohne Schwierigkeiten durch die Paßkontrolle. Ich hatte wenig Gepäck mit, und die Zollbeamten ließen mich ohne weiteres durch. Erst jetzt fühlte ich mich wirklich frei. Für mich sollte jetzt das größte Abenteuer meines Lebens anfangen!

1. Warum wachte ich auf?
2. Warum mußte ich aussteigen?
3. Weshalb betrat ich die Schnellimbißstube?
4. Warum war es nicht nötig, eine Landkarte zu kaufen?

5. Wozu setzte ich mich hin?
6. Wann brach ich wieder auf?
7. Wo mußte ich durch die Paßkontrolle gehen?
8. Warum ließen mich die Zollbeamten schnell durch?
9. Warum fühlte ich mich wirklich frei?
10. Was glaubte ich jetzt?
11. Aus dem Text suchen Sie Synonyme für:
    (a) einige
    (b) endlich
    (c) beinahe
    (d) nochmals
    (e) nun
    (f) beginnen.

5. Als Rolf am späten Abend in der kleinen Stadt Altheim ankam, regnete es in Strömen. Niemand war auf den Straßen zu sehen, den er nach dem Weg zu einem Hotel hätte fragen können. Auf dem Platz vor dem Rathaus parkte er seinen Wagen, schloß ihn ab und ging zu Fuß die Straße entlang. Dabei schaute er nach rechts und links. Endlich erblickte er ein großes Schild. Er eilte darauf zu und blieb davor stehen. *Zum weißen Rößel* las er darauf.

Durch eine offenstehende Tür trat er in eine Gaststube, wo ein Mann damit beschäftigt war, Tische und Stühle abzuwischen.

„Guten Abend," grüßte Rolf. „Ist der Wirt zu sprechen?"

„Leider ist er zur Zeit verreist. Ich bin der Ober; kann ich irgendwie behilflich sein?" erwiderte er.

„Ich suche Quartier für eine Nacht. Haben Sie vielleicht ein Einzelzimmer frei?" erkundigte sich Rolf.

„Sie haben Glück," antwortete der Ober. „Kommen Sie bitte mal mit!"

Er nahm Rolfs Gepäck und führte ihn in die dritte Etage, wo er Rolf ein geräumiges Zimmer zeigte. Das Zimmer gefiel Rolf, und er nahm es sofort. Bevor der Ober wegging, bat ihn Rolf, „Fahren Sie meinen Wagen, der vor dem Rathaus steht, in die Hotelgarage! Hier ist der Schlüssel. Vergessen Sie nicht, mich morgen früh um halb acht zu wecken!"

1. Was ist Altheim?
2. Warum war niemand auf den Straßen zu sehen?

3. Auf welche Weise war Rolf nach Altheim gekommen?
4. Warum schaute Rolf nach rechts und links?
5. Wo blieb er stehen?
6. Wann wußte Rolf, daß er ein Hotel gefunden hatte?
7. Was tat der Mann, gerade als Rolf eintrat?
8. Welche Person wollte Rolf sprechen?
9. Warum war diese Person nicht zu sprechen?
10. Warum hatte Rolf Glück?
11. Was wollte Rolf im Hotel tun?
12. Wo im Hotel lag das Zimmer, das Rolf bekam?
13. Warum nahm Rolf sofort das Zimmer?
14. Weshalb gab Rolf dem Ober den Schlüssel?
15. Was sollte der Ober am nächsten Tag tun?

6. Punkt 22.00 Uhr begann die lange Bahnfahrt von Flensburg in die Schweiz. Alfred war froh, als der überfüllte D-Zug den hellerleuchteten Bahnhof verließ. Im Schlafwagenabteil war die Luft unerträglich schlecht, daher machte Alfred das Fenster auf. Zuerst packte er einige für die Nacht nötige Sachen aus, dann trat er auf den Gang hinaus, wo einige Reisende auf ihrem Gepäck hockten. Sie hatten wohl in den überfüllten Abteilen keinen Platz bekommen. Unter diesen Passagieren befanden sich zwei junge Mädchen, die sich leise lachend unterhielten. Alfred blieb noch eine Zeitlang auf dem Gang stehen, um eine Zigarette zu rauchen, ehe er schlafen ging. Im Schlafabteil zog er sich aus, ehe er sich hinlegte. Bald schlief er ein.

Am nächsten Morgen wachte Alfred früh auf. Im Abteil nebenan störte ihn ein Reisender, der beim Aufstehen furchtbar viel Lärm machte und laut vor sich hin pfiff. Bald hatte Alfred sich fertiggemacht und trat auf den Gang hinaus. Als er zum Fenster hinausblickte, konnte er statt der flachen norddeutschen Landschaft hohe Berge sehen. In kurzer Zeit würde Alfred am Reiseziel sein.

1. Woher wissen wir, daß Alfred nachts fuhr?
2. Warum hatte Alfred eine lange Fahrt vor sich?
3. Warum machte Alfred das Fenster auf?
4. Wann trat Alfred auf den Gang hinaus?
5. Warum hatten einige Reisende keinen Platz bekommen?
6. Wann ging Alfred schlafen?
7. Wann legte er sich hin?

8. Wen konnte Alfred nebenan hören?
9. Was für eine Landschaft konnte Alfred sehen?
10. Wo lag Alfreds Reiseziel?
11. Wo liegt Flensburg?

7. Nach einem anstrengenden Arbeitstag bei einer Exportfirma war Franz Klein abends immer sehr müde. Trotzdem ging er ziemlich spät schlafen, denn er blieb gern auf, um sein Lieblingsprogramm im Fernsehen anzuschauen.
Einmal war seine Frau bei Verwandten in Bremen und Franz war allein im Haus. Nach Sendeschluß legte er sich erst gegen Mitternacht ins Bett. Am nächsten Morgen hörte er den Wecker nicht, da er immer noch fest schlief. Endlich wachte er aber doch auf, blickte auf die Uhr und sprang erschrocken aus dem Bett, denn es war schon halb acht. Er sollte spätestens um acht Uhr in der Fabrik sein, wo er als Buchhalter angestellt war.
Er eilte ins Badezimmer, um sich zu waschen. Leider war das Wasser noch ganz kalt und er konnte sich nur schlecht rasieren. Im Schlafzimmer zog er sich möglichst schnell an und lief dann die Treppe hinunter. Unten in der Küche machte er sich etwas zum Frühstück. Zehn Minuten nachdem er aufgewacht war, verließ er das Haus, das er hinter sich abschloß, ehe er zur Bushaltestelle eilte. Er hatte großes Glück, denn ein Bus stand schon da. Glücklicherweise war der Verkehr nicht besonders stark, und der Bus konnte fast unbehindert durchkommen.
In der Nähe der Fabrik sprang Franz aus und ging an das Fabriktor, vor dem er überrascht stehenblieb, denn es war zu. Außerdem war niemand zu sehen: alles war wie ausgestorben. Während er noch überlegte, was eigentlich los sein könnte, hörte Franz eine Glocke läuten. Erst jetzt wurde ihm klar, daß es Sonntag war.

1. Warum war Franz abends immer müde?
2. Was tat er, wenn er spät aufblieb?
3. Weshalb war Frau Klein verreist?
4. Weswegen schlief Franz so spät?
5. Wieviel Zeit hatte Franz, die Fabrik zu erreichen?
6. Was für eine Stellung hatte Franz?
7. Warum mußte er schlecht rasiert bleiben?
8. Wann lief er die Treppe hinunter?

9. Um wieviel Uhr verließ Franz das Haus?
10. Warum ging er zur Haltestelle?
11. Warum konnte der Bus ziemlich schnell fahren?
12. Wann wußte Franz, daß es Sonntag war?

8. Am ersten Dienstag in den Osterferien sagte Frau Meyer zu ihren Kindern Anna und Werner: „Morgen essen wir früher als gewöhnlich zu Mittag, denn wir wollen mit Vater nach Hamburg fahren. Ihr sollt mal den Hafen kennenlernen." Natürlich freuten sich die beiden sehr.

Am nächsten Tag fuhren sie um ein Uhr los und nach anderthalbstündiger Fahrt hatten sie die Anlegestelle für Motorboote erreicht. Vor ihnen lag die breite Elbe. „Kommt!" sagte Herr Meyer, „wir wollen zum Auskunftsbüro gehen: ich möchte mich erkundigen, wann die nächste Hafenrundfahrt stattfindet." Im Büro sagte das Fräulein am Schalter: „Wenn Sie sich beeilen, erreichen Sie noch das nächste Boot."

Schnell kaufte Herr Meyer die Fahrscheine und alle vier eilten zum Boot, das abfahrbereit war. Ein Matrose in Uniform legte ab und sie fuhren los. Sobald das Boot die offene Elbe erreicht hatte, begann der Fremdenführer den Fahrgästen alles durch den Lautsprecher zu erklären, was zu sehen war. An Bord waren einige Ausländer. Für sie wurde alles in ihrer Landessprache wiederholt. Da Anna und Werner Fremdsprachen lernen, konnten sie mal nachprüfen, ob sie irgendetwas von dem verstehen konnten, was auf Englisch oder Französisch durchgegeben wurde.

Werner wollte wissen, warum man keine großen Passagierdampfer sah. „Solche Dampfer können nicht in den Hamburger Hafen einfahren," erklärte der Fremdenführer. „Statt nach Hamburg zu kommen, müssen die Dampfer in Cuxhaven anlegen und ihre Passagiere da absetzen."

1. Wer sind Anna und Werner?
2. An welchem Tag besucht die Familie Meyer Hamburg?
3. Warum waren die Kinder nicht in der Schule?
4. Um wieviel Uhr erreichte die Familie Hamburg?
5. An welchem Fluß liegt Hamburg?
6. Warum ging Herr Meyer zum Auskunftsbüro?
7. Mit wem sprach Herr Meyer im Büro?
8. Warum mußten sie sich beeilen?

9. Was mußte ein Matrose tun?
10. Warum konnten sie alles klar hören?
11. Warum wurde alles auf Englisch und Französisch wiederholt?
12. Wozu benutzen die Passagierdampfer Cuxhaven?

SECTION 7B

MULTIPLE-CHOICE EXERCISES

A. *In diesem Teil müssen Sie entscheiden, wer spricht.*

1. „Was soll dir denn der Weihnachtsmann bringen? Ein Brüderchen oder ein Schwesterchen?"
   „Ich habe ihm doch schon geschrieben—einen Fußball und eine elektrische Eisenbahn!"
   A. Reisender und Lokomotivführer
   B. Manager und Fußballspieler
   C. Mutter und Sohn
   D. Arzt und Frau

2. „Wem bringst du denn diesen schönen Blumenstrauß?"
   „Na, wem schon! Meiner Zukünftigen, natürlich!"
   A. Ein Gärtner und ein Gärtnerjunge
   B. Ein Mann und seine Frau
   C. Ein junger Mann und sein Freund
   D. Ein Musiker und ein Komponist

3. „Sagen Sie mir bitte, was ich gegen meine Kurzatmigkeit tun muß"
   „Nun ja! Erstens müssen Sie zwanzig Pfund abnehmen."
   A. Eine Frau und ein Metzger
   B. Ein Arzt und seine Patientin
   C. Ein Kunde und ein Bankangestellter
   D. Eine Dame und ein Optiker

4. „Warum haben Sie mir einen falschen Namen angegeben, als ich Sie festnahm?"
   „Ja, ich war zuerst so verwirrt, daß ich mich selbst nicht mehr kannte."

A. Ein Hoteldiener und ein Gast
B. Ein Student and ein Professor
C. Ein Reisender und ein Angestellter im Reisebüro
D. Ein Polizist und ein Verhafteter

5. „Soweit wir feststellen können, handelt es sich um einen ziemlich großen, schlanken Mann."
„Ja, ich wollte, wir hätten bei jedem Straßenüberfall solche guten Hinweise."
A. Zwei Detektive
B. Zwei Händler
C. Schneider und Kunde
D. Bankier und Assistant

6. „Es steht hier: ,Die Leistungen Ihres Kindes lassen leider nach!' Was soll das heißen?"
„Du weißt, ich habe nachmittags immer Sport getrieben."
A. Mann und Frau
B. Vater und Sohn
C. Angler und Polizist
D. Sportler und sein Manager

7. „Rühr in der Küche nichts an! Ich bin dort noch nicht fertig."
„Du brauchst dir keine Sorgen zu machen, Liebling."
A. Ein Ehepaar
B. Mutter und Tochter
C. Detektiv und Journalist
D. Oberkoch und Lehrling

8. „Ja, ich hab's gesehen. Der Junge lief aus dem Haus und auf die Straße, gerade als das rote Auto um die Ecke sauste."
A. Zuschauer bei einem Autorennen
B. Augenzeuge eines Straßenunfalls
C. Beobachter eines Bombenangriffs
D. Teilnehmer an einer Bergwanderung

9. „Gehen Sie vor mir ins Haus! Und vor allem, schreien Sie nicht! Benehmen Sie sich ganz, als sei ich ein alter Bekannter, der zu Besuch kommt!"

A. Krankenpfleger und Patient
B. Ein zorniger Vater und sein Sohn
C. Zwei Freunde
D. Verbrecher und Hausbesitzer

10. ,,Münzendorf, bitte. Hin und zurück."
    ,,Das macht drei Mark fünfzig."
    A. Bahnbeamter und Fahrgast
    B. Zwei Astronome
    C. Zwei Fußballspieler
    D. Postbeamter und Kunde

11. ,,In dem Aufsatz, ,Meine Ferien' hast du das gleiche wie Fritz geschrieben. Wie erklärst du das?"
    ,,Durch Zufall waren wir am gleichen Ort."
    A. Zeitungsredakteur und Journalist
    B. Pilot und Stewardeß
    C. Lehrer und Schüler
    D. Hotelchef und Feriengast

12. ,,Die Tür der Bank wurde aufgerissen, und ein Mann mit einem Revolver in der Hand stürzte heraus..."
    ,,Und was haben Sie gemacht?"
    ,,Na ja, ich bin kein Held..."
    A. Ein Mann und ein Polizist
    B. Ein Bankdirektor und ein Kunde
    C. Ein Filmregisseur und ein Filmstar
    D. Ein Offizier und ein Soldat

13. ,,Was ist denn los? Ist etwas kaputt?"
    ,,Ich glaube, die Kerzen sind verschmutzt." Er blies auf die Zündkerzen.
    A. Priester und Kirchendiener
    B. Ein Ehepaar
    C. Juwelier und Kunde
    D. Autobesitzer und Mechaniker

14. ,,Gehen Sie essen, ich bleibe solange hier. Er schläft, und das ist ein gutes Zeichen. Und daß es ja ganz still im Hause ist!"

A. Koch in der Küche
B. Professor im Studierzimmer
C. Arzt im Krankenzimmer
D. Lehrer in der Schule

15. „Ich möchte schnell zum Hauptbahnhof. Was kostet das?"
„Das kostet etwa fünf Mark."
„Gut. Aber schnell."
„Bitte schön. Steigen Sie ein!"
A. Schaffner und Fahrgast
B. Taxifahrer und Kunde
C. Pilot und Fluggast
D. Reisender und Gepäckträger

B. *In diesem Teil müssen Sie entscheiden, wo die Sprechenden sind.*

1. „Wie spät ist es denn, Junge?"
„Zehn vor neun."
„Und wie weit ist's zum Bahnhof?"
„Ein Kilometer."
A. In einem Flugzeug
B. In einem Zug
C. Auf der Straße
D. Auf einem Schiff

2. „Da drüben haben meine Eltern gewohnt. Du kannst das Dach des Hauses sehen. Früher konnte man in zehn Minuten zu Fuß hingehen. Aber jetzt nicht mehr. Sie haben die Mauer gebaut."
A. Auf dem Rhein
B. In Berlin
C. Auf einem Bauernhof
D. Auf der Heide

3. „Nun, lassen Sie uns bitte für kurze Zeit allein."
„Das geht gegen meine Befehle. Ich darf niemanden ohne Aufsicht im Sitzungssaal lassen."
A. In einer Bank

B. Im Bundestagsgebäude
C. In einem Warenhaus
D. Auf der Polizeiwache

4. „Der erste Akt ist jetzt zu Ende. Er war schrecklich. Gehen wir nach Hause!"
„Das können wir doch nicht! Wir haben Freikarten."
A. Im Hotel
B. Im Konzert
C. Im Kino
D. Im Theater

5. „Meine Damen und Herren, in einer Minute werden wir starten. Bitte, schnallen Sie sich an."
A. In der U-Bahn
B. Im Bus
C. Im Flugzeug
D. Auf einem Schiff

6. „Herr Ober! Zahlen bitte."
„Sehr wohl, mein Herr. Ich komme gleich."
A. Auf der Rennbahn
B. An der Tankstelle
C. In der Mathematikstunde
D. In einem Restaurant

7. „Wohin so eilig, gnädige Frau? Warum rennen Sie so?"
„Ich muß schnell für meinen Mann den Arzt anrufen."
A. Auf der Straße
B. An der Haltestelle der Straßenbahn
C. Im Schwimmbad
D. Im Auto

8. „Meine Dame, kann ich Ihnen behilflich sein?"
„Ich suche etwas Passendes für meine Tante."
A. Auf der Bühne
B. In einer Buchhandlung
C. In der Metzgerei
D. Im Krankenhaus

9. „Haben Sie etwas zu verzollen?"
„Ja. Ich habe diesen Pelzmantel in München gekauft."
A. Bei der Damenschneiderin
B. Bei der Gepäckkontrolle
C. Auf der Jagd
D. In einem Warenhaus

10. „Warum fahren Sie jetzt immer so langsam?"
„Man darf hier nicht mehr als 40 Km. die Stunde fahren."
A. Auf Fahrrädern
B. Auf einem Schiff
C. Im Wagen
D. Auf einem Pferd

11. „Ist noch jemand ohne Fahrschein?"
„Ja, einmal Stadion, bitte."
A. Auf der Autobahn
B. Auf dem Markt
C. In der Straßenbahn
D. In der Fahrschule

12. „Sehen Sie! Sesselbahnen und Schlepplifte bringen die Leute dort in wenigen Minuten auf die Höhen. Dann jagen sie auf ihren Brettern wieder herunter."
„Herrlich! Wollen wir es mal versuchen?"
A. Im Zug
B. Auf der Jagd
C. Am Bahnhof
D. In den Alpen

13. „Was wollen Sie, mein Herr? Ist etwas geschehen?"
„Es ist unerhört! Dieser Mensch hier raucht in einem Nichtraucherabteil!"
A. Im Zug
B. Im Theater
C. An der Tankstelle
D. Im Konzert

MULTIPLE-CHOICE EXERCISES 185

14. „Jetzt wollen wir Beethovens Geburtshaus besichtigen."
„Oh ja! Deswegen sind wir hierher gekommen."
Touristen in. . .
A. Wien
B. Jena
C. Bonn
D. Weimar

15. „Ich möchte diese beiden Platten hören, bitte."
„Gerne, Fräulein. In dieser Kabine können Sie alles ungestört hören."
A. Im Fernsehen
B. In der Telefonzelle
C. Beim Spülen des Geschirrs
D. Im Musikgeschäft

16. „Herr und Frau Menzel. Ja, bitte sehr. Zimmer 402."
"Sie haben auch ein Einzelzimmer für meine Mutter, nicht wahr?"
A. In einer Jugendherberge
B. Im Wirtshaus in einem Dorf
C. In einem Hotel
D. Bei Freunden

17. „Haben Sie Ihren Führerschein bei sich, bitte?"
„Jawohl. Hier haben Sie ihn."
A. Während der Bahnfahrt
B. Bei der Straßenwacht
C. Vor der Waschmaschine
D. Bei einer Fabrikführung

18. „Und hier, meine Damen und Herren, sehen Sie das bekannteste Bild in Deutschland."
„Von wem ist es denn?"
A. In einer Bildergalerie
B. In einem Seehafen
C. In einer Bäckerei
D. In einem Modehaus

19. „Passagiere für den Flug BE 270 nach London bitte zum Ausgang 28."
   A. Im D-Zug
   B. In einem Warenhaus
   C. In einer Autofabrik
   D. Auf dem Flughafen

20. „Schnell! Dort steht schon der Zug."
   „Aber Rudi! Es ist streng verboten, die Gleise zu überschreiten."
   A. Auf dem Bahnsteig
   B. Vor der Verkehrsampel
   C. Beim Fahrkartenschalter
   D. Im Park

C. *Suchen Sie den Satz aus, der dieselbe Bedeutung hat wie die in Kursive gedruckten Worte*

1. *Ich wünsche dir viel Vergnügen* heißt:
   A. Hoffentlich genügt es dir
   B. Ich will, daß du viel Spaß hast
   C. Ich hoffe, daß du genug bekommen hast
   D. So etwas ist sehr wünschenswert

2. *Wir freuen uns sehr auf die Ferien* heißt:
   A. Wir nehmen gern an den Ferien teil
   B. Die Ferien machen uns immer große Freude
   C. Wir sehen begeistert den Ferien entgegen
   D. Die Ferien waren höchst erfreulich

3. *Er sitzt gern vor dem Bildschirm* heißt:
   A. Es freut ihn, die Illustrierten zu lesen
   B. Er sitzt stundenlang im Kino
   C. Er macht gern Aufnahmen
   D. Er sieht gern fern

4. *Wofür halten Sie mich?* heißt:
   A. Warum fassen Sie mich an?
   B. Was ist Ihre Meinung über mich?
   C. Warum darf ich nicht weiterfahren?
   D. Weshalb nehmen Sie mich bei der Hand?

5. *Wir wollen bald aufbrechen* heißt:
   A. Bald beginnen die Schulferien
   B. Wir wollen möglichst schnell alles zerschlagen
   C. Wir sind im Begriff, uns auf den Weg zu machen
   D. Wir planen bald zu entkommen

6. *Ich wunderte mich sehr* heißt:
   A. Ich überlegte mir alles
   B. Es schien mir ganz wunderschön zu sein
   C. Es wirkte wie ein Wunder
   D. Ich war ganz überrascht

7. *Ich habe mich dazu entschlossen* heißt:
   A. Ich habe die Sache abgeschlossen
   B. Ich habe mich dafür entschieden
   C. Ich habe damit Schluß gemacht
   D. Es ist ausgeschlossen, daß ich das mache

8. *Mich geht es nichts an* heißt:
   A. Es geht mir nicht besonders gut
   B. Es bleibt mir nichts übrig
   C. Es ist nicht meine Angelegenheit
   D. Ich interessiere mich nicht dafür

9. *Es gelang uns endlich* heißt:
   A. Es langweilte uns endlos
   B. Endlich verlangten wir es
   C. Es dauerte unendlich lange
   D. Schließlich hatten wir Erfolg

10. *Warum hörst du nicht auf?* heißt:
    A. Warum machst du nicht Schluß?
    B. Weshalb gehorchst du nicht?
    C. Warum bist du so unaufmerksam?
    D. Warum paßt du nicht auf?

11. *Sie hatte sich in der Stadt verirrt* heißt:
    A. Sie war zu weit durch die Stadt gebummelt
    B. Sie war in die Stadt einkaufen gegangen
    C. Sie hatte sich in der Stadt verlaufen
    D. Sie war in der Stadt verunglückt

12. *Sind Sie damit einverstanden?* heißt:
    A. Haben Sie es verstanden?
    B. Stimmen Sie damit überein?
    C. Haben Sie lange dagestanden?
    D. Haben Sie Verständnis dafür?

13. *Er machte sich große Sorgen darum* heißt:
    A. Er war sehr darum besorgt
    B. Es tat ihm sehr leid
    C. Er handelte höchst sorgfältig
    D. Er achtete sehr darauf

14. *So etwas ist manchmal vorgekommen* heißt:
    A. Etwas Ähnliches ist oft passiert
    B. So etwas ist mehrere Male erschienen
    C. Derartiges ist öfters erreicht worden
    D. Ich habe schon mehrmals etwas Ähnliches abgeholt

D. *Suchen Sie die passendste Fortsetzung aus!*

1. *Notbremse! Griff nur bei Gefahr ziehen!* liest man
   A. in der Straßenbahn
   B. an einer Verkehrsampel
   C. rechts an der Autobahn
   D. in einem Flugzeug

2. „*Wieviel kostet das Auslandsporto?*" fragt man
   A. wenn man mit dem Bahnbus aufs Land fährt
   B. bei der Gepäckaufbewahrung
   C. beim Abschicken eines Päckchens
   D. beim Empfang eines Briefes aus Deutschland

3. „*Die Nachfrage ist sehr groß. Nehmen Sie lieber drei Dosen!*" hört man
   A. beim Eierkaufen auf dem Markt
   B. wenn man hohes Fieber hat
   C. wenn man sich hinlegen will
   D. beim Einkaufen im Lebensmittelladen

4. „*Können Sie mir helfen? Ich habe eine Reifenpanne,*" sagt man
   A. wenn man etwas auf den Küchenherd setzen will
   B. zum Tankwart
   C. wenn man Angst hat
   D. zum Zahnarzt

5. *„Was für Tabletten wünschen Sie?"* wird gefragt
   A. sobald man eine Gaststätte betritt
   B. im Süßwarengeschäft
   C. in der Apotheke
   D. im Schreibwarenladen

6. *„Darf ich dich um Feuer bitten?"* sagt man
   A. zu einem Verwandten, der ein Feuerzeug besitzt
   B. wenn man den Elektroherd anschalten will
   C. zu einem Fremden, wenn man rauchen möchte
   D. zu jemandem bei sehr kaltem Wetter

7. *Fremdenzimmer frei!* heißt:
   A. Fremde können kostenlos Unterkunft bekommen
   B. Touristen können hier untergebracht werden
   C. Es dürfen nur Ausländer hier wohnen
   D. Verwandte sind unerwunscht

8. *„Auf Wiederhören! Ich lege jetzt auf,"* sagt man
   A. beim Abschiednehmen
   B. nach einem Besuch beim Arzt
   C. beim Schlafengehen
   D. wenn man ein Telephongespräch beendet

9. *„Sammeln Sie Rabatmarken,"* fragt man mich
   A. am Postschalter
   B. auf dem Fundbüro
   C. beim Einwechseln von Reiseschecks
   D. an der Ladenkasse

10. *„Achtung! Frisch gestrichen!"* schreibt man,
    A. wenn man Butter auf frisches Brot schmiert
    B. wenn etwas eben bemalt worden ist
    C. sobald Arbeiter in den Streik treten
    D. wenn man einen Streich gespielt hat

11. *„Wo liegt die nächste Wechselstube?"* fragt man,
    A. wenn man Geld eintauschen möchte
    B. weil man Erfrischung sucht
    C. wenn man Kleingeld haben möchte
    D. wenn man jemanden anrufen will

12. „*Haben Sie etwas zu verzollen?*" wird gefragt,
    A. wenn man das Restaurant verläßt
    B. wenn man über die Grenze fährt
    C. wenn man ein Schuhgeschäft betritt
    D. wenn man vor dem Gericht erscheint

13. „*Einmal einfach mit Zuschlag,*" sagt man,
    A. wenn man Fußball spielt
    B. wenn man ein Speiseeis kauft
    C. wenn man eine Fahrkarte löst
    D. wenn man etwas Einfaches vorschlägt

14. „*Ich möchte mich nach einer Unterkunft am Meer erkundigen,*" sagt man
    A. zu einem Kunden im Reisebüro
    B. zum Beamten, wenn der Zug Verspätung hat
    C. wenn man in Urlaub fahren will
    D. wenn man ein paar Tage an der See verbringen möchte.

E. *Suchen Sie die passendste Fortsetzung aus!*

1. Der Rhein fließt
   A. durch das Harzgebirge
   B. an Wuppertal vorbei
   C. in die Ostsee
   D. durch den Bodensee

2. Das deutsche Frühstück besteht gewöhnlich aus
   A. Kaffee, Brötchen, Butter und Marmelade
   B. Wein, Wienerschnitzel und Bratkartoffeln
   C. Bier, Frankfurter Würstchen und Brötchen
   D. Tee, Speck, Ei und Toast

3. Wenn man den Fasching sehen will, fährt man am besten nach
   A. Koblenz
   B. Hamburg
   C. Köln
   D. München

4. Der Nürburgring ist
   A. eine Stadt in Bayern
   B. eine Rennstrecke
   C. eine Oper von Richard Wagner
   D. ein wertvolles Schmuckstück

5. In Garmisch-Partenkirchen lernt man oft gut
   A. skilaufen
   B. turnen
   C. segeln
   D. segelfliegen

6. Auf der Reise von Hamburg nach Frankfurt am Main fährt man im Auto am besten über
   A. Heidelberg
   B. Leipzig
   C. Kassel
   D. Mainz

7. Köln ist berühmt wegen
   A. des Biers
   B. des Doms
   C. einer Abtei
   D. der schönen Frauen

8. Heidelberg liegt
   A. am Rhein
   B. an der Elbe
   C. an der Donau
   D. am Neckar

9. Die Stadt Meißen ist berühmt wegen
   A. ihres Porzellans
   B. ihres Orchesters
   C. ihres Weins
   D. ihres Museums

10. Die Stadt Bayreuth ist berühmt wegen
    A. ihrer arabischen Einwohner
    B. des Volkswagenwerkes
    C. ihrer Weingärten
    D. Wagners Festspielhauses

11. Das Passionspiel von Oberammergau ist
    A. ein Kartenspiel
    B. ein christliches Drama
    C. ein deutscher Liebesfilm
    D. ein Kinderspiel

12. München ist die Landeshauptstadt von
    A. Schleswig-Holstein
    B. Bayern
    C. der Pfalz
    D. Hessen

13. „*Ritter Tod und Teufel*" ist
    A. ein Bild von Albrecht Dürer
    B. ein Drama von Schiller
    C. ein Gedicht von Goethe
    D. eine Symphonie von Mozart

14. *I.G. Farben* ist
    A. ein Bund deutscher Maler
    B. eine Bildergalerie
    C. ein industrieller Großbetrieb
    D. eine Textilfabrik

15. Der Gemeinsame Markt heißt auch
    A. CDU
    B. DDR
    C. EG
    D. FBI

16. Essen liegt
    A. im Taunus
    B. im Ruhrgebiet
    C. im Schwarzwald
    D. im Elsaß

17. Der Bundestag ist
    A. ein jährliches Fest
    B. der 1 Januar
    C. eine Tagung der Gewerkschaften
    D. Das Parlament der Bundesrepublik

18. Das Brandenburger Tor findet man in
    A. Potsdam

MULTIPLE-CHOICE EXERCISES

    B. Berlin
    C. Hannover
    D. Ostpreußen

19. Die Deutsche Lufthansa ist
    A. eine Schiffahrtsgesellschaft
    B. ein Bund deutscher Städte an der Ostee
    C. ein deutscher Flugzeugtyp
    D. eine Fluggesellschaft

20. Berlin liegt
    A. an der Spree
    B. an der Oder
    C. an der Elbe
    D. am Main

21. Wolfgang von Goethes Geburtsort heißt
    A. Nürnberg
    B. Jena
    C. Weimar
    D. Frankfurt am Main

22. Die Frankfurter Messe ist
    A. ein Kirchenfest
    B. eine industrielle Ausstellung
    C. ein Werk von Bach
    D. eine Art Wurst

23. Ein Gymnasium ist
    A. ein Klub für Leichtathletik
    B. eine Turnhalle
    C. eine Schule
    D. ein Gefängnis

24. Eine Hochschule ist
    A. eine Universität
    B. eine Bergschule
    C. eine sehr große Schule
    D. eine Fliegerschule

25. Ein Rathaus ist
    A. das Haus des Rattenfängers
    B. ein Geschäft, wo man auf Raten kauft
    C. ein Gebäude im Zoo
    D. ein Verwaltungsgebäude

GERMAN—ENGLISH VOCABULARY

1. It is assumed that the pupil has some knowledge of German. Very common words (*e.g.* **das Haus, geben**) have been omitted except in their compounds.
2. The genitive singular and nominative plural are indicated after all masculine and neuter nouns but the genitive is not given after feminine nouns, as it is, of course, the same as the nominative.
3. The vowel changes in the strong verbs are indicated. For a fuller conjugation of the strong verbs, see § 3 and § 5 of the grammar.
4. (*sep.*) shows that the verb is separable, (*insep.*) that it is inseparable; (*v.t.*) that it is transitive and (*v.i.*) intransitive.

das **Abendblatt, -(e)s, ¨er,** evening newspaper
das **Abendbrot, -(e)s,** supper
die **Abenddämmerung,** twilight, dusk
die **Abendmahlzeit,** supper
der **Abendschimmer,** evening glow
der **Abendsonnenschein,** evening sunshine
die **Abendtasche, -n,** evening bag
die **Abenteuergeschichte, -n,** adventure story
abfahren (ä, u, a) (*sep.*), to drive away, to go away, to leave
abfallen (ä, ie, a) (*sep.*), to slope, to fall away
der **Abhang, -(e)s, ¨e,** slope, cliff
abholen (*sep.*), to call for, to fetch
ablassen (ä, ie, a) (*sep. v.i.*), to cease
abnehmen (i, a, o) (*sep. v.i.*), to decrease; (*v.t.*) to take off
abnutzen (*sep.*), to wear out

der **Absatz, -es, ¨e,** pause; sale
der **Abschied, -s,** departure; **Abschied nehmen,** to say good-bye, to leave
die **Absicht, -en,** intention
der **Absprung, -s, ¨e,** leap, jump
absteigen (ie, ie) (*sep.*) to dismount, to climb down
abstellen (*sep.*), to put on one side
sich abtrocknen (*sep.*), to dry oneself
abwerfen (i, a, o) (*sep.*), to throw off
die **Abwesenheit,** absence
achten (auf), to pay attention (to), to heed; to regard, to esteem
ächzen, to groan
die **Allee, -n,** avenue, walk
allerhand, all sorts of
allerlei, all sorts of
allmählich, gradually
allzumal, all together
die **Alpen** (*plur.*), the Alps
alsdann, then

das **Alter, -s, -,** age, epoch
der **Amtsrichter, -s, -,** district judge
der **Anbeginn, -s,** beginning
der **Anblick, -s,** sight, view
andrehen (*sep.*), to switch on
anfassen (*sep.*), to seize, to grasp
angehen (**i, a**) (*sep.*), to concern
angenehm, pleasant
das **Angesicht, -s, -er,** face; presence
die **Angst, ⸚e,** anxiety, worry, fear
ängstlich, anxious, fearful
der **Anker, -s, -,** anchor
sich anklammern (**an**) (*sep.*), to cling (to)
sich ankleiden (*sep.*), to dress
ankommen (**a, o**) (*sep.*), to arrive
anlangen (*sep.*), to arrive
anlegen (*sep.*), to put on, to apply
anliegen (**a, e**) (*sep. v.i.*), to adjoin; (*v.t.*) to concern; **es liegt ihm viel daran,** it means a great deal to him
anmelden (*sep.*), to announce
annehmen (**i, a, o**) (*sep.*), to accept
der **Anreiz, -es,** charm
anrühren (*sep.*), to touch
anschreien (**ie, ie**) (*sep.*), to shout at
ansehen (**ie, a, e**) (*sep.*), to look at
ansetzen (*sep.*), to take a run before jumping (No. 48)
der **Anspruch, -s, ⸚e,** claim; **in Anspruch nehmen,** to claim

anspruchslos, modest
die **Antenne, -n,** aerial
das **Antlitz, -es, -e,** face
die **Anzahl,** number
sich anziehen (**o, o**) (*sep.*), to dress
der **Anzug, -s, ⸚e,** approach; suit, dress
anzünden (*sep.*), to light, to set on fire
die **Apotheke, -n,** chemist's shop
das **Appartement, -s, -s,** apartment
ärgerlich, irritable, cross
der **Ärmel, -s, -,** sleeve
die **Art, -en,** kind; way, manner
der **Artikel, -s, -,** article
der **Ast, -es, ⸚e,** branch
der **Atem, -s,** breath; **Atem holen,** to get one's breath
atemlos, breathless
atmen, to breathe
der **Aufenthalt, -s,** stop, stay
auffallen (**ä, ie, a**) (*sep.*), to strike, to astonish
auffressen (**i, a, e**) (*sep.*), to eat up
aufführen (*sep.*), to perform (a play)
die **Aufführung, -en,** performance (of a play)
aufgehen (**i, a**) (*sep.*), to rise (of sun, moon)
aufheben (**o, o**) (*sep.*), to lift up, to raise
aufhorchsam, attentive
aufhören (*sep.*), to cease
sich aufklären (*sep.*), to brighten (of weather)
aufmachen (*sep.*), to open
aufmerksam, attentive
aufnehmen (**i, a, o**) (*sep.*), to accept, to receive
aufrecht, upright
aufreißen (**i, i**) (*sep.*), to tear open

aufschrecken (*sep. v.t.*), to frighten
aufsitzen (**a, e**) (*sep.*), to mount
aufstehen (**a, a**) (*sep.*), to stand up
der **Aufstieg, -s, -e,** climb, ascent
aufsuchen (*sep.*), to call on; to seek out
auftauchen (*sep.*), to appear, to come to the surface
aufwachen (*sep. v.i.*), to wake up
der **Augenblick, -s, -e,** moment
ausbreiten (*sep.*), to spread out
ausdehnen (*sep.*), to extend, to stretch
ausdrücken (*sep.*), to express
ausführen (*sep.*), to carry out, to execute
ausfüllen (*sep.*), to fill up
ausholen (*sep.*), to raise the arm to strike
auspressen (*sep.*), to crush, to squeeze out
ausruhen (*sep.*), to rest
aussehen (**ie, a, e**) (*sep.*), to look, to appear, to seem
außer (*dat.*), except for, besides
äußerst, extreme(ly)
die **Aussicht, -en,** view
ausstellen (*sep.*), to issue (a pass)
ausstoßen (**ö, ie, o**) (*sep.*), to utter
ausstrecken (*sep.*), to stretch out, to extend
der **Ausweg, -(e)s, -e,** way out, issue
der **Autofahrer, -s, -,** car-driver
die **Axt, ⸚e,** axe

der **Bach, -es, ⸚e,** stream
das **Bächlein, -s, -,** little stream
der **Badeanzug, -s, ⸚e,** swimming-costume
baden, to bathe
die **Badekabine, -n,** bathing-hut
der **Bahnhof, -s, ⸚e,** station
der **Bahnsteig, -s, -e,** platform
der **Bahnübergang, -s, ⸚e,** railway (level) crossing
bald, soon
ballen, to clench
sich ballen, to bank (of clouds)
das **Band, -es, ⸚er,** ribbon
barfuß, barefooted
die **Barriere, -n,** barrier
der **Bart, -es, ⸚e,** beard
der **Basar, -s, -e,** bazaar
der **Bau, -s, -ten,** building
der **Bauer, -n, -n,** peasant, farmer
die **Bäuerin, -nen,** peasant, farmer's wife
der **Bauernhof, -es, ⸚e,** farm
baumeln, to dangle, to swing
beachten, to heed
der **Beamte, -n, -n,** official
beängstigen, to worry
der **Becher, -s, -,** goblet, glass
bedecken, to cover
sich bedenken (**a, a**), to consider, to think about
bedeuten, to mean
die **Bedingung, -en,** condition
beenden, to end, to terminate
befehlen (**ie, a, o**) (*dat.*), to command, to order
sich befinden (**a, u**), to feel; to be situated
sich begeben (**i, a, e**), to betake oneself, to go
begegnen (*dat.*), to meet
die **Begegnung, -en,** meeting, appointment

begleiten, to accompany
begrüßen, to greet
behaglich, comfortable
beiderseitig, mutual
beinahe, almost
beischaffen (*sep.*), to bury
beiseite, aside
beißen (i, i), to bite
bejahen, to affirm, to say "yes"
bekannt, known
der **Bekannte, -n, -n,** acquaintance
bekommen (a, o), to receive, to obtain
sich **bekümmern,** to sorrow, to grieve
belehren, to instruct, to teach
beleidigen, to insult
bellen, to bark
die **Belohnung, -en,** reward
bemannen, to man
bemerken, to notice, to note
sich **bemühen,** to strive, to try
benachbart, neighbouring
sich **benehmen (i, a, o),** to behave
benutzen, to use
bequem, comfortable
bereit, ready
bereits, already
bergauf, uphill
der **Bergesabhang, -s, ̈e,** mountain slope
der **Berggipfel, -s, -,** mountain top
der **Bericht, -s, -e,** report
berichten, to report
beritten, mounted
beruhigen, to pacify
berühmt, famous
berühren, to touch; to move
sich **beschäftigen (mit),** to occupy oneself (with)
beschließen (o, o), to decide
beschreiben (ie, ie), to describe
beschreiten (i, i), to bestride
beschweren, to burden, to encumber
sich **besinnen (a, o),** to remember
besinnungslos, unconscious
der **Besitz, -es,** possession
besonders, especially
besorgt, worried
besprechen (i, a, o), to discuss
bestellen, to order, to reserve
bestrafen, to punish
bestreuen, to strew, to scatter
der **Besuch, -s, -e,** visit; company, visitors
besuchen, to visit
betäuben, to stun, to stupefy
betrachten, to observe, to watch
sich **betragen (ä, u, a),** to behave oneself
betreten (i, a, e), to enter; to step on
betrunken, drunk
sich **beugen,** to bend down, to bow
bewahren, to keep, to preserve
bewegen (*weak*), to stir, to move; **(o, o)** to move, to induce
die **Bewegung, -en,** movement
bewegungslos, motionless
beweisen (ie, ie), to prove
der **Bewohner, -s, -,** occupant
bewußtlos, unconscious
das **Bewußtsein, -s,** consciousness

GERMAN-ENGLISH VOCABULARY

bezahlen, to pay
sich bezeigen, to show oneself
biegen (o, o), to bend
billig, cheap
binden (a, u), to bind, to tie
binnen (*dat.*), within; **binnen kurzem,** in a short time
die **Binnenseite, -n,** inner side
das **bißchen,** little bit
der **Bissen, -s, -,** morsel, bit
bitten (a, e), to beg, to pray, to plead, to ask
blank, bright, polished
blasen (ä, ie, a), to blow
blaß, pale
das **Blatt, -es, ⸚er,** leaf, paper, sheet
das **Blau,** blue
die **Blaukittel** (*plur.*), 'Bluesmocks' (name given to band of men, No. 35)
bleich, pale
der **Blick, -es, -e,** glance, look
bloß, mere(ly)
blühen, to bloom, to flourish
die **Blume, -n,** flower
die **Blumenau, -en,** flower-field
das **Blut, -es,** blood
die **Blütenflocke, -n,** blossom
der **Bock, -es, ⸚e,** ram
der **Boden, -s, ⸚,** floor; valley bottom; attic
die **Bodentreppe, -n,** attic stairs
der **Bord,** board (ship); **an Bord,** on board
böse, angry
der **Branntwein, -s,** brandy
brausen, to roar
brechen (i, a, o), to break
breit, broad
die **Breite, -n,** breadth; open plain
breitschultrig, broad shouldered

die **Bremse, -n,** brake
bremsen, to brake
brennen (a, a), to burn
die **Brillengläser** (*plur.*), glasses
die **Brücke, -n,** bridge
brüllen, to roar, to bellow
der **Brunnen, -s, -,** well
die **Brust,** chest
das **Büblein, -s, -,** little boy
der **Bücherschrank, -s, ⸚e,** book-case
sich bücken, to bend down
die **Bude, -n,** booth, stall; small hut (Nos. 15 and 27)
die **Bugleine, -n,** bow-painter
bunt, motley, many-coloured
der **Bürger, -s, -,** citizen

das **Dach, -es, ⸚er,** roof
die **Dachkammer, -n,** attic
die **Dachluke, -n,** dormer-window
dahinterkommen (a, o) (*sep.*), to get to the bottom of
damals, then, at that time
dämmerig, dusk
dämmern, to grow dusk
der **Dampf, -(e)s,** steam
dankbar, grateful
die **Dankbarkeit,** gratitude
darben, to starve
dauern, to last
die **Decke, -n,** ceiling; covering
der **Degen, -s, -,** sword
der **Deich, -(e)s, -e,** dyke
denken (a, a), to think
deutlich, clear
dicht, dense, thick; **dicht an,** close to
der **Dichter, -s, -,** poet
der **Dieb, -(e)s, -e,** thief
dienen, to serve

der **Dienst,** -es, -e, service; **außer Dienst,** retired
dienstfertig, obliging; officious
diesmal, this time
das **Doppelbett,** -(e)s, -en, double bed
das **Dorf,** -es, ̈er, village
der **Dorn,** -es, -en, thorn
der **Drachen,** -s, -, kite
das **Drama,** -s, **Dramen,** drama, play
sich **drängen,** to crowd, to press
draußen, outside
drehen, to turn
dreinsehen (ie, a, e) (*sep.*), to look
drohen (*dat.*), to threaten
dröhnen, to thud, to roar
der **Druck,** -(e)s, ̈e, pressure
drücken, to press
der **Dschungel,** -s,- jungle
der **Duft,** -(e)s, ̈e, scent, fragrance
dumm, stupid
das **Dunkel,** -s, darkness
dünn, thin
der **Dunst,** -(e)s, ̈e, vapour, steam
durchbohren, to penetrate
durchdringen (a, u) (*sep.*), to penetrate
durchfahren (ä, u, a), to go through
durchqueren, to cross
durchschneiden (i, i) (*sep.*), to cut through
dürfen (*modal*), to be allowed
dürr, withered, dry
der **Durst,** thirst; **den Durst stillen,** to quench the thirst
durstig, thirsty
das **Dutzend,** -s, -e, dozen

die **Ebene,** -n, plain
die **Ecke,** -n, corner
ehe, before
die **Ehre,** -n, honour
die **Eiche,** -n, oak
eigen, own
eigenartig, peculiar
eigentlich, real(ly), actual(ly)
eilen, to hurry
eiligst, in a great hurry
einbiegen (in) (o, o) (*sep.*), to turn (into)
eindringen (a, u) (*sep.*) to penetrate, to surge
der **Eindruck,** -s, ̈e, impression
einfach, simple
einfallen (ä, ie, a) (*sep.*), to fall in; to occur to
der **Eingang,** -(e)s, ̈e, entrance
einholen (*sep.*), to catch up, to overtake
einkaufen (*sep.*), to go shopping, to shop
die **Einkehr,** putting up at an inn
einladen (ä, u, a) (*sep.*), to invite
die **Einladung,** -en, invitation
einlassen (ä, ie, a) (*sep.*), to admit
einläuten (*sep.*), to ring in, to announce by ringing
einsam, lonely
einschlafen (ä, ie, a) (*sep.*), to fall asleep
einschrumpfen (*sep.*), to shrink, to shrivel
einst, formerly
einsteigen (ie, ie) (*sep.*), to get in, to climb in
einstellen (*sep.*), to put in; to discontinue
einstürzen (*sep.*), to fall in
eintreten (i, a, e) (*sep.*), to enter

der **Eintritt, -s, -e,** entrance
einwerfen (i, a, o) (*sep.*), to smash in
der **Einwohner, -s, -,** occupant
einziehen (o, o) (*sep.*), to move in
einzig, single, only
das **Eis, -es,** ice
eisern, iron
elend, miserable, wretched
elfenbeinern, ivory
empfangen (ä, i, a), to receive
empfehlen (ie, a, o), to recommend
empfinden (a, u), to feel
endlich, finally
eng, narrow
entbrennen (a, a), to take fire
entdecken, to discover
die **Entdeckung,** discovery
entfalten, to unfold, to develop
sich **entfernen,** to go away, to move away
entfernt, distant
entfliehen (o, o), to flee
entführen, to carry off, to abduct
entgegenlaufen (ä, ie, au) (*sep.*), to run to meet
entgegnen, to retort, to reply
entgehen (i, a), to escape
enthalten (ä, ie, a), to contain
entkommen (a, o), to escape
entlang, along
entnehmen (i, a, o), to take away
entreißen (i, i), to tear away, to snatch
entschlafen (ä, ie, a), to fall asleep; to die

entsetzlich, horrible, terrible
entzünden, to light, to set on fire
erbauen, to build; to edify
erblicken, to catch sight of, to espy
die **Erde,** earth
das **Erdgeschoß, -sses, -sse,** ground-floor
erfahren (ä, u, a), to get to know; **erfahren** (*past part.*), experienced
der **Erfolg, -s, -e,** success
erfolgreich, successful
erfreulich, delightful
erfreut, glad, joyful
erfüllen, to fulfil
sich **ergießen (o, o),** to gush forth, to overflow
ergreifen (i, i), to seize, to grasp
erhalten (ä, ie, a), to receive; to maintain
sich **erheben (o, o),** to rise
erhellen, to brighten, to light up
sich **erholen,** to recover, to get better
erkennen (a, a), to recognize, realize
erkiesen (erkor, erkoren), to choose
die **Erklärung, -en,** explanation
erleuchten, to light up, to brighten
erlöschen (o, o), to be extinguished
ermorden, to murder
ermüden, to tire, to fatigue
die **Ermüdung,** fatigue
ernst, earnest, serious
erquicken, to refresh, to revive
erreichen, to reach

erschlagen (ä, u, a), to slay, to kill
erschrecken, to frighten
erspähen, to espy, to catch sight of
erst, first; **das erstemal**, the first time
erstarrt, benumbed, petrified
das **Erstaunen, -s**, astonishment
erstaunlich, astonishing
erstaunt, astonished
ertränken (*v.t.*), to drown
ertrinken (a, u), (*v.i.*), to be drowned
erwachen (*v.i.*), to wake up
erwarten, to expect, to await
die **Erwartung, -en**, expectation
erweisen (ie, ie), to show
erzählen, to relate, to tell
die **Erziehung**, education
der **Esel, -s, -**, ass, donkey
europäisch, European
ewig, eternal

der **Faden, -s, ¨**, thread, string, twine
die **Fahne, -n**, flag
fahren (ä, u, a), to drive, to travel, to go, to ride
der **Fahrer, -s, -**, driver
die **Fahrkarte, -n**, ticket
der **Fahrkartenschalter, -s, -**, ticket-office
der **Fährmann, -leute**, ferryman
der **Fahrplan, -s, ¨e**, time-table
falb, fallow, dim, pale
der **Fall, -es, ¨e**, case; incident; fall
falsch, false
falten, to fold
famos!, fine!
fangen (ä, i, a), to catch
die **Farbe, -n**, colour
färben, to dye, to stain, to colour
die **Färbung, -en**, colouring, hue
fassen, to seize, to grasp; **den Plan fassen**, to plan; **auf etwas gefaßt**, prepared for something
fast, almost
faul, lazy
die **Feder, -n**, feather; pen
fegen, to sweep, to clean out
fehlen, to be lacking, to be missing
der **Fehler, -s, -**, mistake
der **Fehltritt, -s, -e**, false step
feiern, to celebrate
fein, fine, delicate
der **Feind, -es, -e**, enemy
das **Fell, -es, -e**, skin, hide
der **Fels, -en, -en**, der **Felsen, -s, -**, rock
die **Felsenschluft, -en**, ravine, gorge
das **Fensterkreuz, -es, -e**, window-crossbar
die **Fensteröffnung, -en**, window-opening
der **Fensterrahmen, -s, -**, window-frame
die **Fensterscheibe, -n**, window-pane
die **Ferien** (*plur.*), holidays
die **Ferne, -n**, distance
fest, firm, solid
das **Fest, -es, -e**, festival, banquet
festhalten (ä, ie, a) (*sep.*), to hold firm
die **Festung, -en**, fortress
der **Feuerschein, -s**, firelight, glow
die **Feuersglut**, fiery glow

der **Feuerstrahl, -s, -en,** flash of a shot
das **Fieber, -s, -,** fever
fieberhaft, feverish
findig, sharp, resourceful
finster, dark, gloomy, sombre
die **Finsternis,** gloom, darkness
fixieren, to fix the eyes on
flach, flat, shallow
der **Flachs, -es,** flax
die **Flamme, -n,** flame
flattern, to flutter, to wave
fleißig, diligent
fliehen (o, o), to flee
fließen (o, o), to flow
flimmern, to twinkle, to sparkle
die **Flinte, -n,** flintlock, musket
die **Flocke, -n,** flake
der **Flug, -es, ⸚e,** flight
der **Flügel, -s, -,** wing
das **Flugzeug, -s, -e,** aeroplane
der **Flur, -es, -e,** entrance hall
der **Fluß, -sses, ⸚sse,** river
flüstern, to whisper
die **Flut, -en,** flood, tide, deluge
fortschlüpfen (*sep.*), to slip away
fortschweben (*sep.*), to float away
fortsetzen (*sep.*), to continue
das **Frauenzimmer, -s, -,** young girl
frech, cheeky, impertinent
freilich, admittedly, certainly
der **Fremde, -n, -n,** stranger
die **Freude, -n,** joy
sich freuen (auf), to look forward (to)
freundlich, friendly, kind
der **Friedenstag, -s, -e,** day of peace
friedlich, peaceful

frieren (o, o), to freeze
fröhlich, joyful, merry
fromm, pious
das **Frühlingslaub, -s, -e,** Spring foliage
der **Frühlingsschmaus, -es, ⸚e,** Spring feast
das **Frühstück, -s, -e,** breakfast
fühlbar, perceptible
fühlen, to feel
führen, to lead, to guide, to take
füllen, to fill
funkeln, to sparkle
furchtbar, fearful, terrible
sich fürchten (vor), to be afraid (of), to fear
fürchterlich, frightful, dreadful
der **Fußboden, -s, ⸚,** floor
der **Fußgänger, -s, -,** pedestrian
das **Futteral, -s, -e,** case

der **Gang, -es ⸚e,** walk; passage, corridor; **in Gang bringen,** to start (a machine)
ganz, quite; whole
die **Gasse, -n,** side-street, narrow street
der **Gast, -es, ⸚e,** guest
das **Gebirge, -s, -,** mountain range, mountains
der **Geburtstag, -s, -e,** birthday
das **Geburtstagsfest, -s, -e,** birthday party, celebration
das **Gebüsch, -es, -e,** bush, shrubs, thicket
der **Gedanke, -ns, -n,** thought
gedenken (a, a), to think, to bear in mind, to remember
das **Gedicht, -s, -e,** poem
die **Geduld,** patience

die **Gefahr, -en,** danger
gefährlich, dangerous
gefallen (ä, ie, a) (*dat.*), to please
das **Gefühl, -s, -e,** feeling
die **Gegend, -en,** area, region
gegenüber (*dat.*), opposite
gegenüberliegend, opposite
der **Gegenwind, -s, -e,** counterwind, headwind
der **Gegner, -s, -,** opponent
gehorchen (*dat.*), to obey
gehören (*dat.*), to belong to
der **Geist, -es, -er,** spirit, mind
geistig, intellectual; spiritual
die **Gelegenheit, -en,** opportunity
der **Gelehrte, -n, -n,** scholar
das **Geleise, -s, -,** railway lines, rails
gelingen (a, u), to succeed
gellend, shrieking, shrill
gemäß (*dat.*), according to
gemessen, measured, sedate, calm
gemütlich, cosy, comfortable, nice
gen (shortened form of **gegen**), towards
genau, exact(ly)
Genezareth, Lake of Gennesaret (Sea of Galilee or Lake Tiberias)
der **Genosse, -n, -n,** companion
das **Gepäcknetz, -es, -e,** luggage rack
der **Gepäckträger, -s, -,** porter
gerade, straight
geraten (ä, ie, a), to fall
das **Geräusch, -es, -e,** noise, bustle
das **Gericht, -es, -e,** court of justice, tribunal
der **Gerichtsschreiber, -s, -,** clerk of the court

geschehen (ie, a, e), to happen
das **Geschenk, -s, -e,** present, gift
die **Geschichte, -n,** story, history
das **Geschirr, -(e)s, -e,** harness
das **Geschrei, -s, -e,** shouting, screams
geschwind, quick
die **Geschwindigkeit, -en,** speed
der **Geselle, -n, -n,** companion
die **Gesellschaft, -en,** party, society, company
das **Gesicht, -s, -er,** face; **-s, -e,** vision, apparition
gespannt, tense
das **Gespenst, -s, -er,** ghost
die **Gestalt, -en,** figure
das **Gestein, -s, -e,** stone
gesund, healthy
gewähren, to give, to grant, to guarantee
gewaltig, powerful, mighty
das **Gewehr, -s, -e,** gun, rifle
gewiß, certain, sure
der **Gewissensbiß, -sses, -sse,** prick of conscience
gewöhnt (an), accustomed, used (to)
der **Giebel, -s, -,** gable
glänzen, to shine, to gleam
das **Gläschen, -s, -,** little glass
glatt, smooth
glauben (*dat.*), to believe
gleich, equal, like, similar; **(so)gleich,** immediately; **gleich darauf,** immediately afterwards
gleichgültig, indifferent
gleiten (i, i), to glide
das **Glied, -(e)s, -er,** limb, member
glitzern, to glitter, to sparkle
die **Glocke, -n,** bell

das **Glück,** -(e)s, happiness, good fortune
glücklich, happy, fortunate
glücklicherweise, fortunately
glühen, to glow
die **Gnade,** -n, grace, mercy, pardon
der **Granitblock,** -s, ¨e, block of granite
gräßlich, horrible
grau, grey
grausam, cruel
das **Grautier,** -s, -e, ass, donkey
greifen (i, i), to hold; **greifen nach,** to snatch at
grell, shrill, sharp
die **Grenze,** -n, frontier
grob, coarse, crude
die **Größe,** -n, size
der **Grund,** -es, ¨e, reason; bottom
grüngekleidet, dressed in green
die **Gruppe,** -n, group
grüßen, to greet
der **Gummiball,** -s, ¨e, rubber ball
die **Gunst,** favour
günstig, favourable

die **Habe,** property, goods
hager, haggard, thin, lean
halb, half
halbwüchsig, half-grown
die **Halle,** -n, hall
hallen, to echo, to resound
der **Hals,** -es, ¨e, neck, throat
halten (ä, ie, a), to hold
die **Haltung,** attitude
hämmern, to hammer, to throb
die **Handtasche,** -n, handbag
das **Handtuch,** -(e)s, ¨er, towel

hängen (v.t.), to hang
der **Hanswurst,** clown
hart, hard
häßlich, ugly
die **Hast,** haste, hurry
hastig, hasty, hurried
der **Haufen,** -s, -, heap, pile
das **Haupt,** -es, ¨er, head
der **Hausflur,** -(e)s, -e, entrance hall
die **Hauswand,** ¨e, wall of a house
heben (o, o), to lift, to raise
die **Heckleine,** -n, stern-painter
heftig, violent
das **Heil,** -s, salvation
heimhelfen (i, a, o) (sep.), to rebuke, to tick off
heimlich, secret; comfortable
die **Heimatstadt,** ¨e, native town
heiraten, to marry
heißen (ie, ei), to call; to be called; to order; to mean
der **Held,** -en, -en, hero
hell, bright, clear
das **Hemd,** -es, -en, shirt
der **Henkel,** -s, -, handle
herablassen (ä, ie, a) (sep.), to let down, to lower
heranbrausen (sep.), to approach with a roar
herankommen (a, o) (sep.), to approach
heranrollen (sep.), to roll up, to roll along
herauflangen (sep.), to reach up, to stretch up
herausbekommen (a, o) (sep.), to find out
herb, bitter
herbeirufen (ie, u) (sep.), to evoke
der **Herbstnachmittag,** -s, -e, autumn afternoon

der **Herd,** -es, -e, hearth, home
herrichten (*sep.*), to fix up, to prepare, to arrange
herrlich, glorious, wonderful
die **Herrlichkeit, -en,** glory
die **Herrschaft, -en,** rule; **meine Herrschaften!** Gentlemen!
herrschen, to reign, to prevail
herübertönen (*sep.*), to sound (towards the speaker)
herumdrehen (*sep.*), to turn round
herunterholen (*sep.*), to fetch down
herunterstürzen (*sep.*), to rush down
hervorragen (*sep.*), to tower
das **Herzklopfen, -s,** beating of the heart
die **Herzogin, -nen,** duchess
heulen, to howl
hienieden, down here (on earth)
hierauf, thereupon
hilflos, helpless
der **Himmel, -s, -,** sky, heaven
hinablassen (**ä, ie, a**) (*sep.*), to lower
hinabsteigen (**ie, ie**) (*sep.*), to descend
hinaufsteigen (**ie, ie**) (*sep.*), to climb, to mount
hinauslehnen (*sep.*), to lean out
hinausleuchten (*sep.*), to shine out
hinausschmeißen (**i, i**) (*sep.*), to throw out
sich **hinausschwingen** (**a, u**) (*sep.*), to swing oneself out
hinausstürzen (*sep.*), to rush out

hinlegen (*sep.*), to put down
hinsetzen (*sep.*), to put down
hintereinander, one after the other
hinterher, along behind
der **Hinterteil, -s, -e,** back end, rear
hintreiben (**ie, ie**) (*sep.*), to drive along, to drive away
hinunterfahren (**ä, u, a**) (*sep.*), to take down (in a lift)
sich **hochrecken** (*sep.*), to stretch up
der **Hof, -es, ̈e,** court; farm; yard
die **Hoffnung, -en,** hope
hoffnungsreich, hopeful
höflich, polite
die **Höhe, -n,** height; **in die Höhe,** upwards
die **Hoheit, -en,** Highness
der **Höhepunkt, -(e)s, -e,** top, zenith
hohl, hollow
die **Höhle, -n,** cave
holen, to fetch
das **Holz, -es, ̈er,** wood
die **Holzbank, ̈e,** wooden bench
hölzern, wooden
die **Holzrippe, -n,** wooden rib
der **Hörer, -s, -,** receiver (of telephone)
der **Horizont, -s, -e,** horizon
der **Hufschlag, -s, ̈e,** hoofbeat
der **Hügel, -s, -,** hill
die **Hügelkette, -n,** chain of hills
die **Hühnerjagd,** partridge-shooting
der **Hut, -es, ̈e,** hat
die **Hut,** guard, watch, care

die **Idee, -n,** idea
immerdar, always
der **Inhalt, -s,** contents
innehalten (ä, ie, a) (*sep.*), to stop, to pause
das **Innere, -n,** inside, interior
die **Insel, -n,** island
das **Interesse, -s, -n,** interest
inzwischen, in the meantime
irren, to make a mistake

jagen, to hunt
jahraus; jahraus jahrein, year in, year out
die **Jahresziffer, -n,** date
das **Jahrhundert, -s, -e,** century
jährlich, annual, yearly
der **Jammerblick, -s, -e,** pitiful look, sight
jauchzen, to rejoice, to shout for joy
jedenfalls, in any case
die **Jugend,** youth
die **Jungfrau, -en,** maiden
just, just, exactly
das **Juwel, -s, -en,** jewel, precious stone

kahl, bald, bare
der **Kahn, -es, ̈e,** boat, rowing-boat
kaltblütig, cold-blooded
der **Kamm, -es, ̈e,** comb
die **Kammer, -n,** room, bedroom
der **Kampf, -es, ̈e,** fight, struggle
der **Kanal, -s, ̈e,** canal
kaputt, broken
die **Katze, -n,** cat
kauern, to squat, to cower
der **Kaufmann, -s, -leute,** merchant

kaum, scarcely
die **Kehle, -n,** throat
der **Keller, -s, -,** cellar
der **Kellner, -s, -,** waiter
der **Kerl, -s, -e,** fellow
der **Kies, -es,** gravel; pebbles
die **Kinderfreundin, -nen,** friend of children
die **Kinderwiege, -n,** cradle
das **Kinn, -es, -e,** chin
die **Kirche, -n,** church
der **Kirchhof, -s, ̈e,** churchyard, graveyard
der **Kirchturm, -s, ̈e,** church tower
der **Kirschbaum, -s, ̈e,** cherry-tree
die **Kirsche, -n,** cherry
das **Kissen, -s, -,** cushion
die **Kiste, -n,** box, chest
der **Klang, -es, ̈e,** sound, tone
das **Klappern, -s,** clatter, rattling
das **Kleid, -es, -er,** dress, article of clothing
klettern, to clamber
klingen (a, u), to sound
klinken, to clink, to click
die **Klippe, -n,** cliff, rock
klirren, to clink, to clatter
klopfen, to knock
die **Kluft, ̈e,** chasm, ravine
knacken, to crack, to crunch
knallen, to snap, to explode, to crash
knapp, close fitting; barely sufficient; in short supply
knarren, to creak, to screech
knicksen, to curtsey, to bow
der **Knopf, -es, ̈e,** button, knob
kochen, to cook, to boil
die **Köchin, -nen,** cook
der **Koffer, -s, -,** trunk, case
die **Kohle, -n,** coal, charcoal

kontrastieren, to contrast
der **Korb, -es, ⸚e,** basket
der **Körper, -s, -,** body
die **Kost,** food
kostbar, precious, valuable
krabbeln, to crawl
krach! crash!
der **Krach, -s, -e,** crash
die **Kraft, ⸚e,** strength, force, power
kräftig, powerful
kränken, to hurt, to insult
das **Krankenhaus, -es, ⸚er,** hospital
kraus, irregular (of writing)
das **Kreuz, -es, -e,** cross
kreuz und quer, zig-zag, in all directions
kriechen (o, o), to creep, to crawl
kriegen, to get, to obtain, to receive
der **Kriegsdienst, -s,** military service
der **Kriminalkommissar, -s, -e,** Detective Inspector
die **Krone, -n,** crown; top (of tree)
das **Krümchen, -s, -,** little crumb
die **Küche, -n,** kitchen
der **Kuchen, -s, -,** cake
die **Kugel, -n,** bullet
kühlen, to cool
kühn, brave
die **Kunst, ⸚e,** art; trick
kurieren, to cure
der **Kurs, -es, -e,** course; direction
die **Küste, -n,** coast, shore
der **Kutscher, -s, -,** coachman, driver

lächeln, to smile
lachen, to laugh
lächerlich, ridiculous

die **Lade, -n,** box, chest
der **Laden, -s, ⸚,** shop; shutter
laden (ä, u, a), to load
die **Lage, -n,** position, situation
das **Lampenöl, -s,** lamp-oil
der **Landsmann, -s, -leute,** fellow-countryman
die **Landschaft, -en,** scenery, landscape
die **Landstraße, -n,** highway
die **Landung, -en,** landing
langerwünscht, long-awaited
langsam, slow
der **Lärm, -es,** noise, uproar
lärmen, to create a noise, an uproar
die **Last, -en,** burden, load
die **Laterne, -n,** lantern, lamp
lau, tepid, lukewarm, warm
die **Laube, -n,** bower, arbour
der **Lausbube, -n, -n,** cheeky boy
lauschen, to listen, to eavesdrop
laut, loud
der **Laut, -es, -e,** sound, tone
die **Laute, -n,** lute
läuten, to ring; **Sturm läuten,** to ring the alarm
lauter (*indeclinable adj.*), pure, genuine
lebhaft, lively, gay
lecker, delicate, dainty, tasty
leer, empty
sich legen, to subside (of a storm)
lehnen, to lean
der **Lehnstuhl, -s, ⸚e,** armchair
der **Lehrling, -s, -e,** apprentice
das **Leib, -es, -er,** body
die **Leibeskraft, ⸚e; aus Leibeskraft** or **aus Leibeskräften,** with all one's strength
die **Leiche, -n,** corpse

der **Leichnam, -s, -e,** corpse
leicht, easy, slight
leiden (i, i), to suffer
leise, soft, quiet
die **Leiter, -n,** ladder
die **Leitung, -en,** leadership, management
lenken, to guide
die **Lerche, -n,** lark
der **Leuchtturm, -s, ⸚e,** lighthouse
licht, light, bright
der **Lichtschalter, -s, -,** switch
der **Lichtschimmer, -s,** gleam, shimmer
der **Liebhaber, -s, -,** lover; amateur
lieblich, charming, lovely
linde, soft, gentle
lindern, to soften, to allay, to assuage
die **Linke, -n,** left hand
das **Loch, -es, ⸚er,** hole
die **Loge, -n,** lodge; office
los; was ist los? what's the matter?
losbinden (a, u) (*sep.*), to untie, to loosen
lösen, to untie, to loosen; **eine Karte lösen,** to buy a ticket
losfahren (ä, u, a) (*sep.*), to start off, to drive off
loslassen (ä, ie, a) (*sep.*), to free, to let go
sich **losreißen (i, i)** (*sep.*), to tear oneself loose
der **Löwe, -n, -n,** lion
die **Luft, ⸚e,** air
lüften, to raise (a hat)
lustig, merry, joyful

mächtig, mighty, powerful
das **Mahl, -es, -e,** meal
Makedonien, Macedonia
malen, to paint
mancherlei, many kinds of
manchmal, often
die **Mandel, -n,** almond
der **Mantel, -s, ⸚,** cloak, overcoat
der **Marktplatz, -es, ⸚e,** market-place
marmelsteinern, marble
das **Marmorbild, -s, -er,** marble statue
der **Marsch, -es, ⸚e,** march
die **Masse, -n,** mass
der **Matrose, -n, -n** sailor
die **Mauer, -n,** wall
der **Mauerrand, -s, ⸚er,** rim, edge of wall
die **Maus, ⸚e,** mouse
das **Meer, -es, -e,** sea
der **Meeresboden, -s,** bottom of the sea
das **Mehl, -(e)s, -e,** flour
meinen, to think, to have or to express an opinion
melden, to announce
die **Menge, -n,** crowd, amount
der **Mensch, -en, -en,** human being
das **Menschentum, -s,** humanity
die **Menschlichkeit,** kindness, humaneness
merken, to notice, to note
die **Milch,** milk
die **Milde,** kindness, mildness
mindest, least; **im mindesten,** in the least
missen, to miss
mitfahren (ä, u, a) (*sep.*), to travel with
die **Mitte, -n,** middle, centre
die **Mitteilung, -en,** communication
das **Mittelalter, -s,** Middle Ages
die **Mittelgröße,** medium height

der **Mond, -es, -e,** moon
mondhell, lit up by the moon, moonlit
das **Mondlicht, -s,** moonlight
der **Mörder, -s, -,** murderer
das **Morgenrot, -s,** dawn
die **Morgenröte,** dawn
der **Motor, -s, -en,** motor
die **Motorkraft,** engine power
die **Möwe, -n,** seagull
die **Müdigkeit,** fatigue, tiredness
die **Mühe, -n,** trouble, pains
der **Mühlstein, -s, -e,** millstone
murmeln, to murmur
der **Mut, -es,** courage
die **Mütze, -n,** cap

nachdem, after
nachfolgen (*sep.*), to follow after
der **Nachmittag, -s, -e,** afternoon
das **Nachtgebet, -s, -e,** evening prayer
nachziehen (o, o) (*sep.*), to go after; to pull after
die **Nähe,** neighbourhood, nearness
nahen, to approach
sich **nähern,** to approach
nähren, to feed, to nourish
die **Nahrung, -en,** food, nourishment
der **Nähtisch, -es, -e,** sewing-table
nämlich (*adj.*), same; (*adv.*) namely, that is to say
die **Narbe, -n,** scar
der **Nebel, -s, -,** mist
nebenan, adjacent, close by
das **Nebenbett, -s, -en,** next bed

nennen (a, a), to call, to name
das **Netz, -es, -e,** net
neuentdeckt, newly discovered
neugierig, curious, inquisitive
neulich, recent(ly)
nicken, to nod
nie, never
niedergeschlagen, dejected
sich **niederstrecken** (*sep.*), to lie down, to stretch out
niedrig, low
niemand, nobody
nirgends, nowhere
nirgendwo, nowhere
die **Nordsee,** North Sea
die **Not, ⸚e,** need, want, necessity, misery
nötig, necessary
der **Notpfiff, -(e)s, -e,** alarm (emergency) whistle
notwendig, necessary
Nu; im Nu, suddenly, in no time
die **Nummer, -n,** number
nützen (*v.t.*), to use; (*v.i.*), to be of use
nutzlos, useless

oben, upstairs, up above
die **Oberfläche, -n,** surface
der **Oberst, -en-, en,** colonel
der **Ochs, -en, -en,** ox, bull
der **Ofen, -s, ⸚,** stove, oven
offenbaren, to reveal
öffnen, to open
ordentlich, orderly, proper
die **Ordnung, -en,** order, arrangement
der **Ort, -es, ⸚er** or **-e,** place, spot
der **Osten, -s,** east
österreichisch, Austrian

ein paarmal, a few times
packen, to pack; to grab, to snatch
das **Paket, -s, -e,** packet, parcel
der **Palast, -s, ¨e,** palace
Palästina, Palestine
der **Paß, -sses, ¨sse,** passport
passen (*dat.*), to suit
die **Pause, -n,** interval, break
peinlich, painful
die **Peitsche, -n,** whip
peitschen, to whip
die **Persönlichkeit, -en,** personality
das **Petroleum, -s,** paraffin, oil
pfeifen (i, i), to whistle
das **Pferd, -es, -e,** horse
der **Pfiff, -es, -e,** whistle; trick
die **Pflanze, -n,** plant
pflegen (*v.t.*), to tend, to nurse; (*v.i.*), to have the habit
die **Pflicht, -en,** duty
der **Pflug, -es, ¨e,** plough
der **Pilot, -en, -en,** pilot
die **Pistole, -n,** pistol
die **Planke, -n,** plank
platschen, to splash
die **Platzkarte, -n,** ticket for a seat
plaudern, to chat
plötzlich, sudden(ly)
pochen, to knock
der **Portier, -s, -s,** porter (of an hotel)
der **Posten, -s, -,** post, station; sentry
das **Posthorn, -s, ¨er,** posthorn
prächtig, magnificent
der **Prädikant, -en, -en,** preacher
der **Preis, -es, -e,** price, cost; prize
preisen (ie, ie), to praise
pressen, to press

die **Probe, -n,** rehearsal, experiment
probieren, to try, to test
der **Promenadenquai, -s, -s,** promenade
prügeln, to thrash
der **Pudel, -s, -,** poodle
der **Puls, -es, -e,** pulse
der **Punkt, -es, -e,** point, dot
das **Püppchen, -s, -,** little doll
die **Puppe, -n,** doll, puppet
die **Puppentaufe, -n,** doll's baptism

der **Qualm, -(e)s,** thick smoke
die **Quelle, -n,** spring, fountain, source
quer, athwart, across
quirlen, to whirl

der **Rabe, -n, -n,** raven
sich ranken, to creep, to climb (of tendrils)
der **Ranzen, -s, -,** knapsack
rascheln, to rustle
die **Raschheit,** speed
rasen, to rage, to roar
die **Ratte, -n,** rat
der **Rattenfänger, -s, -,** ratcatcher
der **Räuber, -s, -,** robber, brigand
der **Rauch, -es,** smoke
rauchen, to smoke
die **Rauchwolke, -n,** cloud of smoke
rauh, rough, coarse
der **Raum, -es, ¨e,** room; space
rauschen, to rush; to rustle
die **Rebe, -n,** vine
die **Rechte, -n,** right hand
das **Reich, -(e)s, -e,** empire
reichen, to suffice; to reach, to hand; **sich die Hände reichen,** to shake hands
reichlich, plentiful, ample

die **Reihe, -n,** row, line
die **Reise, -n,** journey
der **Reisende, -n, -n,** traveller
der **Reiter, -s, -,** rider
das **Reitergeschwader, -s, -,** cavalry squadron
rennen (a, a), to run
der **Rennschlitten, -s, -,** sleigh
respektiv, respective
retten, to save
der **Retter, -s, -,** saviour, rescuer
die **Reue,** contrition, regret
die **Rheinlegende, -n,** Rhine legend
der **Richter, -s, -,** judge
richtig, right, correct
die **Richtung, -en,** direction
riechen (o, o), to smell
der **Riegel, -s, -,** bolt, bar
der **Riese, -n, -n,** giant
die **Riesenkraft,** great strength
die **Riesentochter, ¨,** giant's daughter
das **Riff, -es, -e,** reef, ridge
ringsher, round about
der **Ritt, -es, -e,** ride
der **Ritz, -es, -e,** tear, crack
die **Rolle, -n,** rôle; roll
die **Rosine, -n,** raisin
rostig, rusty
der **Ruck, -es, -e,** jolt, jerk
der **Rücken, -s, -,** back
der **Rücksitz, -es, -e,** rear-seat
rückwärts, backwards
die **Ruderbank, ¨e,** rowing-seat
rudern, to row
der **Ruf, -es, -e,** call, cry
rufen (ie, u), to call
die **Ruhe,** rest, peace, calm
ruhig, quiet, peaceful
rühren, to touch, to stir
die **Ruine, -n,** ruin
der **Rumpf, -es, ¨e,** fuselage
rund, round

die **Runde; die Runde machen,** to go the rounds
rüstig, robust, vigorous
rütteln, to shake, to rattle

die **Sache, -n,** affair
sacht, soft, gentle
der **Sack, -es, ¨e,** sack, bag
Salonichi, Salonika
die **Sandbank, ¨e,** sandbank
der **Sandpfad, -s, -e,** sandy path
sanft, soft, gentle
satt, satisfied, filled
der **Sattelgurt, -s, -e,** girth, belly-band
sausen, to roar
der **Schaden, -s, ¨,** damage, injury
schaden (*dat.*), to harm, to hurt, to damage
das **Schaf, -es, -e,** sheep
schaffen, to procure, to get; to do
der **Schaffner, -s, -,** ticket collector, conductor
schallen (*weak*, but imperf. **scholl** also exists), to sound
scharf, sharp
der **Scharfblick, -s, -e,** acuteness; piercing look
der **Schatten, -s, -,** shadow, shade
der **Schatz, -es, ¨e,** treasure
das **Schätzel, -s, -,** sweetheart
der **Schatzgräber, -s, -,** treasure-seeker
die **Schaufel, -n,** shovel; paddle
das **Schauspiel, -s, -,** play, drama
die **Scheibe, -n,** pane of glass
scheiden (ie, ie), to depart; to die
der **Schein, -es, -e,** gleam, light
scheinbar, apparent(ly)

scheinen (ie, ie), to shine; to seem
schenken, to give, to present
schicken, to send
sich schicken, to be fitting, to be suitable
schielen, to squint
die **Schiene, -n,** rail, railway line
schießen (o, o), to shoot
die **Schießscharte, -n,** loophole, embrasure
die **Schildwacht,** sentry
der **Schimmel, -s, -,** white horse
schimmern, to shimmer, to gleam
der **Schlag, -es, ⸚e,** blow, stroke
die **Schlange, -n,** snake
sich schlängeln, to meander, to wind
schlau, cunning
schlecht, bad
schleichen (i, i), to creep, to crawl, to slip
schlesisch, Silesian
schleudern, to hurl
schließlich, final(ly)
schlingen (a, u), to tie, to wind
der **Schlitten, -s, -,** sleigh
Schlittschuh laufen (äu, ie, au), to skate
das **Schloß, -sses, ⸚sser,** castle
schluchzen, to sob
schlummern, to slumber
der **Schlüssel, -s, -,** key
der **Schlüsselbund, -s, -e,** bunch of keys
schmal, narrow
die **Schmalseite, -n,** narrow end
das **Schmalz, -es,** fat, grease
schmecken, to taste

schmeicheln (dat.), to flatter
schmelzen (i, o, o), to melt
der **Schmerz, -es, -en,** pain, sorrow
die **Schmucksachen (plur.),** ornaments, jewels
schneebedeckt, covered with snow
die **Schneedecke, -n,** covering of snow
schneiden (i, i), to cut
die **Schnelligkeit,** speed, quickness
der **Schnellzug, -s, ⸚e,** express train
die **Schnur, ⸚e,** string, cord, line
der **Schoß, -es, ⸚e,** lap
der **Schrank, -es, ⸚e,** cupboard
der **Schrecken, -s, -,** fright
schrecklich, terrible, frightful
die **Schreibmaschine, -n,** typewriter
der **Schreibtisch, -es, -e,** desk
schreien (ie, ie), to shriek, to shout
schreiten (i, i), to step, to stride
die **Schrift, -en,** writing, script
schrill, shrill
der **Schritt, -es, -e,** step, stride
schrumpfen, to shrivel, to shrink
der **Schuh, -es, -e,** shoe
die **Schuld, -en,** debt; guilt, fault
schuld sein, to be guilty
der **Schuldiener, -s, -,** school porter
die **Schuldigkeit,** duty, due; guilt
die **Schulter, -n,** shoulder
der **Schupo** (colloquial for **der Schutzpolizist),** policeman

der **Schuppen, -s, -,** shed
die **Schürze, -n,** apron, pinafore
der **Schuß, -sses, ⸚sse,** shot
die **Schüssel, -n,** dish
schütteln, to shake
schütten, to spill, to empty, to pour out
der **Schutzmann, -s, -leute,** policeman
die **Schwägerin, -nen,** sister-in-law
die **Schwalbe, -n,** swallow
der **Schwarm, -es, ⸚e,** swarm
schweigen (ie, ie), to be, to become, silent
der **Schweiß, -es, -e,** sweat, perspiration
die **Schweiz,** Switzerland
der **Schweizer, -s, -,** Swiss
die **Schwelle, -n,** threshold
das **Schwert, -es, -er,** sword
der **Schwiegersohn, -s, ⸚e,** son-in-law
der **Schwiegerpapa,** father-in-law
schwindeln, to be dizzy
schwinden (a, u), to disappear
sich **schwingen (a, u),** to spring, to bound
schwirren, to whir
der **Schwung, -es, ⸚e,** swing, bound, spring
der **See, -s, -n,** lake
die **See, -n,** sea
die **Seele, -n,** soul
der **Seemann, -s, -leute,** sailor
das **Seeufer, -s, -,** shore of lake or sea
segeln, to sail
segnen, to bless
das **Seil, -es, -e,** rope
die **Seite, -n,** side; page
selten, rare, scarce; seldom
seltsam, strange
senden (*weak* or **a, a**), to send

sich **senken,** to sink
der **Seufzer, -s, -,** sigh
die **Sicht,** sight
sichtbar, visible
das **Sieb, -es, -e,** sieve
silbern, silver
der **Sinn, -es, -e,** sense; mind; **zu Sinnen kommen,** to recover consciousness
sobald (wie), as soon (as)
soeben, just, only just
sofort, immediately
sogar, even
sogleich, immediately
die **Sommerferien** (*plur.*), summer holidays
sonderbar, strange
die **Sonne, -n,** sun
sonnig, sunny
sonst, otherwise; formerly
die **Sorge, -n,** sorrow, care
sorgen (*v.t.*), to look after; (*v.i.*), to be anxious, to worry
sorgfältig, careful
spähen, to spy, to observe
spannen, to span, to stretch; to make tense
spärlich, sparse, bare
der **Spaß, -es, ⸚e,** joke, fun
der **Spaßmacher, -s, -,** joker
der **Spaten, -s, -,** spade
das **Spätzchen, -s, -,** little sparrow
der **Spaziergang, -s, ⸚e,** walk
der **Spazierstock, -s, ⸚e,** walking-stick
der **Speer, -es, -e,** spear
der **Speisesaal, -s, -säle,** dining-room
der **Sperling, -s, -e,** sparrow
die **Sperrstange, -n,** barrier
der **Spiegel, -s, -,** mirror
das **Spielzeug, -s, -e,** toy
spinnen (a, o), to spin
die **Spitze, -n,** point, top (of a mountain)

die **Spritze, -n,** fire-engine
spritzen, to spurt, to splash
der **Spritzer, -s, -,** splash
der **Sprung, -(e)s, ⸚e,** jump, leap
die **Spur, -en,** trace, track
spurlos, without trace
der **Stab, -es, ⸚e,** staff, stick
die **Stahlrute, -n,** steel rod
der **Stall, -es, ⸚e,** stable, shed, stall
der **Stallmeister, -s, -,** riding-master
der **Stamm, -es, ⸚e,** trunk; tribe
stampfen, to stamp
die **Stange, -n,** pole
stark, strong
stärken, to strengthen
statt (*gen.*), instead (of)
die **Statt, ⸚e,** stead, place
der **Staub, -es, -es,** dust, powder
steil, steep
der **Stein, -es, -e,** stone
der **Steinblock, -s, ⸚e,** block (mass) of stone
die **Steinhütte, -n,** stone hut
die **Steinmasse, -n,** pile of stones
der **Steinwurf, -s,** stone's throw
die **Stelle, -n,** place; **auf der Stelle,** immediately
stemmen, to stem, to prop
der **Stengel, -s, -,** stalk, stem
der **Stern, -es, -e,** star
stets, always
steuern, to steer, to guide
der **Stiefel, -s, -,** boot
still, quiet, silent
die **Stille,** silence
stillschweigen (ie, ie) (*sep.*), to be, to become, silent
die **Stimme, -n,** voice
die **Stirn, -en,** forehead, brow
der **Stock, -es, ⸚e,** stick, cane; storey
das **Stockwerk, -s, -e,** storey

stolpern, to stumble
stopfen, to stuff, to fill
stören, to disturb
stoßen (ö, ie, o), to push, to thrust
der **Strahl, -s, -en,** ray, beam, flash
der **Strand, -(e)s, -e,** beach, strand
die **Straßenlaterne, -n,** street-lamp
das **Straßenpflaster, -s, -,** pavement; roadway
sich sträuben, to resist, to oppose
die **Strecke, -n,** stretch, distance; railway line (Nos. 15, 17)
streicheln, to stroke
streichen (i, i), to stroke
streifen (mit einem Blick), to glance at
der **Streifen, -s, -,** strip, stripe
streiten (i, i), to quarrel, to fight
streuen, to strew, to scatter
strohgedeckt, thatched
das **Strohlager, -s, -,** mattress, bed of straw
der **Strom, -(e)s, ⸚e,** stream
der **Strumpf, -(e)s, ⸚e,** stocking
die **Stube, -n,** little room, room
studieren, to study
der **Stuhl, -(e)s, ⸚e,** chair
die **Stunde, -n,** hour
stundenlang, for hours
der **Sturm, -(e)s, ⸚e,** storm
der **Sturz, -es, ⸚e,** crash; fall
stürzen, to hurl, to plunge, to crash
suchen, to look for, to seek
Süddeutschland, Southern Germany
südlich, southern
die **Summe, -n,** sum, total

summen, to hum, to buzz
die **Szene, -n,** scene

der **Tagesanbruch, -s,** dawn
täglich, daily
der **Takt, -(e)s,** time, rhythm
das **Tal, -es, ⸚er,** valley
der **Talar, -s, -e,** robe
die **Tankstelle, -n,** petrol-station
der **Tankwart, -s, -e,** garage man
die **Tanne, -n,** fir
tanzen, to dance
die **Tasche, -n,** pocket; bag
das **Taschentuch, -s, ⸚er,** handkerchief
das **Täßchen, -s, -,** little cup
die **Tasse, -n,** cup
die **Tätigkeit, -en,** activity
der **Tau, -s,** dew
die **Tauchart, -en,** kind of dive
tauchen, to dive
die **Taufe, -n,** baptism
taufen, to baptise
taumeln, to stagger
das **Taurusgebirge, -s,** Taurus Mountains
die **Taxistelle, -n,** taxi rank
der **Teich, -(e)s, -e,** pond
teilen, to divide, to share
teilnehmen (i, a, o) (*sep.*), to participate, to take part
die **Telefonzelle, -n,** telephone kiosk
die **Terrasse, -n,** terrace
die **Tiefe, -n,** depth
das **Tier, -es, -e,** animal
der **Tierarzt, -es, ⸚e,** veterinary surgeon
der **Tintenklecks, -es, -e,** ink-blot
toben, to rage, to roar
der **Tod, -es, Todesfälle,** death
die **Todesangst,** deadly fear
todeskrank, sick unto death, dying

tödlich, fatal, deadly
der **Ton, -es, ⸚e,** sound, tone
der **Topf, -es, ⸚e,** pot
das **Tor, -(e)s, -e,** gate, gateway
der **Tor, -en, -en,** fool
die **Torheit,** folly
der **Tote, -n, -n,** dead man
der **Totenarm, -s, -e,** arm of a dead person
totenstill, deathly silent
die **Totenstille,** deathly silence
der **Trab,** trot
träg, lazy, idle
tragen (ä, u, a), to carry
tränenfeucht, wet with tears
das **Tränlein, -s, -,** tear
der **Traum, -(e)s, ⸚e,** dream
träumen, to dream
traurig, sad
treffen (i, a, o), to meet; to hit
treiben (ie, ie), to drive; to do
trennen, to divide, to part
die **Treppe, -n,** stair
treten (i, a, e), to step, to tread
treu, faithful, loyal
treulos, disloyal, faithless
trocken, dry
die **Trommel, -n,** drum
tropfen, to drip
trotz (*gen.*), in spite (of)
trotzdem, in spite of the fact that
trotzen (*dat.*), to defy, to resist
türkisch, Turkish
das **Türschloß, -sses, ⸚sser,** door lock
die **Tüte, -n,** paper-bag

überall, everywhere
überfahren (ä, u, a) (*insep.*), to run over

die **Überfahrt, -en,** crossing
der **Überfall, -s, ⸚e,** surprise attack
überfallen (ä, ie, a), to overcome (of feeling)
übergehen (i, a) (*insep.*), to pass over, to omit
überhaupt, generally, on the whole; at all
überlassen (ä, ie, a), to leave (to someone else); to give up
übernachten, to spend the night
überreichen, to hand over, to reach
überschauen, to overlook, to command a view over
das **Ufer, -s, -,** shore, bank
sich umdrehen (*sep.*), to turn round
umfangen (ä, i, a), (*sep.*), to encircle, to surround
umgehen (i, a) (*sep.*), to go round, to make a detour; (*insep.*) to avoid, to evade
umher, round about
sich umkleiden (*sep.*), to change (clothes)
umringen (*insep.*), to surround
umschlagen (ä, u, a) (*sep.*), to throw (a cloak, etc.) round one
umschlingen (a, u) (*sep.*), to wind round; (*insep.*) to embrace, to cling to
umschnallen (*sep.*), to buckle on
sich umsehen (ie, a, e) (*sep.*) to look round
umsonst, in vain
umstürzen (*sep.*), to overturn, to knock over
der **Umweg, -s, -e,** detour
sich umwenden (a, a or *weak*) (*sep.*), to turn round

die **Unachtsamkeit,** carelessness
unähnlich, dissimilar
unanständig, improper, unmannerly
unbekannt, unknown
der **Unbekannte, -n, -n,** stranger
die **Unbequemlichkeit,** discomfort, inconvenience
unbeschreiblich, indescribable
undurchdringlich, impenetrable
unerwartet, unexpected
die **Ungeduld,** impatience
das **Ungetüm, -s, -e,** monster
ungewiß, uncertain
ungewöhnlich, unusual
das **Unglück, -s,** misfortune, accident
unglücklich, unhappy, sad, unfortunate
unglücklicherweise, unfortunately
unheimlich, uncomfortable, sinister
unmöglich, impossible
unregelmäßig, irregular
unsanft, rough
unsicher, uncertain, unsure
unten, down below, downstairs
unterdes, meanwhile
untereinander, among themselves
unterirdisch, subterranean
untermischen, to mix
unterscheiden (ie, ie), to differentiate
sich unterstehen (a, a), to dare, to presume
unterwegs, on the way, en route
unverständlich, incomprehensible

vatergleich, like a father
väterlich, fatherly
verändern, to change, to alter
veranstalten, to institute, to organise
verantwortlich, responsible
verbergen (i, a, o), to hide
verbinden (a, u), to tie, to bind
verbleiben (ie, ie) to remain
sich verbreiten, to spread
verbrennen (a, a), to burn, to scorch
verbringen (a, a), to spend (time)
vereinen, to unite, to join
verfault, rotting
sich verfinstern, to grow dark
verfolgen, to persecute; to follow
vergebens, in vain
vergehen (i, a), to pass (of time)
vergessen (i, a, e), to forget
vergittern, to cover with trellis; to board up
vergraben (ä, u, a), to bury
sich vergrößern, to increase, to grow bigger
die **Verheiratung,** marriage
verkaufen, to sell
der **Verkehrsunfall, -s, ⸚e,** road accident
verkehren (mit), to be connected (with), to have contact (with)
verlangen, to demand
verlassen (ä, ie, a), to leave, to desert
verletzen, to hurt
verlieren (o, o), to lose
vermeiden (ie, ie), to avoid

vernehmen (i, a, o), to hear
vernichten, to destroy
verräterisch, treacherous
verreisen, to go away
verriegeln, to bolt
verschieden, different
verschlafen, sleepy
verschlingen (a, u), to swallow up
verschlucken, to swallow
verschwinden (a, u), to disappear
versetzen, to reply
versorgen, to supply, to provide
die **Verspätung; Verspätung haben,** to be late
versprechen (i, a, o), to promise
verspüren, to feel, to be aware of
verstehen (a, a), to understand
verstohlen, stealthy
verstorben, late, dead
verstreuen, to scatter, to strew
verstricken, to ensnare, to entangle
der **Versuch, -s, -e,** attempt, try
versuchen, to attempt, to try
versunken, sunk; engrossed
verteidigen, to defend
vertieft, engrossed; **in Gedanken vertieft,** lost in thought
vertraulich, intimate, familiar
verwelken, to wither, to wilt
verwildern, to become wild
verwunden, to wound
verwundert, astonished

der **Verwundete, -n, -n,** wounded man
verzaubert, enchanted
verzweifelt, despairing, in despair
die **Verzweiflung,** despair
das **Vieh, -s,** cattle
der **Viehhändler, -s, -,** cattle-dealer
viereckig, four-cornered
der **Vogelkäfig, -s, -e,** bird-cage
der **Vogt, -(e)s, ¨e,** overseer, governor
völlig, complete
vollständig, complete
vorangehen (i, a) (*sep.*), to precede, to go in front
vorbeifahren (ä, u, a) (*sep.*), to travel past
vorbeifliegen (o, o) (*sep.*), to fly past
vorbeiführen (*sep.*), to lead past, to take past
vorbeigehen (i, a) (*sep.*), to go past
sich **vorbeugen** (*sep.*), to bend forward
vorder, front
das **Vorderbein, -s, -e,** front foot
vorfahren (ä, u, a) (*sep.*), to drive up
vorfallen (ä, ie, a) (*sep.*), to fall forward; to occur, to happen
die **Vorhalle, -n,** porch, entrance hall
der **Vorhang, -s, ¨e,** curtain
vorher, previously
vorig, previous
vorlesen (ie, a, e) (*sep.*), to read aloud
die **Vorliebe,** preference
vorn, at the front; **nach vorn,** to the front
vornehm, distinguished
sich **vornüberbeugen** (*sep.*), to bend forward
der **Vorschein; zum Vorschein kommen,** to appear
vorsichtig, cautious, careful
die **Vorstadt, ¨e,** suburb
vortreten (i, a, e) (*sep.*), to step forward
vorwärtsstreben (*sep.*), to strive, to press forward
vorziehen (o, o) (*sep.*), to prefer

wachsen (ä, u, a), to grow
die **Wacht,** sentry; watch
der **Wächter, -s, -,** watch, guard, attendant
wagen, to dare
der **Wagen -s, -,** coach, car
der **Wagenbesitzer, -s, -,** coach-owner, car-owner
wählen, to choose
wahr, true
wahrnehmen (i, a, o) (*sep.*), to perceive, to become aware of
wahrscheinlich, apparent(ly)
der **Wald -es, ¨er,** wood, forest
waldbedeckt, covered with woods
der **Waldesrand, -s, ¨er,** edge of a forest
der **Walnußbaum, -s, ¨e,** walnut-tree
walten, to rule, to command, to govern
sich **wälzen,** to revolve; to wallow
die **Wand, ¨e,** wall
der **Wanderbursch, -en, -en,** travelling journeyman or apprentice
der **Wanderer, -s, -,** wanderer, traveller

die **Wandkarte, -n,** wall-map, chart
die **Wange, -n,** cheek
wanken, to reel, to stagger; to come slowly
die **Wanze, -n,** bug
wärmen, to warm
warnen, to warn
warten, to wait
der **Wärter, -s, -,** keeper, attendant; signalman
die **Wärterbude, -n,** signalman's cabin
der **Wartesaal, -s, -säle,** waiting-room
die **Wäsche,** washing
die **Wasserlilie, -n,** water-lily
der **Wasserspiegel, -s,** surface (of water)
der **Wasserstrahl, -s, -en,** jet of water
waten, to wade
wecken, to waken
wedeln, to wag
der **Weg, -es, -e,** way, path
wegreisen (*sep.*), to go away
wegschicken (*sep.*), to send away
wegschieben (**o, o**) (*sep.*), to push away
wegschleppen (*sep.*), to drag away
wehen, to wave, to flutter
das **Wehr, -(e)s, -e,** weir
weh tun (**a, a**) (*dat.*), to hurt
das **Weib, -(e)s, -er,** woman
weiden, to graze
weihen, to dedicate
die **Weile,** while, time
der **Weinberg, -s, -e,** vineyard, vine-hill
weinen, to weep
die **Weise, -n,** way, method
weisen (**ie, ie**), to show, to indicate, to point
weit, far, distant

weiterreiten (**i, i**) (*sep.*), to ride on, to continue riding
sich **weitertasten** (*sep.*), to feel one's way forward
welk, withered
die **Welle, -n,** wave
wenden (**a, a** or *weak*), to turn
die **Wenigkeit,** smallness
werfen (**i, a, o**), to throw
wertvoll, valuable
das **Wesen, -s, -,** being, existence
die **Weser,** River Weser
weshalb, why
das **Wetter, -s,** weather
der **Wicht, -(e)s, -e,** creature, child, wight
wichtig, important
die **Wichtigkeit,** importance
wickeln, to wrap, to wind
widerhallen (*sep.* and *insep.*), to echo, to resound
der **Widerschein,** reflection
wiehern, to neigh, to whinny
die **Wiese, -n,** meadow
das **Wiesenland, -s,** meadow, grassland
wieviel, how much
der, das **Willkommen,** welcome
der **Winkel, -s, -,** corner, spot
winken, to wave, to sign
der **Winzer, -s, -,** vintager, vine-dresser
winzig, tiny
wirken, to effect, to have an effect
wirklich, real(ly)
der **Wirt, -(e)s, -e,** host, innkeeper
die **Woche, -n,** week
wohlgekleidet, well-dressed
die **Wohltat, -en,** kindness, kind action
die **Wohnstube, -n,** living-room

GERMAN-ENGLISH VOCABULARY

das **Wohnzimmer, -s, -,** living-room
die **Wolke, -n,** cloud
das **Wolkenhaus, -es, ̈er,** house in the clouds
die **Wolkenmasse, -n,** bank of clouds
das **Wort, -es, -e** or **̈er,** word
die **Wunde, -n,** wound
das **Wunder, -s, -,** surprise, wonder; miracle
wunderbar, wonderful
wunderlich, strange, queer
wundermild, very gentle, mild
wundern, to astonish
der **Wunsch, -es, ̈e,** wish
wünschen, to wish
die **Wurzel, -n,** root
die **Wut,** rage
wüten, to rage

zäh, tough
der **Zahn, -(e)s, ̈e,** tooth
das **Zahnweh, -s,** tooth-ache
zart, tender, gentle
das **Zeichen, -s, -,** sign
zeigen, to show
die **Zeitlang,** time, period
die **Zeitung, -en,** newspaper; news
das **Zelt, -(e)s, -e,** tent
zerbrechen (i, a, o), to break, to smash
zerreißen (i, i), to tear in pieces; **zerrissen** (*past part.*), gloomy, melancholy
zerschneiden (i, i), to cut in pieces
zersplittern, to splinter, to smash
zerstampfen, to stamp on
zerstören, to destroy
zertrümmern, to destroy, to ruin

ziehen (o, o), to pull, to draw; to go
zielen, to aim
die **Zier,** ornament
zierlich, ornamental, pretty, decorative; dainty; fragile
der **Zirkus, -, -se,** circus
zischen, to hiss
zittern, to tremble
zögern, to hesitate
der **Zöllner, -s, -,** customs officer
zornig, angry
zubringen (a, a) (*sep.*), to spend (time)
der **Zucker, -s,** sugar
zuerst, first of all, at first
zufrieden, satisfied, contented
der **Zug, -es, ̈e,** train; feature
der **Zugführer, -s, -,** guard (of a train)
zugleich, at the same time
zuhalten (ä, ie, a) (*sep.*), to hold shut, to keep closed
zuletzt, finally, in the end
zurückbiegen (o, o) (*sep.*), to bend back
zurückkehren (*sep.*), to return
zurückreißen (i, i) (*sep.*), to snatch back
zurückschrecken (i, a, o) (*sep.*), to start back
zurückstürzen (*sep.*), to rush back; to hurl back
zurückverlangen (*sep.*), to demand back
sich **zurückziehen (o, o)** (*sep.*), to withdraw, to retire
zusammenhängen (mit) (*sep.*), to be connected (with)
zusammenraffen (*sep.*), to collect together, to gather
zuschlagen (ä, u, a) (*sep.*), to shut with a bang

zusehen (ie, a, e) (*sep.*), to watch, to look on
zuvor, previously, formerly
zwar, it is true
der **Zweig,** -(e)s, -e, twig; branch
zweisitzig, having two seats
zweistündig, two-hour
der **Zwerg,** -(e)s, -e, dwarf
zwischen (*dat.* or *acc.*), between

ENGLISH—GERMAN VOCABULARY

1. Nationalities and countries have not been given in this vocabulary, since they will be found in § 30 of the grammar.
2. (*s.*) = strong verb.

about; to be just about, im Begriff sein; eben wollen
abroad; to be abroad, im Ausland sein; **to go abroad,** ins Ausland reisen (gehen)
accident, der Unfall (⸚e)
account; on account of, wegen (*gen.*)
accommodation, die Unterkunft
to **accompany,** begleiten
address, die Adresse (-n)
to **address,** adressieren
to **admire,** bewundern
to **admit,** gestehen (*s.*) (*see* stehen)
advice, der Rat
to **advise,** raten (*s.*) (*dat.*)
aeroplane, das Flugzeug (-e)
affair, die Angelegenheit (-en)
afraid; to be afraid of, fürchten (*acc.*); sich fürchten vor (*dat.*)
afternoon, der Nachmittag; **this afternoon,** heute nachmittag
again, wieder
ago; two days ago, vor zwei Tagen
air, die Luft (⸚e); **in the open air,** im Freien
to **allow,** erlauben (*dat.*); **to be allowed,** dürfen (*modal*)
almost, beinahe, fast

alone, allein
along; along the river, den Fluß entlang, am Fluß entlang
already, schon
although, obgleich
always, immer
to **announce,** melden
to **answer,** antworten
answer, die Antwort (-en)
to **appear;** (to **seem**) scheinen (*s.*); (to **come into view**) erscheinen (*s.*)
to **applaud,** Beifall klatschen
apple, der Apfel (⸚); **appletree,** der Apfelbaum (⸚e)
to **approach,** sich nähern (*dat.*)
area, die Gegend (-en); die Umgebung (-en)
arm, der Arm (-e)
army, das Heer (-e); die Armee (-n)
to **arrive,** ankommen (*s. sep.*)
artist, der Künstler (-)
as, *see* § 28
ashamed; to be ashamed of, sich schämen (über etwas, vor einer Person)
ashore; to go ashore, ans Land gehen
asleep; to fall asleep, einschlafen (*s. sep.*)
to **ask,** *see* § 28
to **attend; to attend a party,** eine Gesellschaft besuchen

to **attract,** anziehen (*s. sep.*)
aunt, die Tante (-n)
away; to go away, weggehen (*s. sep.*), fortgehen (*s. sep.*), abreisen (*sep.*); **to be away,** verreist sein
axe, die Axt (⸚e)

back; at the back, hinten
bad, schlecht
bag, der Sack (⸚e); (**hand**) **bag,** die Tasche (-n)
baker, der Bäcker (-)
ball, der Ball (⸚e)
bank (**money**), die Bank (-en); (**of a river**), das Ufer (-)
to **bark,** bellen
to **bathe,** schwimmen (*s.*), baden
bathing-costume, der Badeanzug (⸚e)
bathroom, das Badezimmer (-)
beach, der Strand
beautiful, schön
because (*sub. conj.*), weil, da; (*co-ord. conj.*), denn
to **become,** werden (*s.*)
bed, das Bett (-es, -en)
before, *see* § 28
to **beg,** *see* § 28
beggar, der Bettler (-)
to **begin,** beginnen (*s.*), anfangen (*s. sep.*)
behind (*prep.*), hinter (*acc.* or *dat.*)
to **believe,** glauben (*dat.*)
bell, die Glocke (-n)
to **belong** (**to**), gehören (*dat.*)
below (*prep.*), unter (*acc.* or *dat.*); (*adv.*), unten
to **bend,** biegen (*s.*); **to bend down,** sich bücken
between, zwischen (*acc.* or *dat.*)
bicycle, das Fahrrad (⸚er)
bill, die Rechnung (-en)

bird, der Vogel (⸚)
birthday, der Geburtstag
to **bite,** beißen (*s.*)
bitter, bitter
Black Forest, der Schwarzwald
bomb, die Bombe (-n)
book, das Buch (⸚er)
to **borrow,** borgen
bottle, die Flasche (-n)
box, der Kasten (⸚)
boy, der Junge (-n, -n)
branch, der Ast (⸚e)
bread, das Brot
to **break,** brechen (*s.*); **broken,** kaputt
breakfast, das Frühstück
bride, die Braut (⸚e)
bridge, die Brücke (-n)
bright, hell
to **bring,** bringen (*s.*)
to **build,** bauen
building, das Gebäude (-)
bullet, die Kugel (-n)
to **burn,** brennen (*s.*)
bus, der Autobus (-se)
busy, beschäftigt, geschäftig
butcher, der Metzger (-), der Fleischer (-)
butcher's shop, die Metzgerei, der Fleischerladen
to **buy,** kaufen
by, von (*dat.*), bei (*dat.*); **by train,** mit dem Zug

cage, der Käfig (-e)
to **call,** rufen (*s.*); **to call out,** ausrufen (*s. sep.*)
call, der Ruf (-e)
to **camp,** lagern
camp, das Lager (-)
cap, die Mütze (-n)
captain (**at sea**), der Kapitän (-e); (**military**), der Hauptmann (-leute)

car, das Auto (-s); der Wagen (-)
cart, der Karren (-); das Fuhrwerk (-e)
to **carry,** tragen (*s.*)
case (**in which to carry things**), der Koffer (-); (**incident**), der Fall (⸚e); **in any case,** jedenfalls
castle, das Schloß (⸚sser)
cat, die Katze (-n)
to **catch,** fangen (*s.*); (**a train,** etc.), erreichen
century, das Jahrhundert (-e)
chair, der Stuhl (⸚e)
chance (**opportunity**), die Gelegenheit (-en); **by chance,** durch Zufall
to **change,** ändern, sich ändern; **to change one's clothes,** sich umziehen, sich umkleiden
chemist, der Apotheker (-)
child, das Kind (-er)
chimney-sweep, der Schornsteinfeger (-)
Christmas, Weihnachten; **at Christmas,** zu Weihnachten
church, die Kirche (-n)
cinema, das Kino (-s)
citizen, der Bürger (-)
class, die Klasse (-n); **classmate,** der Klassenkamerad (-en, -en)
clerk, der Angestellte (-n, -n); der Beamte (-n, -n)
clever, klug
to **climb,** steigen (*s.*)
to **close,** schließen (*s.*), zumachen (*sep.*)
coast, die Küste (-n)
coat, der Mantel (⸚); der Rock (⸚e)
coffee, der Kaffee

cold, kalt; **to catch a cold,** sich erkälten
Cologne, Köln
to **come,** kommen (*s.*)
comfortable, bequem
to **compel,** zwingen (*s.*); **to be compelled,** müssen
confidence, das Vertrauen
to **consist** (**of**), bestehen (aus) (*s.*)
content, zufrieden
to **continue** (*with object*), fortsetzen (*sep.*); (*without object*), fortfahren (*s. sep.*)
cook, der Koch (⸚e); die Köchin (-nen)
cool, kühl
corn, das Korn
corner, die Ecke (-n); **corner-seat,** der Eckplatz (⸚e)
to **cost,** kosten
country, das Land (⸚er); **to go into the country,** aufs Land gehen (*s.*)
courage, der Mut
cousin, der Vetter (-s, -n); die Kusine (-n)
to **cross,** kreuzen, hinübergehen (*s. sep.*)
crossing (**at sea**), die Überfahrt
crowd, die Menge (-n)
to **cry** (**weep**), weinen; **to cry out,** ausrufen (*s. sep.*)
cunning, schlau
cup, die Tasse (-n)
cupboard, der Schrank (⸚e)
customer, der Kunde (-n, -n); die Kundin (-nen)
customs, der Zoll

to **dance,** tanzen
dance, der Tanz (⸚e)
dark, dunkel; **to get dark,** dunkeln, dunkel werden (*s.*)
day, der Tag (-e)
deal; a great deal, viel

death, der Tod
to **decide,** beschließen (*s.*), sich entschließen (*s.*)
deck, das Deck (-e)
deep, tief
to **demand,** verlangen
departure, die Abfahrt (-en) die Abreise (-n)
to **descend,** hinuntersteigen (*s. sep.*)
deserted, unbewohnt, öde, verlassen
to **deserve,** verdienen
destination, das Ziel (-e)
to **die,** sterben (*s.*)
different, ander (*adj.*)
difficult, schwer
difficulty, die Schwierigkeit (-en)
dining-room, das Eßzimmer (-)
dinner, das Abendessen; das Mittagessen
to **direct,** richten
to **disappear,** verschwinden (*s.*)
to **discover,** entdecken
distance, die Ferne
to **disturb,** stören
to **dive,** springen (*s.*), tauchen
to **do,** tun (*s.*), machen
doctor, der Arzt (⁼e)
dog, der Hund (-e)
door, die Tür (-en)
dormitory, der Schlafsaal (Schlafsäle)
down; down the hill, den Berg hin-(her-)unter
downstairs, *see* § 28
drama, das Drama (Dramen)
to **draw (pull),** ziehen (*s.*); **(sketch),** zeichnen
to **dream,** träumen
dream, der Traum (⁼e)
to **dress,** sich anziehen (*s. sep.*); sich ankleiden (*sep.*)
dress, das Kleid (-er)
to **drink,** trinken (*s.*)

to **drive,** treiben (*s.*); **(a vehicle)** fahren (*s.*)
drive, die Fahrt (-en)
driver, der Fahrer (-)
dry, trocken
to **dry,** trocknen
duke, der Herzog (⁼e)
during, während (*gen.*)

early, früh
to **earn,** verdienen
to **eat,** essen (*s.*)
edge, der Rand (⁼er)
else; or else, sonst; **something else,** noch etwas
empty, leer
end, das Ende (-s, -n)
engine, der Motor (-s, -en); **(of a train),** die Lokomotive (-n)
to **enjoy,** *see* § 28
enough, genug
to **enquire (about),** fragen (nach)
to **enter,** (hin-, her-)eintreten (*s. sep.*)
envelope, der Umschlag (⁼e)
especially, besonders
Europe, Europa
evening, der Abend (-e); **this evening,** heute abend
ever, je
every, jeder, -e, -es
everywhere, überall
examination, die Prüfung (-en)
except (for), außer (*dat.*)
excited, aufgeregt
to **expect,** erwarten
expensive, teuer, kostspielig
to **explain,** erklären
to **express,** ausdrücken (*sep.*)

face, das Gesicht (-er)
factory, die Fabrik (-en)
faithful(ly), treu

ENGLISH-GERMAN VOCABULARY

to **fall**, fallen (s.); **to fall asleep**, einschlafen (s. sep.)
fall, der Fall (⸚e); der Sturz (⸚e)
family, die Familie (-n)
far, weit, fern
farm, der Bauernhof (⸚e)
farmer, der Bauer (-s, -n)
fast, schnell
father, der Vater (⸚)
to **feel**, fühlen
to **fell**, fällen
fellow, der Kerl (-e)
to **fetch**, holen
few, see § 28
field, das Feld (-er)
fierce, wild
to **fight**, kämpfen
film, der Film (-e)
finally, endlich
to **find**, finden (s.)
fine, schön
to **finish**, beendigen, fertig machen, fertig sein; **finished**, fertig
to **fire**, schießen (s.)
fire, das Feuer (-), der Brand (⸚e)
fire-brigade, die Feuerwehr
firm, die Firma (Firmen)
first, erst; **at first**, zuerst
to **fish**, fischen, angeln
fish, der Fisch (-e)
flame, die Flamme (-n)
flood, die Überschwemmung (-en)
flower, die Blume (-n)
to **fly**, fliegen (s.)
to **follow**, folgen (dat.)
fond; to be fond of (things), gern haben; **(persons)**, lieben, lieb haben
foolish, dumm, töricht
foot, der Fuß (⸚e)
football, der Fußball
for (prep.), für; (conj.), denn, weil, da

to **forbid**, verbieten (s.)
to **forget**, vergessen (s.)
Frankfurt on the Main, Frankfurt am Main
to **free**, befreien
free, frei
to **freeze**, frieren (s.)
fresh, frisch
frequently, oft, öfters
Friday, Freitag
friend, der Freund (-e); die Freundin (-nen)
from, von (dat.)

game, das Spiel (-e)
garage, die Garage (-n)
garden, der Garten (⸚)
gardner, der Gärtner (-)
to **gaze**, blicken, starren
general, der General (-e)
gentle, sanft
gentleman, der Herr (-n, -en); **gentlemen!** meine Herren!
to **get**, see § 28; **to get lost**, sich verlaufen (s.); **to get up**, aufstehen (s. sep.)
ghost, das Gespenst (-er)
gift; (a present), das Geschenk (-e); **(natural gift)**, die Gabe (-n)
girl, das Mädchen (-)
to **give**, geben (s.)
glad, froh
glass, das Glas (⸚er)
to **gleam**, glänzen
to **go**, see § 28; **to go out**, hinausgehen (s. sep.); **to go and meet**, abholen (sep.)
good-bye, auf Wiedersehen
grandfather, der Großvater (⸚)
Grammar School, das Gymnasium
grass, das Gras (⸚er)
grateful, dankbar

great, groß
green, grün
to greet, grüßen
ground, die Erde, der Boden
group, die Gruppe (-n)
to grow, wachsen (*s.*); werden (*s.*)
guard (of train), der Zugführer (-)
guest, der Gast (⸚e)

half, halb; **half an hour,** eine halbe Stunde
hall (of a house), der Flur; **(large room),** der Saal (Säle)
hand, die Hand (⸚e)
to happen, geschehen (*s.*)
happy, glücklich
harbour, der Hafen (⸚)
hard, hart, schwer; **to work hard,** fleißig arbeiten
harvest, die Ernte
hat, der Hut (⸚e)
hay, das Heu
head, der Kopf (⸚e)
healthy, gesund
to hear, hören
heavy, schwer
hedge, die Hecke (-n)
to help, helfen (*s.*) (*dat*); **to help oneself,** sich bedienen
help, die Hilfe
here, hier
to hide, verbergen (*s.*)
high, hoch
hill, der Hügel (-), der Berg (-e)
to hit (strike), schlagen (*s.*); **(hit an object aimed at),** treffen (*s.*)
holidays, die Ferien (*plur.*)
home; at home, zu Hause; **towards home,** nach Hause

homework, die (Schul-)Aufgaben (*fem. plur.*)
honest, ehrlich
to hope, hoffen
horse, das Pferd (-e)
host, der Gastgeber (-); **(of inn)** der Wirt (-e)
hostess, die Wirtin (-nen)
hot, heiß, warm
hotel, das Hotel (-s)
hour, die Stunde (-n)
house, das Haus (⸚er)
how, wie
however, jedoch; wie .... auch
hungry, hungrig
to hurry, eilen
to hurt, verletzen, weh tun (*s.*)

idea, die Idee (-n); **(sudden idea),** der Einfall (⸚e); **he has no idea,** er hat keine Ahnung
if, *see* § 28
ill, krank
illness, die Krankheit (-en)
to imagine, sich einbilden (*sep.*)
immediately, sogleich, sofort
indoors, drinnen
inhabitant, der Einwohner (-)
ink, die Tinte
inn, der Gasthof (⸚e), das Wirtshaus (⸚er)
innkeeper, der Wirt (-e)
insect, das Insekt (-s, -en)
to insist (on), bestehen (*s.*) (auf)
instead (of), anstatt (*gen.*)
intention, die Absicht (-en)
to interest, interessieren; **to be interested in,** sich interessieren für
interest, das Interesse (-n)
interesting, interessant

ENGLISH-GERMAN VOCABULARY

invitation, die Einladung (-en)
to **invite,** einladen (*s. sep.*)
iron, das Eisen
island, die Insel (-n)

John, Johann; (*diminutive*), Hans
journey, die Reise (-n)
joy, die Freude (-n)
judge, der Richter (-)
to **jump,** springen (*s.*)
just (*adv. of time*), gerade; **I was just about to,** ich wollte eben..., ich war im Begriff...

to **kill,** töten
king, der König (-e)
to **knock,** klopfen
to **know,** *see* § 28

to **lack,** fehlen (*impers.*)
ladder, die Leiter (-n)
lack, der Mangel
lady, die Dame (-n), die Frau (-en)
lake, der See (-s, -n)
lamp, die Lampe (-n)
landlord, der Wirt (-e)
lantern, die Laterne (-n)
lark, die Lerche (-n)
to **last,** dauern
last, letzt; **at last,** endlich
late, spät
to **laugh,** lachen
lawyer, der Jurist (-en, -en), der Rechtsanwalt (-̈e)
to **lay** (**a table**), decken
lazy, faul
leaf, das Blatt (-̈er)
to **learn,** lernen
least; at least, wenigstens
to **leave,** *see* § 28
leaving examination, das Abitur

left, link; **on the left,** links
leg, das Bein (-e)
to **lend,** leihen (*s.*)
lesson, die Stunde (-n)
letter, der Brief (-e)
library, die Bibliothek
to **lie,** liegen (*s.*); **to lie down,** sich hinlegen (*sep.*)
to **light,** anzünden (*sep.*)
light, das Licht (-er)
to **lighten,** blitzen
life, das Leben
to **like,** mögen; (**things**), gern haben; (**persons**), lieb haben
to **listen,** zuhören (*sep.*); **to listen to the wireless,** Radio hören
little, klein; **a little,** ein wenig
to **live** (**inhabit**), wohnen, bewohnen; (**be alive**), leben
living-room, das Wohnzimmer (-)
lonely, einsam
long (*adj.*), lang; (*adv.*), lange
to **look,** sehen (*s.*), schauen, blicken; **to look at,** ansehen (*s. sep.*); **to look after,** pflegen; **to look as if,** scheinen (*s.*); **to look for,** suchen; **to look forward to,** sich freuen auf (*acc.*); **to look round,** sich umsehen (*s. sep.*)
to **lose,** verlieren (*s.*); **to get lost,** sich verlaufen (*s.*), sich verirren
lot; a lot, viel; (**fate**), das Los
Louis, Ludwig
lovely, schön
low, niedrig
luggage, das Gepäck
luggage-rack, das Gepäcknetz
lunch, das Mittagessen

machine, die Maschine (-n)
main entrance, der Haupteingang
to **make,** machen
man, der Mann (⸚er *or* Leute)
many, viele
March, März
market, der Markt (⸚e)
marvellous, herrlich
master, der Herr (-n, -en)
match (game), das Spiel (-e), das Wettspiel (-e); das Streichholz (⸚er)
matter; what's the matter? was ist los?; **it doesn't matter,** es macht nichts
may (to be allowed), dürfen (*modal*); **(to be able),** können (*modal*)
May, Mai
mayor, der Bürgermeister (-)
meal, das Essen
to **meet (by chance),** begegnen; **(by arrangement),** treffen (*s.*)
to **mend,** wiederherstellen (*sep.*)
mercy, die Gnade
merchant, der Kaufmann (-leute)
messenger, der Bote (-n, -n)
mile, die Meile (-n)
minute, die Minute (-n)
misfortune, das Unglück
to **miss (a train),** versäumen, verpassen
mistake; to be mistaken, irren, sich irren
mistake, der Fehler (-)
misty, nebelig
moment, der Augenblick (-e)
money, das Geld
monk, der Mönch (-e)
month, der Monat (-e)
moonlight, das Mondlicht

morning, der Morgen; **this morning,** heute morgen
mother, die Mutter (⸚)
motor-bike, das Motorrad (⸚er)
mountain, der Berg (-e)
mouth, der Mund
to **move,** bewegen; **(to another house, town),** übersiedeln (*sep.*), ziehen (*s.*)

nail, der Nagel (⸚)
name, der Name (-ns, -n)
nation, das Volk (⸚er)
naturally, natürlich
nature, die Natur
near, nah
to **need,** brauchen
neighbour, der Nachbar (-s, -n); die Nachbarin (-nen)
never, nie, niemals
new, neu
news, die Nachricht (-en)
newspaper, die Zeitung (-en)
next, nächst
night, die Nacht (⸚e)
nobody, niemand
noise (loud), der Lärm; **(not loud),** das Geräusch
north, der Norden
nothing, nichts
to **notice,** bemerken
novel, der Roman (-e)
now, jetzt, nun

oak, die Eiche (-n)
to **obey,** gehorchen (*dat.*)
object, der Gegenstand (⸚e)
obliged; to be obliged to, müssen (*modal*)
to **obtain,** erhalten (*s.*)
office, das Amt (⸚er), das Büro (-s, -s)
officer, der Offizier (-e)
often, oft, öfters

old, alt
once, einmal; **at once,** sogleich, sofort
only (*adv.*), nur; (*adj.*), einzig
to **open,** öffnen
opera, die Oper (-n)
opinion, die Meinung (-en)
opposite, gegenüber (*dat.*)
or, oder; **or else** (*i.e.* **otherwise**), sonst
orchestra, das Orchester (-)
to **order (command),** befehlen (s.) (*dat.*); **(reserve, ask for),** bestellen
order, der Befehl (-e)
in order to, um ... zu (*infinitive*); so daß (*followed by finite verb*)
outside, see § 28
to **owe,** schulden; schuldig sein
own, eigen

packet, das Paket (-e)
to **paint,** malen
painter, der Maler (-)
painting, das Gemälde (-), das Bild (-er)
paper, das Papier (-e); **(newspaper),** die Zeitung (-en)
to **pardon,** verzeihen (s.) (*dat.*); entschuldigen
pardon, die Verzeihung
parents, die Eltern (*plur.*)
part, der Teil (-e)
party, die Gesellschaft (-en)
to **pass (to go past),** an ... (*dat.*) ... vorbeigehen (s. sep.); **(an examination),** bestehen (s.); **(time),** verbringen (s.), zubringen (s. sep.)
passenger, der Fahrgast (⸚e)
passport, der Reisepaß (⸚sse)
to **pay,** bezahlen
pen, die Feder (-n)
pencil, der Bleistift (-e)

people, die Leute (*plur.*); **(nation),** das Volk (⸚er)
perhaps, vielleicht
person, die Person (-en)
petrol-station, die Tankstelle (-n)
piano, das Klavier (-)
to **pick,** pflücken; **to pick up,** aufheben (s. sep.)
picture, das Bild (-er)
pictures; to go to the pictures, ins Kino gehen (s.)
pilot (aeroplane), der Pilot (-en, en), der Flieger (-); **(ship),** der Lotse (-n, -n)
pity, das Mitleid; **it is a pity,** (es ist) schade!
place, die Stelle (-n)
plane, das Flugzeug (-e)
platform, der Bahnsteig (-e)
to **play,** spielen
playground, der Spielplatz (⸚e)
pleasant, angenehm
to **please,** gefallen (s.) (*dat.*); **to be pleased,** sich freuen; **please!** bitte!
pocket, die Tasche (-n)
poem, das Gedicht (-e)
poet, der Dichter (-)
policeman, der Schutzmann (-leute), der Polizist (-en, -en)
police-station, die Polizeiwache
polite, höflich
pond, der Teich (-e)
porter, der Gepäckträger (-)
poor, arm
to **possess,** besitzen (s.)
possible, möglich
postcard, die Postkarte (-n)
postman, der Briefträger (-)
post-office, das Postamt
to **prefer,** vorziehen (s. sep.); **I prefer to fly,** ich fliege lieber

to **prepare,** vorbereiten (*sep.*)
present; at present, jetzt, zur Zeit
present, das Geschenk (-e)
pretty, hübsch
previous, vorig
price, der Preis (-e)
prisoner, der Gefangene (-n, -n)
prize, der Preis (-e)
professor, Professor (-s, -en)
to **pull,** ziehen (*s.*); **to pull out,** hervorziehen (*s. sep.*)
pupil, der Schüler (-); die Schülerin (-nen)
purse, der Geldbeutel (-), die Geldtasche (-n)
to **put,** see § 28; **to put on a coat,** einen Mantel anziehen (*s. sep.*)

quarter, das Viertel (-)
quay, der Kai
queen, die Königin (-nen)
question, die Frage (-n)
quick, schnell
quiet, ruhig
quite, ganz

railway, die Eisenbahn
railway-engine, die Lokomotive (-n)
to **rain,** regnen
rain, der Regen
rather, ziemlich
to **reach,** erreichen
ready, see § 28
to **realise,** sehen (*s.*), verstehen (*s.*)
really, wirklich
to **receive,** erhalten (*s.*), bekommen (*s.*)
to **recognise,** erkennen (*s.*)
to **recover,** sich erholen
red, rot

region, die Gegend (-en)
to **remain,** bleiben (*s.*)
to **remember,** sich erinnern an (+ *acc.*)
to **repair,** wiederherstellen (*sep.*)
to **reply,** erwidern, antworten; **he replies to me,** er antwortet mir; **he replies to a letter,** er antwortet auf einen Brief
to **report,** berichten; **he is reported to be rich,** er soll reich sein
report, der Bericht (-e)
to **resemble,** gleichen (*s.*) (*dat.*), ähneln (*dat.*)
to **rest,** ruhen, sich ausruhen (*sep.*)
rest, die Pause
to **return,** zurückkehren (*sep.*), zurückkommen (*s. sep.*), zurückgehen (*s. sep.*)
to **reward,** lohnen, belohnen
reward, der Lohn
Rhine, der Rhein
rich, reich
to **ride,** reiten (*s.*); (**a bicycle**), radfahren (*s. sep.*)
ride, die Fahrt (-en)
right, recht; **to the right,** rechts; **he is right,** er hat recht; **it is right,** es ist richtig
to **ring,** läuten
river, der Fluß (⸚sse)
to **roll,** rollen
Rome, Rom
room, das Zimmer (-); (**space**), der Platz (⸚e)
rough (**of sea**), aufgeregt, unruhig
round, rund
route, der Weg (-e)
rucksack, der Rucksack (⸚e)
ruins, die Ruine (-n) (*usually in singular*)
rumour, das Gerücht (-e)

to **run**, laufen (s.), rennen (s.)
to **rush**, stürzen

sailor, der Matrose (-n, -n)
same, derselbe, dieselbe, dasselbe
sand, der Sand; **the sands**, der Strand
sandwich, das Butterbrot (-e)
Saturday, der Sonnabend, der Samstag
to **save** (**rescue**), retten; (**money**), sparen
to **say**, sagen
scarcely, kaum
school, die Schule (-n)
to **scream**, schreien (s.)
sea, das Meer, die See; **seasick**, seekrank; **seaside**, die Küste; **sea-voyage**, die Seereise
seat, der Platz (⸚e); (**in a bus, train**), der Sitzplatz (⸚e)
second (adj.), zweit
secondly, zweitens
to **see**, sehen (s.)
to **seem**, scheinen (s.)
to **seize**, ergreifen (s.)
to **sell**, verkaufen
to **send** (**for**), schicken (nach)
serious, ernst
to **serve**, dienen (dat.)
to **set** (**of sun**), untergehen (s. sep.); **to set out**, sich auf den Weg machen
several, einige; **several times**, oft, manchmal
shadow, der Schatten (-)
shady, schattig
shelter, der Schutz
to **shine**, scheinen (s.), glänzen
ship, das Schiff (-e)
shoe, der Schuh (-e)
shoemaker, der Schuhmacher (-)
shop, der Laden (⸚)
shopkeeper, der Verkäufer (-), der Händler (-)
shopping; to go shopping, Einkäufe machen
shore, die Küste, das Gestade
to **shout**, rufen (s.), schreien (s.)
shout, der Ruf (-e), der Schrei (-e)
to **show**, zeigen
to **shut**, schließen (s.), zumachen (sep.)
sick, krank
sickness, die Krankheit (-en)
side, die Seite (-n)
silent, ruhig, schweigsam; **to be silent**, schweigen (s.)
since, see § 28
to **sing**, singen (s.)
sister, die Schwester (-n)
to **sit; to be sitting**, sitzen (s.); **to sit down**, sich hinsetzen (sep.); **to sit an examination**, eine Prüfung machen
to **skate**, Schlittschuh laufen (s.)
to **sleep**, schlafen (s.)
slope, der Abhang (⸚e)
slow, langsam
to **smoke**, rauchen
smoke, der Rauch
to **snow**, schneien
snow, der Schnee
soldier, der Soldat (-en, -en)
some, einige
someone, jemand
something, etwas
sometimes, zuweilen
son, der Sohn (⸚e)
song, das Lied (-er)
soon, bald
sorry; I am sorry, es tut mir leid

soul, die Seele (-n); (**person**), der Mensch (-en, -en)
sound, das Geräusch (-e); der Ton (⸚e)
south, der Süden
to **speak,** sprechen (*s.*), reden
to **spend** (**time**), verbringen (*s.*); (**money**), ausgeben (*s. sep.*)
spite; in spite of, trotz (*gen.*)
to **spoil,** verderben (*s.*)
square, der Platz (⸚e)
stair, die Treppe (-n); **stairs,** die Treppe
to **start,** beginnen (*s.*), anfangen (*s. sep.*); **to start on a journey,** sich auf den Weg machen, eine Reise antreten (*s. sep.*)
station, der Bahnhof (⸚e)
to **stay,** *see* § 28
to **steal,** stehlen (*s.*)
steamer, der Dampfer (-)
steep, steil
to **step,** treten (*s.*); **to step forward,** hervortreten (*s. sep.*)
stick, der Stock (⸚e)
still (*adv.*), noch; (*adj.*) still, ruhig; **better still,** noch besser
stone, der Stein (-e)
to **stop,** *see* § 28
storm, der Sturm (⸚e), das Gewitter (-)
story, die Geschichte (-n)
strange, fremd, seltsam
stranger, der Fremde (-n, -n)
stream, der Bach (⸚e)
street, die Straße (-n)
to **strike,** schlagen (*s.*)
string, der Bindfaden
to **stroll,** wandeln
strong, stark

student, der Student (-en, -en)
to **study,** studieren
to **succeed,** gelingen (*s.*) (*impersonal*)
success, der Erfolg (-e)
suitcase, der Koffer (-), die Handtasche (-n)
sudden(ly), plötzlich
summer, der Sommer
sun, die Sonne (-n)
sunrise, der Sonnenaufgang
sunshine, der Sonnenschein
to **suppose,** vermuten; **he is supposed to be rich,** er soll reich sein
sure, sicher
to **surprise,** überraschen (*insep.*)
surprise, die Überraschung (-en)
swift, schnell, rasch
to **swim,** schwimmen (*s.*)
swimmer, der Schwimmer (-)
swimming-pool, das Schwimmbad

table, der Tisch (-e)
to **take,** *see* § 28
to **talk,** sprechen (*s.*), plaudern
tall, hoch, groß
task, die Aufgabe (-n)
to **taste,** schmecken
to **telephone,** telephonieren, anrufen (*s. sep.*)
to **tell,** sagen, erzählen
tennis; to play tennis, Tennis spielen
tent, das Zelt (-e)
that (**those**), jener, jene, jenes, jene
to **thank,** danken (*dat.*)
theatre, das Theater (-)
then, *see* § 28
there (*adv. of place*) da, dort

thief, der Dieb (-e)
thing, das Ding (-e), die Sache (-n)
to **think,** denken (*s.*); (**to be of the opinion**), meinen
thirsty, durstig
to **threaten,** drohen (*dat.*)
through, durch (*acc.*)
to **throw,** werfen (*s.*)
thrush, die Drossel (-n)
thunder, der Donner
to **tie,** binden (*s.*)
time (**occasion**), das Mal; **ten times,** zehnmal; (**period**), die Zeit; **in time,** zur Zeit; **what time is it?** wieviel Uhr ist es? **at times,** zuweilen
tired, müde
to-day, heute
to-morrow, morgen; **to-morrow morning,** morgen früh
to-night, heute abend
too, zu; (**also**), auch
top (**of a hill**), der Gipfel (-)
tower, der Turm (⸚e)
town, die Stadt (⸚e)
town-hall, das Rathaus
toy, das Spielzeug (-e)
train, der Zug (⸚e)
tram, die Straßenbahn, die Elektrische
to **travel,** reisen
traveller, der Reisende (-n, -n)
travels, die Reisen (*plur.*)
to **tread,** treten (*s.*)
treasure, der Schatz (⸚e)
tree, der Baum (⸚e)
trip, der Ausflug (⸚e)
truth, die Wahrheit
to **try,** versuchen
to **turn,** wenden (*w.* and *s.*), sich umwenden (*sep.*)
two, zwei; (*adj.*), beide

ugly, häßlich
unable; to be unable, nicht können
uncle, der Onkel (-)
to **understand,** verstehen (*s.*)
to **undress,** sich ausziehen (*s. sep.*)
unfortunate, unglücklich
unfortunately, unglücklicherweise
unhappy, traurig, unglücklich
unpleasant, unangenehm
upstairs, *see* § 28
to **use,** gebrauchen
usual(ly), gewöhnlich

valley, das Tal (⸚er)
vase, die Vase (-n)
vegetable(s), das Gemüse
very, sehr
vicar, der Geistliche (-n, -n), der Pfarrer (-)
view, die Aussicht (-en), die Ansicht (-en)
village, das Dorf (⸚er)
to **visit,** besuchen
visit, der Besuch (-e)
visitor, der Besuch, der Gast (⸚e)
voice, die Stimme (-n)
voyage, die Seereise (-n)

to **wait,** warten
waiter, der Kellner (-)
to **wake,** *see* § 28
to **walk,** gehen (*s.*), wandern, wandeln; **to go for a walk,** einen Spaziergang machen, spazierengehen (*s. sep.*); **to walk on the grass,** das Gras betreten
walk, der Spaziergang (⸚e)
wall (**inside building**), die Wand (⸚e); (**outside building**), die Mauer (-n)

wallet, die Brieftasche (-n)
war, der Krieg (-e)
warden, (of Youth Hostel), der Herbergsvater (⸚)
warm, warm
to **wash,** waschen (s.), sich waschen (s.)
to **watch,** beobachten
watch, die Uhr (-en)
water, das Wasser
to **wear,** tragen (s.)
weather, das Wetter
week, die Woche (-n)
well, gut, wohl
well, der Brunnen (-)
wet, naß
when, see § 28
whenever, see § 28 under **when**
where, wo
which, welcher, welche, welches, welche; (rel. pronoun), der, die, das etc.
while, während (gen.)
while, die Weile
to **whistle,** pfeifen (s.)
whistle, die Pfeife (-n)
white, weiß
who (interrogative), wer?; (rel. pronoun), der, die, das, etc.
whole, ganz
why, warum
wide, breit
wife, die Frau (-en)
wind, der Wind (-e)

window, das Fenster (-)
wine, der Wein (-e)
winter, der Winter
wireless, das Radio; **wireless-set,** der Radioapparat
to **wish,** wünschen, wollen (modal)
wish, der Wunsch (⸚e)
woman, die Frau (-en)
to **wonder,** überlegen; **I wonder,** ich möchte gern wissen
wood, das Holz; der Wald (⸚er)
to **work,** arbeiten
work, die Arbeit (-en); (literary work), das Werk (-e)
world, die Welt
to **worry,** sich kümmern, sorgen
wristlet-watch, die Armbanduhr
to **write,** schreiben (s.)

year, das Jahr (-e)
yesterday, gestern; **yesterday evening,** gestern abend
yet (**still**), noch; (**however**), jedoch, doch; **not yet,** noch nicht
young, jung
Youth Hostel, die Jugendherberge (-n)